Joyce's Uncertainty Principle

Joyce's Uncertainty Principle

Phillip F. Herring

PRINCETON UNIVERSITY PRESS

PRINCETON, NEW JERSEY

Published by Princeton University Press, 41 William Street,
Princeton, New Jersey 08540
In the United Kingdom: Princeton University Press, Guildford, Surrey

Library of Congress Cataloging in Publication Data will be found
on the last printed page of this book

ISBN 0-691-06719-8

This book has been composed in Linotron Palatino type

Clothbound editions of Princeton University Press books are printed
on acid-free paper, and binding materials are chosen for
strength and durability. Paperbacks, although satisfactory
for personal collections, are not usually suitable
for library rebinding

Printed in the United States of America by Princeton
University Press, Princeton, New Jersey

For Paul and Alec

Contents

Preface

In *The Arts Without Mystery*, Denis Donoghue has said:

> I want to reinstate mystery and to distinguish it from mere bewilderment or mystification. One of the strongest motives in modern life is to explain everything and preferably to explain it away. The typical mark of modern critics is that they are zealots of explanation, they want to deny to the arts their mystery, and to degrade mystery into a succession of problems. . . . A problem is something to be solved, a mystery is something to be witnessed and attested." (12)

According to Frank Kermode, the Gospel of St. Mark is just such a mystery, "which cannot be reduced to other and more intelligible forms . . . something irreducible, therefore perpetually to be interpreted; not secrets to be found out one by one, but Secrecy."[1] Should a mystery simply be witnessed, or must it suffer perpetual interpretation? Is there ever validity in interpretation, or must literary critics tackle the same problems generation after generation, oblivious of the question of solvability, examining the same evidence and emerging from the dusty book stacks with interpretations that at best show how imaginative and intelligent they are?

This book grew out of a need to discover the difference between solvable problems and mysteries in Joyce studies, and to satisfy myself and a few others about how we tell the difference. Initially I was more optimistic about validity than I later became, when I gradually discovered (for myself, at least) that every interesting question of interpretation I could ask about Joyce's works, even after twenty-four years of nearly continuous study, was essentially a mystery. This led me to contemplate the care with which, by omitting vital evidence or intro-

[1] Kermode, *The Genesis of Secrecy* (143), quoted by Brivic in his discussion of indeterminacy in Joyce (67). One of the main points of Robert Boyle's *James Joyce's Pauline Vision* is that Joyce "builds on mystery" (11).

ducing ambiguity, Joyce designed his puzzles to be unsolvable.

My thesis is that Joyce formulated an uncertainty principle as early as the first *Dubliners* story, when he included *gnomon* with *paralysis* and *simony* as the three key words to interpretation. These I take to be important not only for the story, but for his *Dubliners* in general; though there is no evidence that this was Joyce's intention, the words are relevant to all his works. *Simony* points to his persistent belief in the Church's role in Ireland's oppression, *paralysis* to the complicity of the Irish in that oppression, or their inability to throw off the fetters that bound them. Few themes in Joyce's works surpass these in importance. With *gnomon,* a Euclidian term meaning an incomplete geometrical structure, he introduced his uncertainty principle, a strategy designed to create mystery.

Epistemological uncertainty is a familiar enough theme in modernist literature, and the major influence was probably Nietzsche, whose works Joyce knew well. As Joseph Valente has written, Nietzsche and Joyce "formulated their skeptical epistemologies with the aim of enriching the prospects of human experience by developing our interpretive capacities" (2). It was the business of Joyce's uncertainty principle to foster the perspectivism Valente describes.

In the library scene of *Ulysses,* Stephen Dedalus says the world was founded "upon the void. Upon incertitude, upon unlikelihood" (*U* 9:842),[2] and he later affirms to Leopold Bloom "his significance as a conscious rational animal proceeding syllogistically from the known to the unknown and a conscious rational reagent between a micro and a macrocosm ineluctably constructed upon the incertitude of the void" (*U* 17:1012-15). In the lines that follow this statement it be-

[2] References to *Ulysses* (*U*) are to the new Garland "Critical and Synoptic" edition prepared by Hans Walter Gabler (New York, 1982). Though the jury is still out, for the foreseeable future it should be the standard edition of *Ulysses.* References are to episode and line number (e.g. *U* 12:436). An added advantage to using it, for those needing a concordance, is the companion volume by Wolfhard Steppe and Gabler, *A Handlist to James Joyce's "Ulysses,"* also published by Garland Publishing, Inc. (New York, 1985).

comes clear that, like many readers, Bloom misapprehends Stephen's meaning in his own way, giving it a perspectival twist. Alone with his thoughts in Ithaca, Bloom imagines himself to be "a conscious reactor against the void of incertitude" (*U* 17:2210-11).

Initially, perhaps, Joyce addressed the problem of validation in reading and interpretation to insure that only initiates could read his revolutionary message; later enigmas simply pleased and amused him, though at the same time he did seriously question the confidence with which we interpret world or text. If Joyce could have impressed upon us one single habit of mind, I think it would have been skepticism, which Sheldon Brivic has rightly called "the contractile force in the fabrication of Joyce's mental world" (25).

There is no evidence that *gnomon* remained of interest to Joyce beyond *Dubliners*, but the uncertainty principle that grew out of this concept never left him. In its more general form it encourages skepticism and fosters the perpetual interpretation of mystery that Kermode associates with the Gospel of St. Mark. From "The Sisters" through *Finnegans Wake*, major issues of interpretation are usually constructed so as to be indeterminate, and the evidence for decidability is normally ambiguous. There are also minor issues and textual cruces that cannot finally be decided, but many can be. Problems of interpretation that hinge upon textual evidence are normally ambiguous, but through research the range of perspectives often may be limited. Where the question is one of textual development, the study of notes, drafts, and sources may tell us much about Joyce's literary works without enabling us to answer undecidable questions of interpretation. Even so, manuscript study is often more rewarding than playing Joyce's games of speculation.

I have tried to avoid the morass of intentionalism. Still, in adding "principle" to "uncertainty" in the title, I admit that my aim was to suggest a devious authorial strategy the Irish have always associated with Joyce. The nod to Werner Heisenberg, discoverer of the uncertainty principle in physics, is not unwarranted. Regarding the difficulties of *Finnegans Wake*,

Clive Hart has written, "As with some questions of modern physical theory, it is not that we could know but don't; it is rather that the information, the certainty, that we are seeking does not exist."[3]

How does an uncertainty principle function? It introduces a range of interpretive possibilities that usually deceive a reader into believing that he/she is engaged in discovering the "true" meaning of a text. In Joyce's case we normally find that an essential piece of evidence is missing that would allow us a measure of security in interpretation; readers are invited to fill the gap by speculating about what is missing, such as what happened in an important scene omitted from a plot sequence.[4] Uncertainty is to a great extent true of all literary texts, but it is untrue that authors before Joyce generally had uncertainty principles.

The terms *uncertainty, ambiguity,* and *indeterminacy* in common parlance have often had much the same meaning, but in this century they have parted ways in literary and scientific theory. *Ambiguity,* some would claim, was appropriated by the New Criticism; *indeterminacy* has led a life of its own in deconstruction, where it is used to indicate a problem besetting all language and all texts. The term *uncertainty,* still in the public domain, points to scientific theories roughly contemporary with Joyce, so to avoid confusion with Derridean principles I prefer that term to *indeterminacy.* What I describe is not a feature of all language or of all literary texts.

If Joyce's principle directs our attention to absence, hence uncertainty, in plot or motivation, it also suggests problems of characterization that I believe we may safely call *indeterminant* or *ambiguous,* depending upon the case. When we ask the broadest, most meaningful questions about nearly any interesting character in Joyce, we immediately encounter Joyce's uncertainty principle, which went beyond the idea of missing pieces to generate unsolvable problems. For instance, a very

[3] Clive Hart, "*Finnegans Wake* in Perspective": 162.

[4] Hugh Kenner probably invented this technique of discovery in Joyce studies. (He even named a book of essays *Gnomon.*) See his "The Rhetoric of Silence."

great amount of effort has gone into trying to decide whether or not Leopold Bloom is really Jewish, when any answer obviously depends on definitions about which there is no consensus and never can be. Close scrutiny will also show that the evidence has been tampered with. This example of indeterminacy of character I find unsolvable and not very interesting.

Nevertheless, I do explore indeterminacy of character in three instances that prove both exemplary and fascinating (to me at least): the mystery of the Man in the Macintosh, which has haunted many readers of *Ulysses;* the Gibraltarian background of Molly Bloom and its indeterminate aspects; and the question of why Stephen Dedalus, the artist-to-be, seems to make so little progress toward becoming an artist, why he is caught fast in a perpetuity of vocational development. In each case we have a literary character who in some sense cannot be what he/she is.

The uncertainty principle affected structure in Joyce's works through his developing sense of closure, eventually resulting in his famous circular endings. As early as the *Dubliners* stories he constructed enigmatic endings that resist interpretation, that seem designed to send the reader back into the text for clarification. The ending of "The Dead," the volume's last story, occurs at the end of the old year and the beginning of the new, when Gabriel Conroy experiences a disintegration of his old personality and the presumed birth of a new one. At the beginning of *A Portrait* Stephen listens to a story he associates with himself, whereas at the end he tells his story to his diary and us. In *Ulysses,* the first and last words of Molly Bloom's monologue are "yes," and circularity is stressed in other ways. Joyce's comic vision in *Ulysses* led him to associate circular endings with human posteriors, perhaps a travesty of the scriptural notion that "in our end is our beginning." Circular endings also remind us of the persistent theme of resurrection in Joyce; from Father Flynn to Humphrey Chimpden Earwicker, the dead live again in memory and imagination.

The most startling examples of Joyce's uncertainty principle are to be found in *Finnegans Wake,* where language, plot, character, and motivation are all destabilized to produce literature's most famous enigma. Implicitly agreeing with Denis Donoghue that while problems may be solvable, mysteries may only be experienced, Wilhelm Füger has summarized Joyce's "creed concerning the fundamental nature of literary art," as expressed in *Finnegans Wake,* in these words: "insofar as literature can be said to be an adequate expression of life . . . it is bound to remain just as enigmatic as life itself. . . . The mystery withstands all efforts of analysis, and there is no use deploying scholarly or scientific endeavors to an excessive extent" (411). Yet all the features of uncertainty in the *Wake* are to some degree present in the earlier works—uncertainty is even the dominant theme in Joyce's play *Exiles.* Of especial relevance to our topic in the *Wake* is ALP's letter, which exists, if at all, outside the text, where its absence generates seemingly endless speculation and reference.

What becomes obvious from such a study is that Joyce's work is all of a piece not merely in autobiographical or thematic terms, but in its certainty and uncertainty as well. But, then, we should not be surprised, for Joyce vowed to keep us busy unravelling his mysteries during the millennium to come.

Acknowledgments

I am indebted to the Graduate School Research Committee of the University of Wisconsin-Madison for two summer grants that helped immeasurably the progress of this book. Of the many people who have helped in the shaping of the book's arguments at one time or another, two colleagues deserve my deepest gratitude—David Hayman, with whom I carry on an intellectual tug-of-war that has been indispensable to my development as a Joycean; and Jay Clayton, who read nearly every chapter of this book, and whose unerring judgment and eclectic knowledge never cease to amaze me. Like so many scholars of modern literature, I am indebted to A. Walton Litz for invaluable advice and continual encouragement. Hugh Kenner and Robert M. Adams I thank for insights of central importance to this book. Wherever critics of modernist literature look, they find that these critics have been there first. Other friends have read individual chapters with careful eye or have given valuable advice: Charles Rossman, Shari and Bernard Benstock, Janet Dunleavy, Florence Walzl, William C. Dowling, John Henry Raleigh, Marjorie Perloff, Patrick A. McCarthy, Cóilin Owens, and E. D. Hirsch. Margaret Walsh contributed a sketch for a *Dubliners* chapter. To John Bishop and Joseph Valente I am indebted for permission to quote from unpublished manuscripts, and to Bishop especially I am grateful for insights that my references probably do not adequately demonstrate.

Joyce's Uncertainty Principle

ONE

Dubliners: The Trials of Adolescence

Gnomon and the Rhetoric of Absence

Joyce's seemingly contradictory strategy of producing both ambiguous texts and the keys to interpreting them may have the effect of keeping professors busy, one of his stated purposes, but it also reveals a genuine skepticism about our ability to get at the truth except in fragments, to understand finally and completely the impressions that our senses bring us, to analyze and interpret experience with a high degree of certainty, and to express ourselves unambiguously in eel-slippery language.

In Joyce's earliest work, however, skepticism was often a less prominent concern than politics, for in *Dubliners* he wrote with great bitterness and in considerable fear a political indictment of his city using a hidden rhetoric of absence. Out of this strategy grew his uncertainty principle, but it was surely no coincidence that it flourished only when he felt safe enough to condemn directly the sources of oppression.

Joyce's rhetoric of absence made its initial appearance on the first page of *Dubliners,* where we find the three words in italics generally accepted as key words for interpretation. (Most critics have said that they are keys to the first story alone; I say they are relevant to the entire collection.) While *paralysis,* the first key word, has been widely discussed, *gnomon,* the second one, has remained murky. The *OED* tells us that it is both a parallelogram with a smaller parallelogram missing in one corner and the pillar of a sundial, which tells time by casting part of a circle into shadow.[1] One should give more

[1] See Euclid, in his *Elements* (Book II, Definition 2), on *gnomon,* and Thomas E. Connolly ("Joyce's 'The Sisters' ": 195), on the edition of Euclid that Joyce probably used. The most authoritative article on *gnomon,* and one to which I am indebted for several ideas, is by Gerhard Friedrich, "The Gnomonic Clue

credence to Euclidian usage, since in the story the boy's understanding is probably restricted to that, but Joyce surely knew that in both definitions the missing part is what is important, either as a space that defines a geometric shape or as a shadow that indicates the time of day. *Gnomon* signaled his creation of absences that readers must make speak if they are to gain insight into character, structure, and narrative technique. In Greek, *γνώμων* means "judge" or "interpreter," which might provide a fanciful etymological link between the reader as interpreter in *Dubliners* and that which is to be discovered—significant but suppressed meaning. The richness of *gnomon* is precisely its vagueness.[2]

"Gnomonic" language may contain ellipses, hiatuses in meaning, significant silences, empty and ritualistic dialogue. We note the continual emphasis on emptiness, incompletion, solitude, loneliness, shadow, darkness, and failure, which so affect the lives of Joyce's Dubliners and allow subtle expression of his political views.

Joyce must have been well instructed in the dictionary meanings of *gnomon,* because the concept is relevant to most of the major concerns of *Dubliners.* It suggests that certain kinds of absence are typical of the whole of Dublin life at a significant *time* in its history. (Here the sundial meaning of the word is applicable.) In effect, a *gnomon* may be a key synecdoche of absence, part of a political rhetoric of silence within a larger framework of language. In general, it indicates how selective examples such as the characters of *Dubliners* define life in their city, how shades illuminate presences, even how abnormality can define the normal.

The third key word in the opening paragraph of "The Sis-

---

to James Joyce's *Dubliners.*" He says that " 'paralysis' means literally a loosening or weakening at the side. . . . Parallelograms that are non-rectangular may be thought of as loosened at the side; and the Euclidean gnomon has moreover the appearance of an impaired, cutaway parallelogram . . ."(422). See also Fabian; Day; and Reid.

[2] For a discussion of the ideological implications of a text's silences or gaps, see Pierre Macherey's *A Theory of Literary Production.* See also Staley.

ters" is *simony*, the buying and selling of ecclesiastical preferment. If *paralysis* describes the moral and physical condition of Dubliners, given their need for freedom, transcendence, and fulfillment, and *gnomon* reemphasizes these absences at a particular time in history, then *simony* points to corruption in high places and illegitimate ecclesiastical authority as the primary obstacles to people's fulfillment. The first two terms describe the condition, telling readers how to arrive at meanings deeper than the textual surface, while the word *simony* places the blame squarely where Joyce thought it belonged—on institutions and their representatives who barter sacred rights Ambition, energy, free will, revolutionary zeal—these forces play no role and could not, Joyce thought, in a city and country where centuries of political and religious oppression had caused a general paralysis of mind and will. Transcendence came only through death or emigration.

John Fowles recently said in an interview that "academic critics seem often to me to be blind to a negative side of the novel: what it does not say, what is left out."[3] A major exception is Hugh Kenner, who has become well known in Joycean circles for his gnomonic perspectives in revealing important textual lacunae, which have sparked both wide interest and controversy.[4] His article "The Rhetoric of Silence" is the pioneering work in this area, and it has given me my chapter subtitle, but my emphasis is on absence rather than silence, and in *Dubliners* at least, politics as often as puzzles.

Bernard Benstock called Kenner "the man in the gap" ("The Kenner Conundrum": 434) for, as Milton's angel Gabriel might have said, "busying his thoughts with matters hid," but Benstock also said that Kenner's

> speculations are important since they open up investigation into the missing sections of *Ulysses* and attempt to account for the events which must have taken place during the hours in which Joyce does not allow us to witness the

[3] In "An Interview with John Fowles," *Modern Fiction Studies* 31 (1985): 189.

[4] See Kenner, "Molly's Masterstroke" and "The Rhetoric of Silence"; see also Wellington.

> progress of his characters. This exercise in gnomonic criticism focuses on the shadows conveniently overlooked by many readers of the novel, and regardless of Kenner's success as a detective of the unsubstantial, his efforts force attention about the neglected pockets of darkness. (ibid., 428)

Benstock points to three examples of gnomonic criticism in Kenner's work: (1) In *The Pound Era,* Kenner discusses a vital bit of information, not present in the story "Eveline," about the boat from the North Wall. Presumably Eveline freezes at dockside because she has been promised that the ship would take her and Frank to Buenos Aires, but she now sees that ships from the North Wall dock sail to Liverpool. I disagree with Kenner's interpretation, but the discovery of a vital missing detail, upon which any convincing interpretation of a story would depend, is a good example of gnomonic criticism. (2) Late in *Ulysses* Stephen complains of an injured hand, but there is scant evidence as to how this injury occurred. In his chapter on "Circe" in the Hart-Hayman book, Kenner recreates for us a missing scene at the end of "Oxen," where Stephen strikes Buck Mulligan at the Westland Row Station. (3) In "Molly's Masterstroke," Kenner sees importance in the fact that the furniture at 7 Eccles Street has been rearranged in Bloom's absence, causing him to bump his head (*U* 17:1275). My view would be that the Greek generals returning from the Trojan War were often startled to find their homes rearranged; Bloom, an Odysseus figure, comes into contact with tangible evidence of this. Kenner imagines a scene in which Molly has Boylan rearrange the furniture in order to tire him out and thus guard her virtue. In any event, Kenner's attempts to recreate missing scenes on the basis of scattered evidence are gnomonic exercises that Joyce would have applauded.

Even Leopold Bloom plays a gnomonic game when at the end of "Nausicaa" he writes with a stick in the sand "I.AM.A.," thus insuring future speculation about both his message and his identity as he sees it (*U* 13:1258-64). The difficulty, of course, comes in knowing which "pockets of darkness" will yield up secrets and which will not, for along with the invitation to probe into absence we have abundant evidence of Joyce's love for trickery. It is finally he who manipulates Bloom's stick, beckoning us to look closer.

Why Joyce should wish to employ subterfuge in *Dubliners* rather than targeting his enemies directly as he did in later works is obvious when one contemplates what actually happened to the collection of stories. Irish publishers such as Grant Richards and George Roberts, with whom Joyce negotiated about publication, anticipated censorship and demanded changes in the text; Roberts's printer John Falconer eventually destroyed the proofsheets. All had good reason to fear litigation that could have landed them in prison. Joyce's broadside "Gas from a Burner" (*CW* 243) was written out of a deep indignation at his treatment by Irish publishers.

Cheryl Herr mentions the heavy-handed intervention of Church and State in matters of publishing (176 n. 12) and clearly demonstrates by reference to "Aeolus" Joyce's "idea that art should not only circumvent the censor wherever possible but also eschew altogether the end-oriented rhetoric of politics, even when the end sought is the alleviation of ideological oppression" (142). Such cunning Stephen Dedalus would vow to practice; "*per vias rectas*" was the motto of the reactionary Garrett Deasy of "Nestor," but Joyce knew from the beginning that straight ways were dangerous. In 1915 Joyce's bitterness over censorship would equal D. H. Lawrence's at the suppression of *The Rainbow*. The key words on the first page of *Dubliners* reveal Joyce's concern with, maybe even his prediction of, censorship and persecution.

As Dubliners seek to fly by nets erected to keep them down, one of the chief benefits of an uncertainty principle emerges: stories may achieve greater depth and complexity and yet seem simple enough to have broad, popular appeal. (They are hence invaluable for teaching close reading to students.) Adopting a gnomonic perspective helps us to see more clearly the nature of Joyce's embittered social commentary, the interplay of presence and absence from the viewpoint of a subversive artist with a social conscience. Readers alerted to the implications of the three key words from the first, "trained" to read the stories skeptically, could feel more deeply the political impact they contain. In theory the author then need not fear censorship because libelous thoughts are in the reader's mind, not in the text. *Gnomon* therefore has the effect of enlisting a reader as co-creator in the production of meanings that are in harmony with the author's political concerns. Joyce thus evoked the odor of corruption that hangs over his stories, pointed the finger at the forces of oppression, and hoped to evade the consequences.[5] "Heard melodies are sweet, but those unheard / Are sweeter," not to mention safer to sing.

About a third of my book concerns *Dubliners* because readers associate Joycean experimentalism with the later works, but seldom if ever see that the uncertainty principle that generated much of the obscurity was in his work from the beginning. Still, such an approach is not without problems. While gnomonic structures often have political implications in *Dubliners*, or at least foster skepticism, some stories obviously fit the pattern better than others. We begin with a story about uncertainty in interpretation from a boy's more mature perspective in later years, and end with the mystery surrounding Gabriel Conroy's fading identity, but in between the three key words were not always uppermost in Joyce's mind. (Of course there is no reason why he should have felt bound by consistency.) But the general neglect of *Dubliners* in theoretical matters of broader scope has prompted me to say something about all the stories, and to argue that gnomonic absence in its early form often has moral and political implications, as when what is missing is some vital human quality such as love or compassion or empathy, emotions consistently absent in *Dubliners*. In some stories absence has little to do with mystery or uncertainty, but everything to do with privation. If this strategy is a weak link in my conceptual chain, then at the least it

[5] If this was Joyce's assumption, it turned out to be false. His publisher Grant Richards and the printer were to demand excisions of essential pieces that would mar his carefully uncompleted texts; i.e., their gnomonic strategy wasn't Joyce's.

provides two useful correctives: it emphasizes the radical politics of Joyce's youth, and it saves us from yet another series of discrete interpretations.

Structure and Meaning in "The Sisters"

On numerous occasions Joyce provided guideposts to interpretation (see Herring, *Joyce's Notes* 121-23), but it has not been generally accepted that "The Sisters" itself functions in that capacity. Still, the story is clearly about ambiguity, about the impossibility of reaching certainty. The reader encounters several barriers to understanding: the text is full of elliptical language filtered through the consciousness of a bewildered youth who broods over the deceased Father Flynn and the meaning of their friendship. Readers are easily deceived into thinking that the boy is merely naive, and that greater maturity would be an advantage to him in wrestling with the holes in meaning, an illusion that should be dispelled at the story's end when we are denied access to the boy's final thoughts. His reaction to new and probably decisive information is cloaked in ellipses, while the reader is left to fill in the gaps. Both reader and boy are frustrated by an unsuccessful exercise in gnomonic interpretation.

The opening lines of the early version of the story, published in *The Irish Homestead* in 1904 (*D* 243) illustrate that the uncertainty principle was already present (italics mine):[6]

> Three nights in succession I had found myself in Great Britain Street at that hour, as if by *providence*. Three nights I had raised my eyes to that lighted square of window and *speculated*. *I seemed to understand* that it would occur at night. But in spite of the providence which had led my feet and in spite of the reverent curiosity of my eyes *I had discovered nothing*.

[6] All references to Joyce's *Dubliners* (*D*) and *A Portrait of the Artist as a Young Man* (*AP*) are to the Viking Critical Editions. An earlier version of this chapter appeared as "Structure and Meaning in 'The Sisters,' " in Benstock, ed., *The Seventh of Joyce*.

This theme of uncertainty was reinforced in the story's final version with the addition of our three key words. Here the boy's interpretative difficulty, first attributed to fickle providence and human frailties, is now located in language itself: "Every night as I gazed up at the window I said softly to myself the word *paralysis*. It had always sounded strangely in my ears, like the word *gnomon* in the Euclid and the word *simony* in the Catechism" (*D* 9).

No logic binds these three italicized words together—only the strangeness of their sounds in the boy's ear. To him the meanings are private ones, perhaps only loosely connected, if at all, to dictionary definitions. The words seem to cast a spell over him and, at the same time, to point to many interpretive possibilities about which the sensitive reader may speculate. Father Flynn was a paralytic; what do *gnomon* and *simony* have to do with him? Can these terms be applied to anyone or anything else? Yet the reader, like the boy, is impelled to seek a truth he can never find: the three words provide no illumination, but neither are they meaningless. This is the dilemma of following the lead of the author-critic-tease who provides keys to understanding an ambiguous text. We shall see how it is possible to use one term—*gnomon*—as an instrument of interpretation within this curious epistemological framework.

Let us take a closer look at the key words. The narrator of *A Portrait* says of young Stephen Dedalus, "Words which he did not understand he said over and over to himself till he had learned them by heart: and through them he had glimpses of the real world about him" (*AP* 62). The comprehension of key concepts is also the primary means of orientation for the boy in "The Sisters," who, with the reader, may see that the magical word that has preoccupied him—*paralysis*—describes considerably more than Father Flynn's physical debility. In the final story of *Dubliners,* "The Dead," the word "dead"—that final paralysis—may refer not only to those faithful departed, but to their survivors; in this first story *paralysis* is applicable both to the priest (it has become his *rigor mortis*) and to those who mourn him, perhaps even his young friend in his interpretive dilemma, or even the reader. Upon reflection we are meant to see that it is epidemic in Ireland's capital (*D* 269; Joyce, *Letters* 1:55; 2:134).

Like most of Joyce's work, "The Sisters" is about transcendence, in this case how a young boy wishes to elude the authority of elders, who unwittingly inhibit the youth's spiritual and intellectual growth, who are instructive only as negative examples. His impatience indicates that his uncle and Mr. Cotter are antagonists, a class eventually to be joined by the sisters of Father Flynn and perhaps the priest himself. More than age, what distinguishes the boy from the others is a condition of mind: the boy knows he knows little and seeks to arrive at understanding through inquiry, while the others think they know and obviously do not, long ago having given up the search for meaning. He is open to learning and experience, they are not. A condition of mind such as the elders have could be called *paralysis*, though, ironically, the boy will approach no nearer the truth than they. Still, his struggle to interpret is more noble than their acquiescence.

Upon reflection, a reader might first be struck with the gnomonic nature of the story's language: it is elliptical, evasive, sometimes mysterious. A mystery is there to be uncovered, but boy and reader will be frustrated by language in their attempts to solve it. We do know that it concerns the priest's vocation, his apparently forced retirement due to the effects of paralysis (however that is defined), and the exact nature of his friendship with the boy, for whom all this is an area of experience cast in perpetual shadow. The boy seems totally dependent on his elders (who won't knowingly cooperate) for information, just as the reader is on the text. Candlelight on a darkened blind (a geometrical form partially cast in light) may tell the boy that the priest is dead, but that will hardly be an issue. Too many pieces are missing from the puzzle for him to see the picture clearly. Even when important pieces are filled in, such as at the story's end, neither boy nor reader is party to any epiphany.

Gnomonic language works as follows: if the boy eschews dictionary meanings, unsympathetic characters in "The Sisters" misuse words and fracture sentence structure. Associated with their narrative style is the ellipsis, which presents hiatuses of meaning that can only be filled in by readers or listeners.[7] The tiresome, pipe-puffing Mr. Cotter, speaking of the dead priest, says, "There was something queer . . . there was something uncanny about him. I'll tell you my opinion . . ." (*D* 9-10), thus producing spaces in meaning while he hints at a clerical weakness that he cannot or will not articulate. Even the boy falters at one point when comparing the atmosphere of his mysterious dream to Persia. Like us, he is baffled by these holes in meaning: "I puzzled my head to extract meaning from his [Cotter's] unfinished sentences" (*D* 11). Ellipses frequently signify euphony, especially in the final section, and at the story's end they could theoretically prod the reader toward eventual illumination.

Questing characters in *Dubliners* are frequently assaulted by something I call a "tyranny of triteness," being vacuous language or malapropisms spoken by people who await them at their destinations. In "The Sisters," the boy hears misnomers like "the *Freeman's General*" for "the *Freeman's Journal*," "rheumatic" for "pneumatic" wheels, and ritual dialogue. These signs of defective language are appropriate to the conversation's subject—a defective priest. Father Flynn "was too scrupulous always," Eliza says. "The duties of the priesthood was too much for him. And then his life was, you might say, crossed." (These hollow phrases, pumped so long for meaning by the critics, are meant to evoke laughter in the reader as they must have in Joyce.) Speaking at cross purposes, the aunt says, "He was a disappointed man. You could see that" (*D* 17).

This exchange occurs as part of a ritual dialogue of condolence that Joyce must have heard at funerals or wakes.[8] It is the gesture that is important, for the ritual words themselves are not really vehicles for direct communication. The dialogue be-

[7] Ellipses are a prominent feature of the epiphanies collected in Scholes and Kain and in other *Dubliners* stories, where they often function merely as pauses in narration. See also Marilyn French.

[8] On the decorum of wake visits, see pages 379-80 of the very thorough article by Florence Walzl, "Joyce's 'The Sisters': A Development."

gins (*D* 15) with the aunt saying "Ah, well, he's gone to a better world." One expects to learn nothing, yet the shocker comes when the sisters deviate from traditional inanity to reveal information about their brother that the priest would have wished left unsaid. This the boy must try to evaluate, but the story's final ellipses prevent readers from gauging his success.

The first sentence of "The Sisters" describes the hopelessness of Father Flynn's physical condition by saying that his time is growing short: "It was the third stroke." Immediately thereafter we are told that the school term is over—"it was vacation time," which here denotes free time within a school calendar and may hint at the story's theme of freedom and bondage. In the night a rectangular window is lighted in the priest's house; if he is dead two candles will illuminate his head, while his feet are cast in relative darkness. If some words or silences are significant, clichés like *"I am not long for this world"* are thought "idle." All this play on light and shadow, presence and absence, is set forth in the first half page of "The Sisters."

As we read along, the word *gnomon* suggests additional possibilities: the boy lacks direction and guidance; he is told to box his corner as if his life had geometric shape; like the story his dream is open-ended; he usually sits in the corner of the priest's room. Father Flynn lacks a whole chalice, an intact vocation, muscular coordination, a confessor to absolve him, an appropriate vehicle in which to revisit the house of his youth. His mourners "gazed at the empty fireplace" in his room (*D* 15); the fallen chalice "contained nothing." An obsolete meaning of *gnomon* is "nose" (*OED*), the cavities of which Father Flynn attempts to fill with snuff, though the greater part falls on his vestments. Boy and priest are counterparts as failed clerics, a small corner in the geometric shape of the Church in Ireland, but one of real significance. Like their fellow Dubliners, they are gnomonic in their needs, gnomonic in their representativeness, and their story is gnomonic in that the precise description of their problems, and the remedies thereof, are left to the reader.

Simony reinforces *gnomon* and *paralysis* as a thematic key for understanding the story's central problem—what the boy and priest meant to each other. The term may be a broad paintbrush for church walls in Ireland, but it also works on the individual level. Father Flynn's own indoctrination program could in part have had personal gain as its motive; having cracked a chalice and lost a vocation, whatever guilt he might suffer could possibly be expiated by providing a clerical replacement. Spiritually, says Thomas E. Connolly, Father Flynn "has become a 'remainder after something else is removed,' a gnomon" (Connolly, " 'The Sisters' ": 195). If, in addition, he is "not all there" mentally as well as physically incapable of coordination, this defective priest who is, after all, defined in terms of vocation, might from impure motives be capable of seeking a replacement for himself. The boy's preoccupation with *simony* might indicate an awareness that this trap has been evaded, but he too suffers from a kind of gnomonic vacancy in terms of vocation and experience.

The boy's dream of the priest trying to confess to him may be the beginning of the boy's awareness of impropriety. To hear the priest's confession is to accept the priestly vocation. Though this happens in a dream, he is aware of coercion and feels his "soul receding into some pleasant and vicious region" (*D* 11), where, unwanted, the priest follows. We cannot know whether or not the priest has committed the sin of simony, but his young friend is definitely suspicious that he has been coerced by an old teacher who at the least has charged a tuition in snuff.

Perhaps not fully aware of these conditions, the boy in "The Sisters" is nevertheless sufficiently repulsed by his world to seek spiritual guidance from an old priest whose physical debility would frighten most children. He has the disconcerting habit, for instance, of uncovering "big discoloured teeth" when he smiles, and draping his tongue over his lower lip (*D* 13). Though by no means homosexual or sado-masochistic, as some critics have suggested, their relationship has become symbiotic: the boy seeks escape and guidance through admission to a new and different world. A Persia of strange customs being unattainable except in dreams, he explores the mysteries, rituals, sacred lore of the Church. The priest, who no longer officially represents the Church in Ireland (critics have mostly said otherwise), takes a disciple as the main reason for his existence and a reliable source of snuff. Fellow Dubliners are conviced that he is defective both mentally and physically, but what life and mind he has left are dedicated to instructing a neophyte. (An early draft reads, "His life was so methodical and uneventful. I think he said more to me than to anyone else" [*D* 247]). Aware of this bond, the boy imagines his "heavy grey face" following him in a dream, desiring to confess something. What secrets he learns, if any, are appropriately unrevealed. Like the story, the dream is gnomonic, or open-ended. The central point, however, is the boy's awareness that he was meant to fill the paralytic's shoes.

The boy's singleminded desire in the story is to understand what this relationship meant—the death of the priest and the process of clarification representing the end of one kind of quest and the beginning of another that we suspect has something to do with language. Freed from the constraints of the classroom (it is vacation time), he will free himself from the effects of a more sinister form of indoctrination, yet will stay to contemplate this strange disease, to "look upon its deadly work" (*D* 9). He senses a mystery here—why does this paralysis suggest to him "some maleficent and sinful being" (*D* 9)? Do Mr. Cotter and his uncle think *any* tutorial relationship between a boy and a priest unnatural, or do they know something, do their ellipses hide unspoken meaning? Their opposition, plus the sinister dream and the boy's sense of newly won freedom prepare him (us) to interpret the concluding scene, where general awkwardness in verbal expression (a function of paralysis?) and a dominant quality of mind as shabby as the setting prepare for what promises to be a moment of illumination.

The structure of a number of the stories in *Dubliners* requires the protagonists to leave their familiar world on quests that end up shocking them into an awareness that life in their city is far uglier than they ever imagined it to be. In his "scrupulous meanness" (*D* 269) Joyce sends them to one destination to have them arrive at another. Epiphany, or clarification, if and when it comes, arrives suddenly and in the oddest circumstances, in the first three stories resulting in the protagonists' frustration with their previous naiveté and a noticeably more cynical attitude. This is the process of maturation for the boys in *Dubliners*.

"The Sisters" sets the stage for epiphany by the ironic fusion of ecclesiastical ritual and the decorum of wake visits. With the priest dead and coffined, the sisters are now in charge (thus the title), and in their benign ignorance they reveal secrets perhaps hinted at by Mr. Cotter and the uncle.

Understandably, the boy cannot pray. The sisters of the priest of the cracked chalice offer a communion of crackers and sherry, unconsecrated yet unmistakable. Ritual questions lead to revelation—to a new knowledge of Father Flynn's paralysis in both the physical and spiritual sense. Reluctant to traffic in secrets, the boy has tried to escape the priest's dream confession, but he has also sought clarification. Now it will come. In the final section, ritual questions about peaceful death, extreme unction, and resignation are followed by a shocking comment (the first in a series) about a woman brought in to wash the corpse, who comments on its beauty (*D* 15). Unwittingly, Eliza betrays her brother's memory as materialist imagery betrays all hope of transcendence. Her vulgarity offends the boy's sense of delicacy and prepares for what promises to be the final rejection of his defunct vocational model.

If "The Sisters" is seen as a geometric structure, then one part of it will always remain in shadow. Indeed, the elusive title suggests that meaning will be displaced. With an uncertainty principle in evidence, interpretation must thus involve speculation about textual meaning, and what follows is mine: If Father Flynn has sought to bind his novice, he has probably freed him instead; if he has wished to indoctrinate him, it is surely the example of what he became that made the more lasting impression. Whatever transcendence the youth has gained, it involves not religion, but a deeper knowledge of what it is to know. Like the boys in "An Encounter" and "Araby," or Little Chandler in "A Little Cloud," the price he pays for such rude instruction will be a sense of humiliation that will not soon fade. The protagonists in all of these stories have sought light, positive images, and have been taught by negatives, shadows, the incomplete geometric shape instead of the whole one. The last sentence of "The Sisters" describes Father Flynn in the confession box; like the coffin that will contain him, it is a rectangular shape, now in shadow, now in light. The door is opened to reveal him laughing to himself, but what precisely causes this laughter, what it means, or what its consequences for his vocation will remain forever in doubt. The story's final ellipses do leave space for our minds to focus on unspoken implications, but the reader must supply the missing pieces for the puzzle to be complete.

Boy and reader in "The Sisters" seem to follow a parallel course in their struggle with meaning, but this is actually an illusion. The boy interprets the world as text, and the reader interprets the text as world. A sophisticated reader, recognizing the self-reflexive qualities of the story, can also read the text as text and consider its playfulness, but whereas there is no limit to the range of readers who may read the story, there is only one protagonist-narrator, and his level of sophistication can be established within a narrow compass. Though he narrates, he cannot read the text, nor can he be responsible for the range of possible meanings there. Though obliged to read the world as text, he cannot read the world as world, and denied a glimpse at that epiphanic moment, the reader cannot know at the story's end how much the boy has learned about his world or even what the more mature narrator knows. Even if both decipher, the nature of their ignorance differs because of a time gap and the struggle of narration, differing as well from that of any reader.

In the end, a potential advantage lies with the reader, for the words of the text, regardless of slippery etymologies, do not change, while the boy-narrator must deal with shifting impressions based on incomplete information about a forbidden subject. Consciously or unconciously, the narrator provides the reader with signposts to meaning, even if nobody in the text's world seems willing to render the narrator a similar service.

Indians and Other Subversives: "An Encounter"

"An Encounter" is the second part of a larger thesis on a boy's frustrated search for transcendence. Religion having been dismissed as a plausible vehicle, the focus is now on adventure. Though there is the familiar pattern of quest followed by disillusionment, the sociological structure is now more complex. Our youth (not necessarily the same one) is still opposed by authority, but with the years his questions about identity have become troublesome as well. He is torn between the need to conform in the classroom and the need to have adventures in the outdoors. With one part of himself he submits, and with another he rebels. In the story this behavior is normal and necessary to growth; the boy's problem, however, is that the avenues of escape he chooses set him apart from other boys. He must define himself in relation to two authority structures—that of the grown-up world and that of his peer group. If he conforms in both ways, he is untrue to himself, yet if he rebels he may become ostracized like the old gentleman he meets later in the story. He realizes the importance of doing well in school and playing those games endorsed by his fellows, but his keenly felt differences cannot so easily be dismissed. Somewhere in between open rebellion and total conformity, the young subversive must find his way.

The atmosphere is quite different from the claustrophobic one of "The Sisters," as if the young boy had indeed decided to "box his corner" and abandon mystic impulses. All avenues lead abroad, outdoors, away from schoolroom, home, introspection, all that is familiar. The story opens with the experiential context that defines both movement and meaning: our model—Joe Dillon—has been so influenced by reading Westerns that he lives the part of an Indian brave, organizing battles in which he always triumphs over the younger boys (*D*

19). Juxtaposed to that imaginary world of the Wild West is the reality of eight-o'clock mass and Dillon's unexpected "vocation for the priesthood," where he will be obliged to lead a life of order and self-discipline. The question implicit in his example is: how does one live freely, passionately, disregarding rules and consequences with one part of the self—the self at play—while with another part embodying those qualities prerequisite for a life of rigid conformity? At the story's opening is Joe Dillon, who succeeds at the integration of these contradictions, while at the conclusion is the example of a haunted figure who has failed.

It surprises the protagonist that this work-play dichotomy seems normal, yet he finds it difficult to conform both to the exigencies of school and to the avenues of escape preferred by his fellows. This is how he knows he is different. Fearing to seem "studious or lacking in robustness," and attracted by the prospect of escape and excitement, the boy becomes a reluctant Indian, as critics have named him, one whose sense of adventure is carefully described by his literary tastes. Preferring detective stories (Wild West adventures being "remote from [his] nature"), he nevertheless acquiesces in the literature of the tribe. Father Butler, a pillar of orthodoxy who takes for his text Roman history, would condemn both genres. Furthermore, his text is as deceptive as the world of Dublin and the lives of its citizens: there is the public face of Rome that boys encounter in expurgated schoolbooks, and a private one of gossip and blacklisted works that hides scandals and orgies perhaps unsurpassed in all the world's histories. Into the classroom where pupils study the ordered, sanitized portion of the history of an empire that was the epitome of the simultaneous triumph of culture and decadence, boys like Joe's brother Leo bring forbidden "chronicles of disorder" (*D* 20-21). Leo's is called *The Apache Chief*, a work that is probably as divorced from reality as his Roman history text. These subversive works obviously satisfy more than a boy's taste for adventure; in the story they challenge orthodoxy, and hint at youth's need to learn about and experience a forbidden world that hypocritical adults want to keep all to themselves, which the boys sense exists not only in books, but all around them. The city has its red-light district, and each person has his hidden lusts.

Emerging ever more clearly in "An Encounter" is the idea of contiguous worlds where one part is decent, ordinary, normal, the world of day—and another the opposite of these, which is hidden from view. Internalized, these dichotomies account for Jekyll-Hyde personalities; society accepts Joe Dillon as normal while abhorring the behavior of the old "pervert." The protagonist suspects that a similar internal tension accounts for his feeling extraordinary, that his bookish taste may indicate hidden unacceptable tendencies. Fearing this, he seeks to merge his life with the dominant group rather than exploring the meaning of his difference in isolation. He suppresses the bookworm in his nature, joins the tribe, genuinely shares in their feeling of alienation in the classroom and, like them, fears the authority of teachers. But the contiguous worlds of classroom and tribe must remain mutually exclusive; when Leo Dillon is caught with *The Apache Chief* in his desk, it is to the protagonist not merely a punishable breach of decorum. For him Indians have come to represent socially acceptable personas he can assume when his conforming self is eclipsed by that hidden side of his nature nourished by hormones and the imagination.

Soon he begins to "hunger again for wild sensations" (*D* 20), to experience in person the full meaning of that world he senses yet cannot see. Literature is no longer enough, nor is the "mimic warfare of the evening" (*D* 21). Since real adventures "must be sought abroad," and during school time, he plans a day's miching with Leo and Mahony. Except in "The Dead," where directional movement is complicated, in *Dubliners* one moves eastward to experience new life, adventure, or the future; thus the boy's destination is the Pigeon House, at Dublin's most easterly point. On the eve of the appointed day the conspirators shake hands; the next morning, appropriately, the unnamed boy hides his books and walks to the rendezvous point. All is joy, sunlight, expectation, undampened by Leo's failure to show. But his absence is the first omen that all will not go according to plan. Two companions appear, one remains hidden; this void will be filled by another who will define the geometric shape of their adventure.

Once out of "public sight" (*D* 22), Mahony asserts his Indian aspect, chasing ragged children who mistake him for a Protestant rather than a warrior brave. One tame event follows another as, the narrator states, "school and home seemed to recede from us and their influences upon us seemed to wane" (*D* 23). Conditions become right for meaningful events. As the day wanes, movement toward the Pigeon House is diverted to the bank of the Dodder—perverted, one almost wishes to say. Darker omens predominate: Mahony is unhappy, clouds obscure the sun, the companions' thoughts have turned jaded and their provisions to crumbs (*D* 24). In the protagonist's imagination green eyes will somehow be a clue to the adventure that eludes him, with the same intuitive logic with which his counterpart in "The Sisters" senses the importance of paralysis in his quest. Just as the protagonist is chewing a green stem, a man approaches, "shabbily dressed in a suit of greenish-black" (*D* 24), one who will peer out of "bottle-green eyes" beneath "a twitching forehead" (*D* 27).

Like the truant boys, this gentleman with the good accent lives in camouflage. He too has gone abroad in search of adventure and, like Father Flynn, will instruct by negative example. The boys use false names; they pretended to go to school, yet went in another direction. The man's movements are equally deceptive: he walks past them slowly, retraces his steps and seems to be looking for something in the grass. What he says is described to us by subject until the first actual line of verbatim dialogue, which speaks directly of the central dichotomies that have caused the protagonist to feel extraordinary: "—Ah, I can see you are a bookworm like myself. Now, he added, pointing to Mahony who was regarding us with open eyes, he is different: he goes in for games" (*D* 25).

The boy cannot contradict this distinction, but is suspicious of the overtures he invites in pretending to have read every book title the stranger mentions. He wishes not to appear as stupid as Mahony, who is satisfied to chase cats (*D* 24), because he also attaches importance to the distinction made.

After some chitchat about the romantic, escapist literature he prefers (it is not the Wild West), the man tantalizes them with a further distinction—between the works of Lord Lytton boys may and may not read. The appropriateness of this point must make the entire conversation seem uncanny to the protagonist, given that his central questions have to do with the relationship between "rubbish" books and acceptable ones, escapist fiction and real adventures, the rote learning of the schoolroom versus the forbidden knowledge gained through truancy or illicit reading.

With his foot in the door, the gentleman turns from literature to life, and with a "strangely liberal" air begins to question the boys about sweethearts. His behavior grows increasingly odd. As he dwells on the sensual details of girls' hands and hair, he shivers. "Magnetised by some words of his own speech, his mind was slowly circling round and round in the same orbit." This hypnotic monologue is very revealing: it seems intended to arouse the boys sexually ("all girls were not so good as they seemed to be if one only knew"), to lull them into complacent intimacy, and to promise secret knowledge such as might be found in banned books (he "spoke mysteriously as if he were telling us something secret" [*D* 26]). His masturbatory incantation serves only to arouse his own feelings, however, and he soon steps into a field, presumably to fondle and exhibit himself.[9]

We have now moved from the realm of books and fantasy to the scene of a visually witnessed act of public conduct far more illicit than miching. Now we are out of the boy's world of make-believe and into an adult one of real psychological depth and complexity. An aggressive tribe of Indians besmeared

[9] In " 'An Encounter,' " Fritz Senn says that the old man definitely masturbates (31). This is anybody's guess, but his subsequent behavior seems to indicate continued sexual excitement.

with warpaint they could understand, but no experience has prepared the boys for this present danger.

The final section of the story corresponds to the female dialogue scene of "The Sisters." While the boy in the first story has sought out a mentor figure, the one in "An Encounter" meets his inadvertently, but the mentor enters at precisely the same moment in their development—when forbidden knowledge is required. If the second story ended where the first one does, there might be a shocking moment of recognition, shared both by reader and presumably by quest figure, that those Dubliners who deviate from the acceptable codes of behavior become outcasts so isolated that their need for love and companionship may express itself in actions that appear normal at one moment and insane in the next. This old man, whose literary tastes the boy shares, is an example of what happens to those who are forced to suppress a dimension of their nature that society considers monstrous. The danger has two aspects: the boy may be attacked physically; or his nonconformity may eventually result in ostracism or homosexuality or some similar "madness." As in "The Sisters," the boy must be wary lest he be compelled to fill the old man's shoes, his life to become a "chronicle of disorder."[10] The structure of "An Encounter" has thus been extended to reveal a more precise definition of the model's defect and the boy's reaction to it.

In "The Sisters" the first dialogue is male and the second is female; here the subject of the first hypnotic monologue is girls, and on the man's return from the field it is boys. When discussing girls, he massages the listener with his words; when he circles around his new subject, as if to pounce, the tone in which he speaks about the necessity of whipping boys

[10] James P. Degnan says that this story emphasizes how overcivilization leads to perversion and decadence; the boy thus sees that "his virtues, sensitivity, intelligence, imagination, and conscientiousness have in them the seeds of the vices the old man embodies" (155). Overcivilization is hardly Joyce's subject; rather it is nonconformity and its consequences. It must be said, however, that Degnan's article is one of the few on this story good enough to argue with.

chastises and threatens. Forgetting "his recent liberalism" (*D* 27) and his view that "every boy . . . has a little sweetheart" (*D* 25), the man now says that "if a boy had a girl for a sweetheart and told lies about it then he would give him such a whipping as no boy ever got in this world. He said that there was nothing in this world he would like so well as that. He described to me how he would whip such a boy as if he were unfolding some elaborate mystery" (*D* 27).

Perhaps too fascinated with the grotesque behavior of his fellow bookworm, the boy fails to sense the danger. When Mahony abandons him to chase a cat, he is alone with this sinister figure. Away from the classroom and public eye, the Dillons and Mahonys of Dublin pretend to be Indians, to play at scalping palefaces, but the sensitive boy's knowledge of the Wild West at play and in books has done little to prepare him for a sadist's ambush. At first the elderly gent is partially in shadow—conventional to the point of boredom in chatting about the weather, his school days, then books. However, literature quickly leads to controversy, to young girls, and, finally, to verbal and manual stroking of self. His stepping into the field is a moment of transformation when Dr. Jekyll seems about to become Mr. Hyde.

Lacking the experience to comprehend the "old josser," the forbidden knowledge he has intuitively awaited in order to fill in a blank area in his understanding proves to be too shocking for the boy. He tries to appear calm as he moves away, but he feels ashamed that he must employ the "paltry stratagem" of calling Mahony to the rescue.

The last line—"And I was penitent; for in my heart I had always despised him a little" (*D* 28)—contains no ellipses, but as a final statement it is certainly elliptical in meaning, and supports the general theme of deception. It is a good example of Joyce's uncertainty principle at work in closure, for readers are invited back into the story on a wild goose chase for evidence that will help them understand what masquerades as an epiphanic moment. But the closural incongruity seems downright flippant, for "An Encounter" is not about how superior the protagonist feels to Mahony, but about how necessary to youth is the bold spirit of adventure that the young "Indian" personifies.[11]

In turning his back on bookish talk and strange behavior to chase cats, Mahony, like Joe Dillon, is, in conventional terms, an example of what a "normal" boy should be. But is it not normal to be inquisitive, the story seems to ask? In probing the more obscure corners of life and literature, the protagonist is unfaithful both to the conventions of his tribe and to the occasion (a day of miching); the result is that he has lost courage (and face) during a short holiday that has turned to nightmare. This attempt at transcendence through adventure having failed, he will henceforth try harder to dominate his rebellious spirit. Beyond the question of courage, which seems here more the product of blindness than insight into the mystery of human nature the story lays bare, Joyce has raised sociological questions for us to explore without giving us direction. Like the boy in "The Sisters," the one in "An Encounter" has received a frightening glimpse into the heart of a Dublin grotesque at an age so impressionable that the experience may safely be termed traumatic. Regardless of their personal sense of identification with the two grotesques, at a premature age they have both gained knowledge of the horrifying isolation that is the lot of Dubliners whose natures make it impossible to conform to the "normal" codes of behavior.

Structurally, the final scene imitates the gnomonic pattern of the larger question asked by the story: what is the relationship of the hidden portion of human experience to the total geometric shape of life and literature in Dublin? (In personal terms, how do square pegs fit into round holes, the only holes

[11] Degnan concentrates on explicating the story's ending as the key to meaning. I think it is indeterminate. He sees the protagonist's contempt for Mahony as the contempt "the man of thought feels for the man of action" (153). True in part, but the problem is of greater complexity since the final statement is basically a non sequitur. The boy has sought to emulate the Mahonys and Dillons; why should he feel penitent that he has depised them? Is there evidence in the story that he has?

society permits to exist?) While the questions are obviously important to the story, all answers would be tainted with uncertainty, especially if formulated by an inexperienced schoolboy recovering from shock.

Structural Balance in "Araby"

"Araby" is the last in a set of three stories about how a youth is thwarted in his quest for transcendence. Each of the stories begins in the tedious surroundings of home or school, in reaction to which boys set for themselves idealized destinations involving eastward journeys: in one case it is a mystical state of mind associated with the priesthood, exotic dreams, and Persia; in the next story it is the Pigeon House at the most easterly point of Dublin's harbor (and anything that might symbolize). In the third story a bazaar named "Araby" casts an eastern enchantment over an adolescent mind. A further common characteristic is that the boys lack a kind of enlightenment necessary for their graduation to a more advanced stage of maturity; this they may eventually achieve, but the greatest benefit of their shocking *rites de passage* will be to illustrate the uncertainty principle of life itself.

"Araby" immediately reveals structural and thematic links to its two predecessors:

> North Richmond Street, being blind, was a quiet street except at the hour when the Christian Brothers' School set the boys free. An uninhabited house of two storeys stood at the blind end, detached from its neighbors in a square ground. The other houses of the street, conscious of decent lives within them, gazed at one another with brown impeturbable faces. (*D* 29)

Metaphorically speaking, the most serious problem for the young boys in *Dubliners* is their blindness, i.e., a youthful naiveté accompanied by introversion, sensitivity, and romanticism (as the protagonists understand the term) that makes them shun the tedious reality of their daily lives. Blindness was, of course, literally Joyce's most enduring affliction, and the biographical strain in the stories is salient enough to remind us that for him this condition had a special meaning. (In *A Portrait*, for instance, the breaking of Stephen's eyeglasses on the cinder path brings him unjust punishment and humiliation, primary determining factors in his evolution as an artist. In the temporary dimness of vision Stephen sees for the first time his powerlessness.)

To describe the boy's street in "Araby" Joyce could have written "cul-de-sac," the standard term on Irish street signs, or even "dead end" in the American sense, equally suggestive, but he used "blind" to foreshadow the boy's fruitless quest. (Later the boy spies on Mangan's sister from beneath a window blind.) This blind street may indeed be a "synecdoche for all the ways of Dublin" as Edward Brandabur suggests (51), but North Richmond was also a real "cul-de-sac," and Joyce lived on it in 1894 when he was twelve, during which time the "Araby" bazaar was a featured attraction in Dublin.[12]

Joyce uses the street to illuminate oppositions in ironic ways. Geometrically it resembles a *gnomon*—a parallelogram disabled at one side for traffic to pass while the other end is closed off.[13] On the blind end of the street is an uninhabited house "in a square ground"; a neighboring house is occupied by surrogate parents apparently blind to the implications of a boy's restless spirit. On the weak, open-ended side of the *gnomon*, facing the vacant house is the exit through which he will travel to "Araby" on an errand that will force him to see that he has been a romantic fool and that the bazaar is a place that caters to such as he.

In addition to blindness and seeing, closed and open, there are other dichotomies. The street is quiet except after school. During school hours the boys are confined, so that when they are released they celebrate their freedom noisily. One house is empty, the others are inhabited. The inhabited houses are conscious of decent lives within, while by implication some Dublin houses must be conscious of indecent lives within, or

[12] See Ellmann, *James Joyce*, 110, Plate III; and Atherton, "Araby" (40).

[13] Cf. Friedrich, "The Perspective": 73.

perhaps some are just unconscious. The strategy of personification may imply that houses must be inhabited to be conscious, since the segregated house seems distinct from its neighbors as much in its lack of awareness as in its location at the blind end. Occupied houses see the reality of their inhabitants' lives; the vacant one has neither inner light nor tenants to be conscious about.

The boy is likewise set apart from his neighbors, oblivious of the inner lives of people he meets—dislocated too through a self-conscious and adolescent romanticism from more typically extroverted boys with whom he has ceased to play. Like the boys in "The Sisters" and "An Encounter," he knows he is different, but unlike them his psychological isolation depends upon blindness to the epiphanies of his world that point vulgarly toward the antiromantic nature of reality. In geometric terms his vision creates gnomonic structures, illuminating one level of experience while blocking out others;[14] if *gnomon* can be a metaphor for inadequacy, as in the case of Father Flynn, then we are dealing with a figure who lacks the vision, experience, and maturity to play the role he has chosen for himself.

The second paragraph reinforces the imagery and opposition of the first by stressing vacancy and decay, and by introducing a protagonist-narrator who seems attracted to the musty smells of vacant rooms. The dead priest, so charitable to institutions, has left behind useless papers, three old books, and a rusty bicycle pump that would fit neatly into T. S. Eliot's "Rhapsody on a Windy Night." Stone (344-67) and Atherton ("Araby") labor to show that each of the books is a thematic key, but the titles probably have just enough relevance to encourage readers to inflate them with meaning. (After all, Joyce supplied the pump.) There is no indication that the boy has read them, especially since he views them as physical objects, preferring the one with yellow leaves. Like his predecessors in

[14] A prerequisite for this selective blindness is isolation, a topic emphasized in Brooks and Warren. Meaningful interaction or communication with others is avoided since apparently the boy believes nobody can help him find his way.

Dubliners, what he seeks is not to be found in books but in the daily life around him.

Despite his affinity for darkness, enclosed spaces, and musty smells, the protagonist enjoys playing outdoors. Yet rough play with the neighborhood children, though exhilarating, loses its appeal as he succumbs to a more mature, more private kind of stimulation. Joyce's imagery of light and darkness, often remarked upon, serves not so much to emphasize the gloom of Dublin seasons as to highlight the confused tensions in the lives of his characters. When dusk falls, the houses grow somber; feeble lanterns stretch out to a violet sky. In this obscurity the children play till their "bodies [glow]." There are "dark muddy lanes," "dark dripping gardens"; "light from kitchen windows" shines through the darkness; when the uncle returns or Mangan's sister appears to call her brother to dinner, the children elude them by hiding in the shadow. From there the protagonist peers at another shadowy figure—Mangan's sister—"her figure defined by the light from the half-opened door." (Voyeuristic scenes in *A Portrait* and *Ulysses* are, of course, foreshadowed.) In door and window Joyce chooses to reemphasize gnomonic shape along with the interplay of light and darkness, vision and blindness, though in the window he has reversed the dark-light aspect to form a shaded rectangle with light entering the lower section: "The blind was pulled down to within an inch of the sash so that I could not be seen" (*D* 30).

Unlike Stephen and Bloom who were only momentarily enchanted, respectively, by the "bird girl" and Gerty MacDowell, the hero of "Araby" feels a passionate commitment of many days duration; but like them he too will find that silent encounters with feminine beauty provide insight, though neither gratification nor commitment. In each case the silent language of adoration is more prayerful Mariology than Petrarchan laudation, with fantasy playing an important role. This somewhat obtrusive religious imagery of "Araby" conforms to the movements of expectation and disappointment, the central journey pattern in the stories of youth (just as it is in most of Joyce's narrative units describing maturation). Imitating a courtly love tradition of which he is presumably ignorant, the boy creates a false madonna and worships her fervently; upon arriving at the bazaar on "this night of Our Lord" (*D* 33), he immediately recognizes "a silence like that which pervades a church after a service" (*D* 34), and might well be reminded of the money-changers in the Temple, as several critics surmise.

Brooks and Warren note that during the latter part of "Araby" the boy's confusion is emphasized. It is a condition he actively magnifies, believing it necessary to romantic euphoria, a confusion of the senses prefigured both by the play upon blindness and by his misuse of the language of prayerful adoration. True, it is the only vocabulary the youth has for praising feminine virtue, but he uses it for self-intoxication rather than wooing: "her name was like a summons to all my foolish blood" (*D* 30); "her name sprang to my lips at moments in strange prayers and praises which I myself did not understand"; "how could I tell her of my confused adoration"; "I was thankful that I could see so little. All my senses seemed to desire to veil themselves"; "when she addressed the first words to me I was so confused that I did not know what to answer" (*D* 31). But like the bird girl and Gerty MacDowell, Mangan's sister hears no words of praise.

Confusion gives way to an intense determination to reach "Araby." Obstacles impede his way, but he completes the third journey of the *Dubliners* collection. His counterpart in "The Sisters" while paying his respects to the dead sought to clarify the nature of his friendship with the priest; in "An Encounter" the boy seeks through adventure to transcend the daily tedium of his life; for his part, the protagonist of "Araby" sets out to purchase a trophy that will make him seem desirable to Mangan's sister. Whether the vehicle for transcendence is religion, adventure, or romantic encounter, the result of each journey is displacement, shock, self-ridicule, and a new awareness of self and world (in "The Sisters" a process implied rather than described).

In "Araby" one sign that the destination is a mirage not of

desert sands but of cityscape is the story's title, with its suggestion of a music-hall backdrop; another is the boy's use of an unexpected bazaar entrance. Clearly he has encountered in the external world a carefully devised confusion to balance the internal one he has nurtured. The purpose of the bazaar is to make money by providing an exotic atmosphere that appeals to the Dubliners' need for adventure or romance, hence the imagery of usury (Mrs. Mercer; the constant clink of coins; the buying and selling of wares). The boy's blindness to reality, his incessant confusion, his use of Mangan's sister to promote a sustained euphoria—the pressures of adolescence have steered him into a very antiromantic, commercial port of call.

In "Araby" Joyce's delicate balancing of the particular elements of the boy's romantic expectation with those present in the bazaar was a brilliant achievement. Quester and goal are each gnomonic shapes that complete each other. The enamored youth deludes himself, the bazaar deludes the populace; the false romance of the youth's delusion encounters the bogus romance of the Café Chantant and "Araby"; his earlier blindness to all that inhibited his romantic vision is finally dispelled by epiphany, the sudden clarity of insight being timed to match his waning view of this darkening vanity fair.

Since the first three *Dubliners* stories form a trilogy of youth, the key words on the first page were made to unlock meanings in all three stories, but they must be stretched slightly to fit the context, just as the boy in "The Sisters" does, until they reinforce a unity of design and help to unravel the three enigmatic endings. Although we are not always told precisely what the boys feel, they seem momentarily to share in the paralysis discovered before turning hurriedly away in a panic of self-awareness. (The ending of "The Sisters" does not show this, but any projection of geometric lines beyond the final ellipses would likely show parallels with the next two endings.) The boys of "The Sisters" and "Araby" obviously have simoniacal relationships, since some kind of commercial exchange is involved in their attachment to priest and madonna figures. As we have seen, gnomonic structures, accompanied by the interplay of light and dark images, become essential components in the boy's "seeing" both sweetheart and bazaar. An incomplete figure himself due to romantic blindness and immaturity, he travels in the rectangular shape of "a third-class carriage of a deserted train" and en route spies "the lighted dial of a clock" (*D* 34), the tardy hour of which forecasts the hopelessness of his journey. No series of ellipses is necessary to call our attention to what is missing in either the romantic impulse or in the structure he imagines to be the instrument of his fulfillment.

"Araby" turns out to be "a large building"; inside is "a big hall girdled at half its height by a gallery"; "the greater part of the hall was in darkness" (*D* 34). It is within this spacious *gnomon*—loosely definable here as an incomplete structure with one section in darkness—that illumination occurs, much as it must have come to Father Flynn in the darkened confessional. As the upper hall gradually darkens, ironically providing the ideal atmosphere for spying on girls and priming the imagination, the boy turns his back on "Araby" now more fully conscious of sight as a faculty that leads one from innocence to experience through disillusionment: "Gazing up into the darkness I saw myself as a creature driven and derided by vanity; and my eyes burned with anguish and anger" (*D* 35). Blindness is no more. This exit from Munsalvaesche should allow our young Parzival eventually to shed his fool's costume.

In the preceding *Dubliners* stories epiphany is accompanied by trite or deceptive language, meaning residing in silence or elliptical language rather than in the verbal camouflage that is the oil of social intercourse. Joycean epiphanies take one unawares, provoked by commonplace events and vacuous language that seem to belie the fact that for the initiate this is a primal scene of discovery. So it is in "Araby":

> "I remarked their English accents and listened vaguely to their conversation:
>
> —O, I never said such a thing!
> —O, but you did!
> —O, but I didn't!

—Didn't she say that?
—Yes. I heard her.
—O, there's a . . . fib!" (*D* 35)

The keenness of the boy's disappointment is commensurate with his sensitivity to language. Like his prototype in "The Sisters," he orients himself by means of totem words that seem to reveal alternative worlds. It is as much the name of "Araby" as the girl's attraction to its wares that lures him to the bazaar.

Brewster Ghiselin is not quite on the mark when he says, "The response of the boy to the name *Araby* and his journey eastward across the city define his spiritual orientation, as his response to the disappointing reality of the bazaar indicates his rejection of a substitute for the true object of the soul's desire (*D* 328)."[15] Such a view diminishes the boy's personal responsibility for his disappointment, and suggests that he is clear about what he expects to find. Harry Stone is similarly wide of the mark in neglecting this aspect of the story. Stone writes convincingly of Yeats's story "Our Lady of the Hills" as a source for Joyce's portrayal of the girl in "Araby" as false madonna, yet it must also be emphasized that no falseness is discoverable in the girl herself as both Stone and Ben L. Collins (97) suggest.

As in the Yeats story, in his imagination the boy makes of the girl something she is not—an unrealistic figure of idolatry. The seven veils of mystery in which the boy cloaks her probably hide an ordinary Dublin girl of her age. Falseness resides, rather, in the voyeurism and mysticism that engender the reaction of an inexperienced lover who must learn about life the hard way, by looking for sustenance to a commercial establishment that matches his own temperament for falseness, a

[15] Like most *Dubliners* stories, "Araby" teaches a lesson: not that lovers are fools, or that romantic feeling is only for experienced lovers, but that love is both spiritual and carnal. In a famous love letter to Nora, Joyce wrote, "One moment I see you like a virgin or madonna the next moment I see you shameless, insolent, half naked and obscene" (*Letters* 2: 243). The boy in "Araby" has been captivated by an illusion that human love is only spiritual.

shabby bazaar that trades on the gullibility of wide-eyed locals by cloaking itself in the name (but not even the borrowed robes) of oriental exoticism. Neither boy nor reader mistakes the facade of Duessa's castle, realizing that falseness lies within both quester and goal, and deliverance is not from any "throng of foes" (*D* 31), but from illusions tenaciously held.

The Hard Life: "Eveline"

So far in the *Dubliners* stories Joyce has been defining the growth of a temperament quite similar to that of the artist in his later works, one that develops by reacting against injustice, hypocrisy, and sordidness, one that defines itself by learning "all the ways of error and glory" (*AP* 172). "Eveline" marks a departure—not thematically, since escape is still the issue as journey is the structure, and at the story's end the protagonist's attitude remains one of confused uncertainty—but now the character has a name, and she is a young woman of about twenty (*D* 37-38). Though she is no less the victim of romantic confusion than the boy in "Araby," she is much less given to insights and epiphanies. In fact her mind is that of a simple shopgirl (the prose reflects this), whose intellectual growth has all but ceased in the oppressive daily tedium of housework and job.

Eveline has the chance to elope with a sailor who says he has "landed on his feet," financially speaking, in Buenos Aires. Yet despite the tedium, the poverty, and dust, and the prospect of becoming a battered daughter, she finds herself at the last minute unable to board the ship with Frank.

> He rushed beyond the barrier and called to her to follow. He was shouted at to go on but he still called to her. She set her white face to him, passive, like a helpless animal. Her eyes gave him no sign of love or farewell or recognition (*D* 41).

If the entire story builds toward this moment of decision, the moment itself seems almost to be a dramatization of a metaphorical idiom: "to miss the boat." The story is about how in love, thus in life, a Dublin girl misses her golden opportunity for certain escape, possible fulfillment (the stakes are decidedly higher than in previous stories). Playing a salty Othello to her Desdemona, Frank offers Eveline a new life in an exotic land, telling her stories of "the terrible Patagonians" and experiences that make her feel she has scarcely lived. She knows too that married women command respect. Yet at times her life seems tolerable, not wholly bleak, and then there is her promise to her dying mother "to keep the home together as long as she could" (*D* 40). The tensions of her decision have been well schematized by Martin Dolch (99) (see diagram).

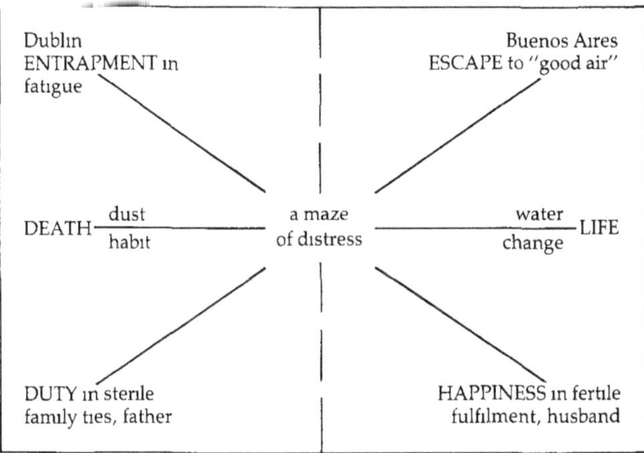

From Martin Dolch, "Eveline," in *James Joyce's "Dubliners": A Critical Handbook*, edited by James R. Baker and Thomas F. Staley (Belmont, Calif.: Wadsworth, 1969), 99.

If Eveline's anguish at her awesome decision is responsible for her frozen posture at dockside, the narrator is careful not to enter her mind at this moment to tell us whether she has actually decided to stay, and is thus paralyzed in her inability to tell Frank he has lost her (as well as the price of a ticket)—or whether she is frozen with indecision to the last minute, unable to act at all. Ultimately it does not matter: the die is cast, but in the process of revelation she undergoes naturalistic depersonalization and becomes "like a helpless animal" (*D* 41).

Joyce's cold, analytical portrayal of her crisis generates in many readers no more sympathy than if she were a calf in a quagmire. Yet the story makes a sociological statement: in class, background, and predicament Eveline is the typical example of perhaps the majority of girls in Ireland. For them the alternative to emigration was often a loveless marriage, or lonely spinsterhood and servility such as Maria of "Clay" knows, or prostitution in Europe's largest red-light district. Having sisters, Joyce knew intimately the prospects of a girl like Eveline, but he makes his point coldly, succinctly, as if he were a dispassionate observer. We return to this theme in a later chapter.

"Eveline" is thus told in the naturalist tradition of Zola's *L'Assommoir* and George Moore's *Esther Waters*, one difference being that it has the more precise economy of a story by Maupassant. It focuses on a single moment of decision, its background and implied consequences, with none of the ugly scenes commonly encountered in naturalist novels. Still, there is a quiet desperation in the Dubliners Joyce portrays; they are intended to be negative portraits that, when developed by means of thought and analysis, lead us to imagine positive models. "Eveline" points to the courage exemplified in many thousands of Irish (including Joyce and Nora) who have emigrated to a life of uncertainty.

Joyce also brings in another literary tradition. He negates the structure of romances or fairy tales where the dashing prince rescues the beautiful princess from an enchanted sleep, domestic bondage, mortal danger, etc., and carries her off to his palace and happiness everlasting. (Such stories are usually climaxed by departure, with or without prior marriage, and practical considerations about what the new life might bring are unimportant.) Seen in this way, the story is in the traditional form of a tale, which must be perceived in positive terms as an archetypal story of transcendence before it can be recognized in the negated form that Joyce employs.

Eveline thus resembles a Cinderella figure of the Dublin slums, held in bondage by a vow that will condemn her to a life of certain frustration—bound too by her fear of the unknown and of breaking convention. She is courted by a nautical prince (her equal in most respects) who has already broken his bonds to the homeland and wishes to return abroad. He is probably sincere, and has at least the price of two boat tickets. Seen from this perspective, it is difficult to accept the thesis of Hugh Kenner, who, affirming the view of Warren Beck, believes Frank to be an imposter out for sexual gratification alone, one who will take Eveline to Liverpool and, when he tires of her, put her on the streets.[16]

The story was written in 1903 and first published in *The Irish Homestead* on September 10, 1904, precisely three months after Joyce met Nora Barnacle. On October 8 of that year he succeeded where Frank had failed: he persuaded his sweetheart to board a ship with him and leave Ireland for a life of exile. Neither the lack of marriage vows, nor job, nor concrete prospects deterred Nora, and Joyce's father was right—being a Barnacle she stuck by him.

One is tempted to read more autobiography into the story than is possibly there in 1903, but "Eveline" seems to be a variation of Joyce's own elopement story. The tyrannical male was a threat to Joyce's sisters as he was to Nora, whose uncle Tommy Healy gave her such a severe beating that a week later she ran off to Dublin and a job as hotel chambermaid. Having faith in her prospects, Nora left Galway for a life of uncertainty; trusting in Joyce's words of affection, she left Ireland with him. If Nora suggests an Eveline who made it on board, Joyce suggests Frank.[17] Joyce was known for his yachting cap and sneakers (a cap he sets on Lenehan of "Two Gallants"). To Eveline's sailor he gives a "peaked cap" and his own taste for music and song; Frank has recently returned from abroad,

[16] If the Liverpool boat left from the North Wall, as Kenner emphasizes in *The Pound Era* (34-39), this does not mean that Frank is selling her into even greater bondage. There were also ships from Liverpool to South America. Furthermore, I have seen in Dublin newspapers of 1903-1904 ads of ships sailing directly to Montevideo, Uruguay from Dublin. Surely ships with destinations other than Liverpool departed from the North Wall occasionally.

[17] In *The Pound Era*, Kenner makes this connection and even has a photo of Joyce entitled "Frank" (36).

where he has had more success than Joyce would recently have had in his medical studies in Paris. Eveline's father has to be deceived about courtship and elopement; Joyce's was led even as far as the dockside bon voyage without being told about Nora. This all has the air of prophecy, as if Joyce were fabricating the scenario of an elopement he foresaw in 1903, many months before he met the girl who would have the faith and courage that Eveline lacks.

Clive Hart and Bernard Benstock agree that Eveline does not love Frank and is using him as a possible ticket out of Dublin.[18] But the rhetoric of the story is entirely supportive of escape; what is at issue is not so much love as her lack of courage to reject the sacrifice that her mother, dying in the line of service, has asked her to make.[19] Joyce clearly puts the welfare of the individual before that of the family here, and freedom before duty to a lost cause. Eveline is clearly meant to cast her bread upon the waters, and place her faith in the possibility of a love that might grow once she is freed of convention and responsibility.

Frank sings to her of the "lass that loves a sailor" (*D* 39), and Eveline believes "he would give her life, perhaps love, too" (*D* 40). Hart is right about love being an absent ingredient in this courtship, but at the same time Joyce is no sentimentalist saying "*amor vincit omnia.*" Eveline's life will never be easy. At this stage mutual affection and the necessity for escape are enough: with Frank she *may* be happy; in Dublin by definition she can never be. In the difficult days of exile Joyce could have shown this story to Nora to reassure her that her decision to elope with him to a life of uncertainty was the correct one.

[18] Hart, "Eveline"; Benstock, "The Kenner Conundrum."

[19] In "final craziness," the mother's insistent words "Derevaun Seraun" (*D* 40) have repeatedly been interpreted (especially as Irish words) and their meaning debated by scholars who seem to feel that their obscurity results not from the mother's delirium, but from mistranscription. The result is a mystery of the class of "M'Intosh" in *Ulysses*. For all their Gaelic flavor, Joyce surely intended the words to be indeterminate in meaning, though he would have delighted in all the fuss.

TWO

Obedientia Civium, Urbis Felicitas: Political Perspectives in *Dubliners*

"After the Race"

In "After the Race" Joyce immediately established political awareness as the most rewarding critical perspective for understanding the story:

> The cars came scudding in towards Dublin, running evenly like pellets in the groove of the Naas Road. At the crest of the hill at Inchicore sightseers had gathered in clumps to watch the cars careering homeward and through this channel of poverty and inaction the Continent sped its wealth and industry. Now and again the clumps of people raised the cheer of the gratefully oppressed. Their sympathy, however, was for the blue cars—the cars of their friends, the French. (*D* 42)

The Continentals own and drive splendid race cars, while the poor Irish gather stupidly to cheer a sport where only foreigners participate.[1] Without the money, skill or technology to build, own or race such cars, these locals nevertheless admire those who do; but, since the poor everywhere are excluded from such frivolities, and yet enjoy races, what is it that makes the Irish different—why are they "*gratefully* oppressed"?

In some ways Jimmy is the Irish exception who proves the rule: first of all he is rich—and had to be to attract Ségouin, Rivière, and Villona—but as Zack Bowen has noted (58), he is also a butcher's son, which means that except for the money he squanders and the superior education that has apparently left him as unenlightened as before, his class and background

[1] Joyce must have felt keenly his own poverty when interviewing the racing driver Henri Fournier, an experience that provided the basis of "After the Race." See Joyce's *Critical Writings*, edited by Mason and Ellmann, 106-108.

hardly differ from those of Polly Mooney of "The Boarding House." After all, Jimmy is not so different from those Irish who gather in clumps to cheer the race or "to pay homage to the snorting motor" (*D* 45).

If Joyce's uncertainty principle trains readers to look for what is missing, in "After the Race" this does not take the puzzle form of structure, but rather one of personal fulfillment. Everybody seems to need something. Jimmy "provides for his father a sort of psychic income because [he] is a living example of conspicuous consumption, and the father is 'covertly proud of the excess' " (Bowen 57). The father is good at making money, but lacks the sophistication necessary to waste it conspicuously. The Continentals seem to have money (except Villona), but would be happy to pick up any loose cash floating around as investment for the auto agency. They, in turn, have something neither Jimmy nor his father can buy: class, style, wit, charm, taste, and intelligence (the father seems shrewd at his business, but at little else).

Jimmy is scarcely bright enough to define his need, but apparently he thinks that sophistication rubs off on people just as does a good education. Attend the right schools, associate with those you wish to emulate, and one transcends the limitations of class and mind. (This is Joyce's judgment on a class of society as well as on a nation.) At the story's end, Jimmy's friends will be richer, but he will be as stupid as ever.

Jimmy's father agrees that Ségouin, reputed owner of some of France's largest hotels, is well worth knowing, though neither knows for a fact that Ségouin is wealthy. This hardly bothers Jimmy, whose central problem is that he walks around in a fog made denser by his naiveté, low intelligence, and taste for alcohol. Cosmopolitan Ségouin's company gives him great pleasure (*D* 43), but in the back seat he cannot understand what the Frenchmen say. Aware that the wealth he controls was amassed by his father's hard work and shrewd capitalism, he nevertheless agrees (with his father's approval) to invest his money in Ségouin's auto dealership in Paris with apparently little more knowledge than the Frenchman's "unmistakable air of wealth" (*D* 45). Surely the money will be lost.

What begins to emerge is the nature of Jimmy's (and by implication the Irish) willing complicity in the exploitation of Ireland by foreigners. This does not, of course, mean that Jimmy is unaware of his homeland's plight. His father started out as "an advanced Nationalist" until his capitalist instincts got in the way and he took police contracts (*D* 43); and Jimmy baits the Englishman Routh in an argument at dinner until his father proposes a toast to "Humanity" and opens the window (*D* 46). Still, talk is cheap, and Irish money remains the quarry.

Jimmy's group of friends grows even more international when the American Farley joins in and invites them to his yacht, where much merriment and drinking is followed by many games of cards. From Jimmy's befuddled viewpoint, he and his companions fling "themselves boldly into the adventure" of gambling (*D* 48), a view that also serves as an implicit commentary on his investment with Ségouin. Ignorant of the rules, mistaking his cards, unable to calculate his I.O.U.'s, unsure of his losses, the Irishman is an easy mark in this international competition; this he vaguely knows, but as Villona opens the cabin door and dawn enters, the more important illumination may be the reader's, in whose ears may echo yet "the cheer of the gratefully oppressed." In cards the Englishman turns out to be the big winner, while in investments the prize goes to the French. As for Jimmy, awash in uncertainty, he is "glad of the dark stupor that would cover up his folly" (*D* 48).

Synge and Social Commentary: "Two Gallants," "The Boarding House," and "Counterparts"

Ireland has emphasized segregation of the sexes from the days when it was a monastic center of Europe to the early part of this century when mixed schooling or bathing or pubs were mostly frowned upon. Physical distance creates psychological distance, which has caused widespread failure of empathy between men and women in Ireland. One can trace this problem far back into Irish history and literature, where it is obvious that men often had great fear of women as sexual creatures—

witness the widespread appearance of the Sheela-na-gig figure in early Irish stone-carvings, a hideous woman who spreads with her fingers an enormous vagina or poses in similarly obscene ways as if to entice men to their perdition.[2]

Surely early Irish monasticism, and its emphasis on celibacy and isolation from the world's temptations, while it made Ireland a center of learning, did little to enhance understanding and trust between the sexes. Stories about St. Kevin's fear of women express a typical attitude. Legend has it that a pretty girl named Kathleen fell desperately in love with St. Kevin, who lived at Glendalough, where he died in 618 A.D. One source says, "Resisting her amorous advances, he cooled her ardour by a good beating with nettles" (Ronan 30). The Irish poet Tom Moore and others tell how the saint dealt with his persistent admirer: when Kathleen climbed a cliff on the lake at Glendalough to his cave above, the outraged Kevin hurled her down into the lake, where she drowned (Bell 212-13).

In a book called *The Irish*, Donald S. Connery begins a chapter entitled "Love and Marriage" by saying:

> Ireland is a country where marriage has been defined as 'permission to sin.' It is a society which has long held the view "that God, in creating desire for woman in man, had been guilty of a lapse of taste." It is a man's country where men are the rulers and mothers enjoy power in a behind-the-scenes matriarchy. Well known for its late marriages and numerous bachelors and spinsters, it is perhaps the one place in the world where men most effectively manage to continue their bachelor pursuits (which have little to do with sex) after marriage. It has the greatest percentage of virgins, the fewest divorces (since divorce is forbidden) and the least-emancipated women in the English-speaking world. (Connery 192)[3]

[2] See Mercier 53-56. Scott also discusses this figure (11-13), where a picture is included. Part of the following chapter was presented as a lecture at the 1979 Modern Language Convention in San Francisco.

[3] See also Fennell.

Connery quotes Monica McEnroy as saying, "We Irishwomen are almost collectors' pieces for sociologists. Irishmen are completely kinked in their attitude to women" (ibid.). He also quotes a Dublin journalist who defined an Irishman as "the only man in the world who will clamber over the bodies of a dozen naked women in order to get to a bottle of stout" (ibid.).

Irish writers have not escaped the consequences of this atmosphere of sexual repression—this we know because we probably have more biographical information about them than any other group of Irish people. From the viewpoint of their sexual attitudes, they are by far the strangest group of writers known to me. A major obsession of Swift was how not to consummate his love for Stella. George Moore pretended to be the age's Don Juan, but a female acquaintance observed, "Some men kiss and tell, Mr. Moore tells but doesn't kiss" (Mitchell 47). Oscar Wilde's preferences are well known. George Bernard Shaw at the age of forty-two married an Irish woman who insisted that their marriage never be consummated. They never had children. Lamenting lost sexual opportunity during later years, Yeats had a Steinach operation and played the wild wicked old man. Patrick Kavanagh's long poem *The Great Hunger* treats of the painful celibacy of a country boy. The political consciousness of Ireland's most famous banned writer—Joyce—was molded principally by the fall of Charles Stewart Parnell due to his affair with a married woman. Sean O'Faolain "was twenty years old and midway through Cork University before he learned how childbirth worked" (Connery 208).

John Millington Synge's play *The Shadow of the Glen* (1903) responds to these social conditions and bears an interesting relationship to *Dubliners* stories about marriage and courtship. Though generally the play has been read as being about a young woman's terrible loneliness, its theme is more precisely loveless marriage and its consequences in a country that was without divorce or equal rights for women. In their biography of Synge, David H. Greene and Edward M. Stephens mention Arthur Griffith's attack on the play as unIrish and a libel on

Irish woman, to which Jack B. Yeats retorted that the play was "a very effective attack on loveless marriages—the most miserable institution so dear to our thrifty elders among the peasants and among their betters, by whom anything like impulse or passion is discredited" (Greene and Stephens 155).[4]

Loveless marriage is a problem in any society, but in Ireland sexual fear combines with economic circumstance and high alcohol consumption to militate against domestic happiness. Women are under strong pressure to marry, yet if they can't they must typically enter the convent, emigrate, or perhaps just stay home and serve the menfolks. As for men, the age at which they marry has long been the most advanced in the world. Greene and Stephens say that "80 per cent of the men between twenty-five and thirty years of age, and more than 63 per cent of those between thirty and thirty-five, are unmarried . . . (158). One explanation for this phenomenon is found in Connery: "In rural Ireland the son who remains on the land after his brothers have gone off to the towns or overseas may be discouraged from seriously contemplating marriage until middle age, or else discouraged from marrying at all, because Mother cannot stand the thought of a rival female in the household with whom she must share her boy's affections" (199).

The Encyclopaedia of Ireland confirms the late age of marriage in Ireland and thus the highly unusual role that sexuality must play in the lives of Irish people:

> The Irish population displays a number of interesting and unusual features. Perhaps the most striking and, along with emigration, the most disturbing, is the very low marriage rate and, combined with this, the late age of marriage. The Republic has the lowest marriage rate in the

[4] Responding to the Jack B. Yeats quotation, Jean Alexander says, "Subsequent critics have agreed without dissent, that Synge's women, in their vigour and independence, present an implicit attack on a traditional conception of womankind. It can certainly be argued also that there is an intentional attack on marriage, lovelessness aside [in *The Shadow of the Glen*], for there is no subsequent play of Synge's which does not mock marriage relationships" (26).

> world. . . . In 1961 over 46% of the males in the Republic between 35 and 44 years in rural areas were single and so were almost 23% of the urban males. In the same year the average age at marriage was 30.6 years for a man and 26.9 for a woman. . . . The peculiar marriage conditions in Ireland have never been completely explained, although one important factor causing postponement of marriage in rural areas is the late age at which many farmers' sons inherit their holdings. Succession is retarded because farmers do not normally retire with advancing years. Of course, sons who do not inherit a holding will very often have to remain celibate or emigrate (107).

These figures for the marriage rate are from the 1960s; they were even more dismal at the turn of the century when Synge was writing his play.

The implications of the sociological context for Synge's play are readily apparent when we look at the plot of *The Shadow of the Glen* with its rural setting. An old farmer named Dan in the Wicklow Hills suspects his young wife Nora of having a lover. He plays dead in order to trap her. A tramp enters and stays to keep them company. Nora goes out and returns with Michael, who suggests that they might marry now that she is free if she inherits Dan's property. Dan awakens, having trapped his wife conversing with Michael, and tells her she must get out of his house for good. Michael won't have her without money, so she leaves with the tramp for the life of a wanderer. Michael and Dan stay behind to drink some whiskey.

In his play Synge grafted together two folktales—the Irish, where the wife is caught in bed with her lover, and the Latin, where the widow of Ephesus, in mourning, allows herself to be seduced by a Roman soldier in the tomb of her husband. Both tales put the wife in the wrong; Synge reverses this and puts the husband in the wrong. But Synge's pessimism requires that meanness and materialism triumph, as it seemed to in his world, so the wife—caught not in adultery but in conversation—must clear out of the house. In conventional terms, for a farmer's wife to be kicked out to wander the roads would be a fate worse than death, yet we are made to feel that her escape from the clutches of this old man is in itself a triumph. Synge thus posits an alternative to loveless marriage that for Irish women in 1903 would have been unthinkable—not emigration or the convent, but freedom from male tyranny and the conventions of a male-dominated society; a loose, natural, amoral relationship with a similar free spirit who happens in this case to be male.

Although Jack Yeats is right in saying the play attacks loveless marriages in Ireland, his view is simplistic. *The Shadow of the Glen* is far more radical: it endorses the tramp's life over farming, wandering and uncertainty over property and staying put, freedom, romance, and spontaneity over housework and status, and free love over loveless marriage.

The traditional Irish folktale Synge chose to dramatize is too paradigmatic of rural life in Ireland for the play not to express social commentary. Old Dan is typical of the very large percentage of rural men unable to marry until advanced middle age; Nora is typical of the young woman who wishes to marry, but whose only proposal and last chance is the old man who says he wants her. Society in a single voice encourages her to choose security and cold feet in her bed; her heart longs for passion and youth. The first view is expressed in her fear of a penniless old age: she says, "What way would I live and I an old woman if I didn't marry a man with a bit of a farm, and cows on it, and sheep on the black hills?" And yet she is trapped by a conflicting impulse, expressed a few lines later: "What way would a woman live in a lonesome place the like of this place, and she not making a talk with the men passing" (Synge 112; 118).

Though Synge heard his story in the Aran Islands, it is international; yet in another sense it is in the mainstream of Irish literary tradition. It deals with the war between the sexes in Ireland, or, more specifically, what often happens when old men marry young wives, a theme in English literature at least as old as Chaucer's "The Miller's Tale." There is no doubt that Synge knew two famous Irish sagas widely discussed during his time: the elopement of Grainne with Diarmid on the eve of her marriage to the older Finn MacCool, and Finn's chasing them around Ireland for years. The story of Deirdre, beloved of the old king Conchubor, was the subject of his last play—*Deirdre of the Sorrows*—unfinished at his death.

The Shadow of the Glen, however, is not meant to remind us of Irish myth, but of Irish reality at the beginning of this century—the all-too-familiar reality of loveless marriage and sterile celibacy. When Dan's parents had passed on, and he was free to bring a wife to his lonely farmhouse, it was a young wife he got—one who married him because he was the only man who asked or was likely to ask. Nora knew the statistics on marriage in Ireland and what her odds were. Security was the common goal—not love, or compatibility—but she could not help recoiling from a husband satisfied merely to possess her as he might one of the sheep who cough on the hillside. Since Nora could not help talking with any young man who could spare the time, she is forced into penury and exile.

In *Joyce and Feminism*, Bonnie Scott dismisses Synge as a feminist influence on Joyce, but a chronology of events will show the parallel lines that Synge and Joyce followed in 1903-1904, especially in *The Shadow of the Glen* and *Dubliners*, and notably in their endorsement of escapes to uncertainty. The play was begun in the summer of 1902, when Synge was also working on *Riders to the Sea*. Some version of it, according to Saddlemyer's chronology (xxiii), was shown to Lady Gregory and Yeats between 8 and 13 October 1902. Joyce and Synge probably first met in November 1902 in Dublin, and met frequently in Paris between 6 and 13 March 1903 to discuss literature and ideas. It is likely that they would have discussed *Shadow* in some detail. First produced in Dublin's Molesworth Hall on 8 October 1903, the play was first printed in *Samhain* in December 1904 and then privately printed by John Quinn in New York. On 8 May 1905, *Shadow* and *Riders* were published in a Vigo edition in London by Elkin Matthews (Saddlemyer xxiv).

During March 1903, Joyce probably became the first person, other than the author, to read *Riders to the Sea*, a play he disparaged to Synge as being overly brief and in violation of Aristotelian rules governing tragedy (*Letters* 2:35; 18; cf. 1:99). Synge was a bit contemptuous of Joyce as well; in a letter to Lady Gregory of 26 March 1903 he says, "I cannot think that [Joyce] will ever be a poet of importance, but his intellect is extraordinarily keen and if he keeps fairly sane he ought to do excellent essay writing" (Saddlemyer 68). Overcoming a sense of rivalry, and perhaps some jealousy of Synge's notoriety during the *Playboy* riots of 1907, with Nicolò Vidacovich, Joyce translated *Riders to the Sea* into Italian in 1909, but was subsequently barred from publishing it by the Synge estate. In 1918 he produced the play for the English Players in Zurich, and even persuaded Nora Joyce to take a part in it. After Synge's death in 1909, Joyce's admiration grew considerably.

In a letter of 7 February 1907, Joyce says, "I have read only one play [of Synge's], *Riders to the Sea*" (Joyce, *Letters* 2:212), but he does not mention whether or not he had seen any performances. A letter by Joyce of that month indicated that he knew Synge had written four one-act plays (Joyce, *Letters* 2:35). They very likely discussed the play in Paris. Since Joyce was in Dublin when *The Shadow of the Glen* was first staged, it is highly unlikely that he would have missed the performance. He was present in June 1904 when Synge announced to the National Theatre Society that *The Well of the Saints* was ready for staging (Ellmann, *James Joyce* 160). At any rate, if he saw *The Shadow*, we can probably speak of influence; if not, then the parallels and coincidences are still interesting enough to warrant juxtaposition of the play with *Dubliners*, which was written 1904-1907.

Joyce, famous for his interest in coincidence, would have found enough of it in *The Shadow of the Glen* to fascinate him. The play's central figure is Nora Burke, who is unjustly evicted by a tyrannical husband for talking with passing men (she possibly did more); in June of 1904 Joyce met a woman similarly treated—Nora Barnacle, who was beaten by her guardian uncle Tommy Healy for walking out with Willie Mulvey [Mulvagh], a Protestant. A week later she left Galway for

Dublin and shortly thereafter met Joyce (Ellmann, *James Joyce* 158-59). Precisely one year to the day after *The Shadow* was first staged, on 8 October 1904, Joyce eloped to the Continent with his Nora, destined for a life of wandering and penury. Like Synge's outcasts, they spurned conventional morality, marital bonds, and the safe life, leaving behind them several burning bridges. This path to uncertainty Eveline rejects.

Central to Joyce's own play *Exiles* is a theme familiar from Synge: Ireland needs a new morality that would allow men and women freely to enter, dissolve, and reevaluate equal partnerships based on love and mutual trust. Like *The Shadow*, and much of the rest of Joyce's work, *Exiles* treats of infidelity, but in each play there remains at the end uncertainty about the wife's actual betrayal. There is also the implication that it might have been justified. In *A Portrait* (182-83), Davin tells a story reminiscent of *The Shadow*'s plot about walking in the lonely Ballyhoura hills, where he stopped for a drink at a cottage and met a young woman "half undressed" whose husband was away and who invited him to stay the night. This happened in the month of October.

In *Dubliners*, Joyce was clearly echoing Synge and George Moore, especially in *The Untilled Field*: in Ireland women and men exploit each other; the state oppresses everybody; the Church is both too powerful and too remote from the lives of the people; sexual attitudes are dangerously unhealthy; marriage is most often a noose; and a life of vitality can only be lived outside social conventions. Joyce's sentiment is reflected in letters of 29 August and 16 September 1904 from Joyce to Nora. He says, "My mind rejects the whole present social order and Christianity-home, the recognized virtues, classes of life, and religious doctrines." He complains that his mother died of his father's ill treatment, and he "cursed the system which had made her a victim" (Joyce, *Letters* 2:48). Shortly thereafter he wrote, "It seemed to me that I was fighting a battle with every religious and social force in Ireland for you and that I had nothing to rely on but myself. There is no life here—no naturalness or honesty . . . " (Joyce, *Letters* 2:53). Joyce could also have mentioned that "the system" of oppression under which women suffered was oiled by the alcoholism of men such as his father. It is a prevalent theme of *Dubliners*.

That his mother's death in 1903 was a main reason for his bitterness in 1904 is easily seen when one adopts the perspective of Edmund Epstein:

> All in all, Mrs. Joyce endured fifteen pregnancies from 1881 to 1894 (or later), with an average time lapse between pregnancies of about fourteen months. In other words, Mary Jane Joyce was allowed five months to recuperate between each birth or miscarriage before she was pregnant again. . . . Mrs. Joyce was crippled indeed, with a calcium drain from her body for each child and a corresponding nutritional loss that was not made up by the family's meager diet. . . . Mary Jane Joyce died on August 13, 1903. She was only forty-four years old, and whatever was the final reason for her death, cancer or cirrhosis of the liver, she died of ill-treatment. (Bowen and Carens 7)

The sociological context provided by *The Shadow* and statistics on the average age at which the Irish marry also enable us to see more clearly one aspect of Joyce's social commentary in *Dubliners*. It seems less remarkable that two elderly women, surely old maids, would live with their brother Father Flynn until he died, or that Frank's proposal of elopement is meant to represent Eveline's one opportunity for happiness. In "Clay," the absurdity of Maria's romantic aspiration is heightened when we have some awareness of her chances of winning a man's heart; it seems more plausible that James Duffy of "A Painful Case" is actually the one man who can fill the emptiness of Mrs. Sinico's life, or that incurable loneliness and alcoholism will be the consequence of his rejection of her. In a country where, by Nuala Fennell's recent count, 11% of the population is admitted "to mental hospital[s] (highest in Europe) and 11% of [the] national income [is] spent on liquor" (4-5), eleven would hardly seem to be the appropriate symbolic number for regeneration, as it is in *Finnegans Wake*. The consequences are seen in the middle stories of *Dubliners*, where structure reinforces meaning to illuminate the desperate conditions of Dublin society. Men and women lead separate lives and are better at entrapment than communication; alcoholism, a major consequence of segregation, accompanies Dubliners through circle after circle of frustration and despair from which labyrinth there seems to be no escape.

In *Dubliners*, men often try to have their fun without paying for it, while women tend to be all business, and yet Joyce tries to keep a balanced perspective. Sexual exploitation in "Two Gallants" is a male strategy, while in "The Boarding House" it is female. Both stories reveal circular patterns in the maze of courtship, entrapment, and alcoholism. As is seen in "Eveline," Sean O'Casey's *Juno and the Paycock*, and many other works of Irish literature, not to mention reality, Irish women are often coerced into supporting on their meager incomes parasitical men who have chosen to view life through the bottom of a beer mug. Mrs. Mooney of "The Boarding House" is strong enough to break the cycle, but she is a rare person; Mrs. Kernan of "Grace" can be more tolerant of her alcoholic husband because he is still the provider. Typically, the men of "Ivy Day" seem more interested in where their next drink is coming from than anything political, while Tom Kernan's friends gather at the alcoholic's bedside to pass the bottle and propose that he amend his life.

Sexual exploitation for the purpose of gaining money for a night of drinking is the theme of "Two Gallants," one of the most successful stories in the collection, and a most bitter comment on male-female relationships. We typically misread the story at the beginning as being about two fellows in search of sexual involvement, with Corley perhaps attempting to bring Lenehan a piece of the action. Only at the end, when Corley walks away with the slavey's gold coin, a princely sum to her, do we realize that the story is yet another indictment of the Irishman's preference for clambering over a woman to get to a bottle of stout.

That Lenehan walks a circular route when he leaves and rejoins Corley has been noticed by many commentators on the story. His route is Joyce's sign that, like Martin Cunningham of "Grace" and *Ulysses*, whose wife repeatedly sells the furniture to buy alcohol, or Farrington of "Counterparts," himself an alcoholic, Lenehan is the Dubliner as Sisyphus. He is a professional cadger of drinks in pubs, and his desire to ultimately break his cycle of despair to find "some good simpleminded girl with a little of the ready" (*D* 58) so that he can live the drinking man's life of leisure will, of course, be unfilled. He must, perforce, continue to be a parasite on males (see Robert Adams Day).

There are no happy marriages in Joyce's works, or even friendships based on mutual trust, and all relationships are potentially adversarial. Being from a family driven into the most appalling poverty by an alcoholic father, having been in daily contact with his seemingly countless deprived brothers and sisters, having seen his mother waste away from disease, neglect, and despair—all this obviously left its mark on Joyce's view of the Irish family. Stephen's anguish at meeting his starving sister in *Ulysses* must have been a shared memory *U* 10:854 ff.; cf. 10:258 ff.); so too the portrait of the niggardly Simon Dedalus, who begrudges his daughter money for food while he spends his day drinking in the pubs.

Like Synge in *The Shadow*, despite the near certainty that marriages of coercion will be disastrous, Joyce sees that Irish women have few alternatives. They entrap and are the victims of entrapment. So it is in "The Boarding House," where Mrs. Mooney, the butcher's daughter, has been shrewd enough to marry her father's foreman; when he becomes a hopeless alcoholic and ruins the business, she obtains a separation, takes what is left, and buys a boarding house. Mooney, cut off *a mensa et thalamo*, becomes a bumbailiff. Now that their daughter Polly is old enough to marry, mother shrewdly keeps silence while daughter seduces a promising man, Bob Doran, who will be coerced into a marriage that will be gossiped about in *Ulysses*, where he is so drunk that he can scarcely remain on a barstool (*U* 12:384 ff.). If history repeats itself, as it seems to be doing here, then it is likely that Mrs. Mooney also used seduction in order to trap her father's foreman, and that the fate of her prospective son-in-law will also be alcoholism, the common refuge for unhappy husbands in Dublin.

Polly, who sings "I'm a . . . naughty girl . . ." (*D* 62), is true to character and plays well the cards her mother deals her. She avoids spinsterhood, emigration, the convent, and the uncertain life of boarding house chambermaid. Doran is also her superior in class and education, a further triumph, but with eligible men in such short supply, it takes the tricks of the Madam's trade to catch one. On the women's side is also conventional morality: though they are the seducers, they will appear to be the victims, and all will sympathize. Knowing his job and reputation are at stake, Doran will be unable to slip the noose. Clearly perceiving the trap, "his instinct urged him to remain free, not to marry. Once you are married you are done for, it said" (*D* 66). It is probably the instinctive fear of many an Irishman.

Farrington of "Counterparts" is another portrait of the husband whose marriage interferes with his bibulous avocation. "His wife was a little sharp-faced woman who bullied her husband when he was sober and was bullied by him when he was drunk" (*D* 97). They are counterparts in divided loyalty: while he is in the pubs, she is at the chapel; she returns home fortified by righteous indignation and he by alcohol. As Robert Scholes shows, Farrington has other counterparts as well (379): he is bullied by his boss, Mr. Alleyne, and he returns home to bully his son, which also makes him the counterpart to Chandler in "A Little Cloud." Yet it is not a simple case of oppression; the nexus of counterpart relationships breaks down when it is pointed out that Farrington deserves no better fate. As a clerk in the law office of Crosbie and Alleyne, he is an intolerable employee who sneaks out for drinks, works inefficiently, makes continual mistakes, lies about having copied letters and contracts, and is disrespectful to his boss, whose bald head he thinks of crushing. He is a bully and a lout who should have been dismissed long ago.

In our first glimpse of Farrington, his alcoholism is clearly noticeable: "He had a hanging face, dark wine-coloured, with fair eyebrows and moustache: his eyes bulged forward slightly and the whites of them were dirty" (*D* 86). Like other *Dubliners* characters, he is caught in a vicious cycle: he drinks, which befuddles his mind; the result is clerical errors, which enrage him; rage produces thirst and so he drinks. The circularity of alcoholism is coupled with another familiar *Dubliners* structure—the series of blows to self-esteem that form a pattern in "Clay" and "The Dead." In Farrington's case, the result of entrapment and defeat is summarized at the beginning of the story's final section (*D* 97):

> He cursed everything. He had done for himself in the office, pawned his watch, spent all his money; and he had not even got drunk. He began to feel thirsty again and he longed to be back again in the hot reeking public-house. He had lost his reputation as a strong man, having been defeated twice by a mere boy. His heart swelled with fury and, when he thought of the woman in the big hat who had brushed against him and said *Pardon*! his fury nearly choked him.

That Farrington has not been previously fired from Crosbie and Alleyne is doubtless due to the widespread view in Dublin that "drink is many a man's weakness," or perhaps it is just due to the equally mistaken view that his large family will suffer less if he drinks his salary than if his alcohol supply is cut off and he becomes really vicious. But the story does really seem to mark the end of his employment, for if he returns to work, he will be driven out for incompetence and for his smart answer to his boss. The scene in which he beats his son for letting the fire go out is surely paradigmatic of what the future holds for the Farrington family, a life of uncertainty by entrapment.

The characters of *Dubliners* seem little more than grotesques when viewed singly, but when seen as forming a gallery of portraits, each is representative of a Dublin type Joyce thought he knew. Though distinct, these Dubliners have in common treacherous attitudes toward each other that constitute a tyranny greater than that of Church and State. In letters Joyce expressed rage against these institutions, rage that will be echoed by Stephen Dedalus; but in the stories he is far more successful in exposing the people themselves, and the atmosphere they create, as the true villains of Dublin. It is in this sense that, like Stephen, Joyce longed to forge the uncreated conscience of his race, something that John Synge, W. B. Yeats, Sean O'Casey, and other Irish writers in their varying ways would also attempt to do. More than one Irish writer would die in exile with the bitter knowledge that he had failed.

"A Little Cloud". Le Poète Manqué

In "A Little Cloud," Joyce returns to the quest structure of earlier *Dubliners* stories and applies his techniques of negation to the story of a youthful, naive figure who believes his artistic nature to be thwarted by the circumstances of his life. Little Chandler is an artiste manqué who defines by negative example the true Irish artist as Joyce imagined him/her to be in 1906. Both Chandler, the shy law clerk, and Ignatius Gallaher, the successful journalist, were conceived not only as polar opposites of each other, but of Joyce as well. They represent two types of Dubliner Joyce despised, but whose vocations he would have been obliged to consider had he not emigrated. In "A Little Cloud" Joyce created two distasteful autobiographical possibilities at a time when the success of his own artistic vocation seemed paralyzed by uncertainty.

Since the story is about how Chandler's positive feelings toward his old friend become negative after their reunion, it is interesting to find in the first paragraph a series of statements about Gallaher that will be contradicted by evidence in the story that follows:

> Eight years before he had seen his friend off at the North Wall and wished him godspeed. Gallaher had got on. You could tell that at once by his travelled air, his well-cut tweed suit and fearless accent. Few fellows had talents like his and fewer still could remain unspoiled by such success. Gallaher's heart was in the right place and he had

> deserved to win. It was something to have a friend like that. (*D* 70)

Gallaher may have "got on" because he has money to spend, but there is no evidence of literary talent given the triviality of his conversation and the triteness of his language.[5] The other judgments are likewise shown to be absurdly wrong. The story will show how appearances deceive, how Gallaher's "heart" was *not* in "the right place" (since he has invited Chandler for drinks solely in order to patronize him), how damaging it is to one's sense of personal esteem to "have a friend like that," and how, if Gallaher has indeed "won," become successful, it speaks rather poorly for his profession.

The opening paragraph is meant to deceive the reader as Chandler has deceived himself about Gallaher: it gives us a false evaluation of the journalist that should eventually lead the reader to question the standard and quality of Chandler's judgment. If the boy in "Araby" is blinded by false love, the little man in this story is blinded by false friendship; the one makes a pilgrimage to a vanity fair and the other to a sham writer who represents all that is vulgar in the Irish who have gone abroad to trade their heritage, or ideals, or integrity for money, men who wallow in the corruption of big cities and brag of it to provincials back home who are primers to their self-esteem. As quest object Gallaher is like the shocking illusions of earlier stories that send protagonists back to a familiar tedium that seems twice as hopeless since they have sought and been denied deliverance.

Specifically, Joyce seems to be saying that a successful journalist like Gallaher prostitutes any literary talent he may have for fame and fortune. Seemingly bothered only by his friend's vulgarity, Chandler is from first to last envious, using materialistic standards for judging a writer's success while, ironically, aspiring to become a kind of Irish Ernest Dowson for British readers of poetry. Joyce must have found considerable humor in Chandler's ridiculous dream that Gallaher might

[5] These linguistic qualities he shares with old Mr. Cotter and the sisters of the first story, the saleslady in "Araby," and other characters in *Dubliners*.

help him to publish in some newspaper as-yet-unwritten verses of melancholy mood as a means to artistic and *thus* financial success. The story's beginning is, in retrospect, a yardstick for measuring both Chandler and Gallaher.

The pervasive monetary images and references in "A Little Cloud," as in "After the Race," support the view that one's attitude toward money is a reliable index to character. Chandler "had never been in Corless's but he knew the value of the name" (*D* 72). If Gallaher marries, "You may bet your bottom dollar there'll be no mooning and spooning about it. I mean to marry money" (*D* 81). Chandler regrets that he has neither married money nor earned enough to hire a servant. In the final scene Annie's thin tight lips and remembered outrage at Chandler's paying 10/11 for a blouse are weighed against his fantasy of rich, voluptuous Jewish women.

If money bedazzles Chandler, bright lights fail to illuminate. Because of the anti-mercenary theme, all that is bright seems to carry negative impact in the story; in fact, "A Little Cloud" could be said to recount how Ignatius Gallaher, formerly shabby and disreputable, and now a "brilliant figure on the London Press" (*D* 71), returns home to Dublin, where on one evening he meets his friend Chandler and blinds him with the radiance of his success as a reporter until Chandler's eyes focus properly. (Similarly, "Araby" could be said to be about the focusing of the eyes of a boy who has been blinded by love.) In *Ulysses,* golden coins of sunlight mock Mr. Deasy (*U* 2:448-49), while here "a shower of kindly golden dust [illuminates] untidy nurses and decrepit old men" (*D* 71). The "golden sunset" is immediately juxtaposed against a "horde of grimy children" (*D* 71), and later it reveals "poor stunted houses," reminding Chandler of "a band of tramps, huddled together along the river-banks," "stupefied by the panorama of sunset" (*D* 73).

When Chandler arrives at Corless's, "the light and noise of the bar held him at the doorway for a few moments. He looked about him, but his sight was confused by the shining of many red and green wine-glasses" (*D* 74). Gallaher's orange tie is one no Irish Catholic would wear: at best it suggests that he has forgotten his origins; at worst the tie is a gold badge indicating his open allegiance to moneyed interests in Britain.[6] It is a clear semiotic message to Chandler's unconscious, which, with the whiskey, the talk of glittering foreign capitals, and the newness of Corless's, seems calculated to hypnotize and disorient him. The last drink is heralded by Gallaher's taking out "a large gold watch" to check the time (*D* 80). Chandler's unhappy marital life emerges in the story's final section, prompted in part by his contemplation of his wife's photograph, as illuminated by a little lamp on the table.

All this blinding glitter emphasizes that "A Little Cloud" treats not of the rejection by a journalist of an aspiring poet, but by a sham writer of another whose values are equally bourgeois. One irony here is that in national terms this meeting in Corless's seems, from the Irish viewpoint, to be the classical one of Ireland, Land of Saints and Sages, with the commercial giant Britannia; in individual terms, it suggests a meeting between the typical Celt who values art, religion, and the life of contemplation with the crass, materialistic Sassenach. That the latter type should be represented here by an ex-Dubliner adds to the irony.

As for Chandler, he is so far from being a portrait of the artist as a little man that one could list his qualities, turn them into opposites, and come close to Joyce's ideal of the artistic temperament. In part this definition is provided by the first three stories of *Dubliners*, where the boys are largely autobiographical—not necessarily proto-artists, but certainly in possession of those qualities of courage, sensitivity, and intellect that could lead them to an artistic vocation. Their problem is that they merely fail to *achieve* a transcendence sought in an early formative experience; Chandler and Eveline are worse off: they fail to *embody* those essential characteristics and thus are doomed to failure before their quests begin. If naiveté remains the pervasive debility of youth, Joyce's Elect seem destined to be cured of it. The Dublin ambience is likewise a gen-

[6] The role of successful exile was one Joyce himself would play during his rare visits to Dublin. Cf. Richard Rowan of Joyce's *Exiles*.

eral problem since it paralyzes free will, but those best equipped to survive have the qualities of the artist-hero: those listed above, plus strength, determination, a contempt for materialism and illegitimate authority, perhaps a satirical strain, and a longing to escape the quagmire of environment. In *Dubliners* this character type is no less visible or definable for being obscured by youthful naiveté, and he exists full-blown in a work Joyce was writing simultaneously—*Stephen Hero*.

Little Chandler, on the other hand, is described as an overly fastidious dandy: "His hands were white and small, his frame was fragile, his voice was quiet and his manners were refined. He took the greatest care of his fair silken hair and moustache and used perfume discreetly on his handkerchief. The half-moons of his nails were perfect and when he smiled you caught a glimpse of a row of childish white teeth" (*D* 70).

As he walks along toward Corless's, we are told that "he watched the scene and thought of life; and (as always happened when he thought of life) he became sad" (*D* 71). Ironically, no connection is made by Chandler between "the scene" and "life" because he thinks only of his own circumstances. The point is crucial. "Life" is to be seen in the "untidy nurses," "decrepit old men," the "horde of grimy children." Yet "Little Chandler gave them no thought. He picked his way deftly through all the minute vermin-like *life*" [italics mine] (*D* 71). Stephen Dedalus, the nearest thing we have to a budding artist in Joyce, seeks out and immerses himself in the life of the city Chandler shuns. In *Ulysses* Stephen says, "History is a nightmare from which I am trying to awake" (*U* 2:377), while for Chandler, "No memory of the past touched him . . ." (*D* 72). He cannot see Dublin's poverty in an historical context or identify with its misery as an Irishman. Rather, as he continues his walk, "For the first time in his life he felt superior to the people he passed . . . his soul revolted against the dull inelegance of Capel Street" (*D* 73).

These Joycean code words—political in nature—have often been ignored, Chandler more than once having been seen as basically sympathetic. For instance, Kenner has said that "given a different ambience, he might indeed have been a sound minor poet" ("Pound on Joyce": 7), a point that Warren Beck finds "hard to determine," feeling that "the chief obstacles to Chandler as poet are his wife and child" (161). Robert Boyle is correct in saying that "Chandler's mind is conventional, limited, insensitive, unperceptive. He is not vigorously alive mentally . . ." ("A Little Cloud": 86), though I would emphasize that the observation makes more sense as an assessment of his potential as an artist. But more than this, the absent ingredient in Chandler (and Gallaher) is social conscience, an essential requisite of the writer, as Joyce implicitly says through his subtle technique of negation.

This quality of mind Joyce satirizes: "He tried to weigh his soul to see if it was a poet's soul. Melancholy was the dominant note of his temperament, he thought, but it was a melancholy tempered by recurrences of faith and resignation and simple joy. . . ." "The English critics, perhaps, would recognize him as one of the Celtic school by reason of the melancholy tone of his poems . . ." (*D* 73-74).

The ending, which follows the familiar ellipses, explores the implications of a marriage and a life gone stale. Gallaher's last recorded words to his friend are unconsciously apt: how stale it must be to be tied to one woman. Chandler is alone with his thoughts: the forgotten coffee, Annie's photograph, his shyness, the meanness of the pretty furniture. Eventually, "a dull resentment against his life awoke within him. Could he not escape from his little house? Was it too late for him to try to live bravely like Gallaher? Could he go to London?" and, immediately, "there was the furniture still to be paid for" (*D* 83), which answers the preceding questions in a subtly humorous way. Owing money, he cannot leave, a circumstance that never stopped Joyce, who owed nearly everybody he knew when he left Dublin in 1904.

Melancholy Chandler takes refuge in Byron's melancholy, oddly appropriate poem "On the Death of a Young Lady." Though its subject is reflected in the title, in the larger sense the poem deals with irrevocable loss, anger, the accusation that God ("the King of Terrors") has seized the young lady "as his prey," and finally consolation. The poet's initial feeling of outrage is swallowed in a line not quoted in the story: "I'll ne'er submission to my God refuse" (*D* 479). The final section of "A Little Cloud" shows us Chandler trapped by convention and especially by his marriage to an ill-tempered wife. His meeting with Gallaher has made very poignant his sense of the irrevocable loss of his personal freedom to choose an alternate life. The die is indeed cast. His rage at the injustice of these circumstances ("he was a prisoner for life") results in an uncharacteristic, intemperate outcry similar to that in the poem. Unable to concentrate on his reading for the crying child in his arms, he shouts "Stop!" thus frightening his son and enraging his wife. Stammering his excuses, the story's end finds him in total submission, "his cheeks suffused with shame" and "tears of remorse" in his eyes (*D* 85). Wanting the courage to sever the chains that bind him to convention, Little Chandler's life threatens to roll "out evenly—an adventureless tale" (*D* 109).

Dubliners was meant to be a revolutionary document, and in few stories does this spirit emerge more perceptibly than in "A Little Cloud." Most readers have missed the point that it contains a political indictment of the paudeen class Yeats so hated, as he eloquently expressed in "September 1913." Whether Chandler and Gallaher have literary talent is not the point, of course; first they must *see* the squalor of Dublin, *feel* the injustice, *know* that the pen can be a mighty weapon. Gallaher is in an excellent position to make an impact upon a British public opinion oblivious to the Irish nationalist press: as a supposedly successful Irish journalist in London he could speak with authority of the "vermin-like life" (*D* 71) of the Dublin streets that produced him, of poverty, oppression, and national frustration. In his own way he plays it as safe as Chandler.

If Gallaher puts behind him his Dublin past and its significance, missing the unique opportunity he might have to write a *Dubliners* of his own, Chandler is callous to the present. An aspiring poet, he has been entertained and humiliated by a journalist of the worst kind; envious of success and money, he turns his back on what from Joyce's viewpoint in 1906 would be an Irish artist's moral responsibility—"the untidy nurses," "the decrepit old men," the "horde of grimy children" (*D* 71), "the poor stunted houses" like "a band of tramps" (*D* 73). These images come to Chandler's mind, but serve only to reinforce his sense of superiority as he walks to the elegant pub called Corless's. Without a social conscience, he will never see as Joyce did that his subject surrounds him at every turn—life in the city of which he is a part. Though he will feel trapped by his job, his marriage, his fastidiousness, and the bourgeois conventions that cushion him against life's inelegance, he will never transcend his individualist viewpoint sufficiently to see the paralysis that entraps his city, or his relationship to this Irish disease. It will be left to other writers to attack the problem.

THREE

Love's Absence: The Later *Dubliners* Stories

"Clay" and "A Painful Case" both employ a strategy familiar from earlier stories: readers are asked to find the missing piece in the geometric shape that is a Dublin life. Though Maria and James Duffy differ markedly from each other as characters, they are both celibates for whose lives the absence of love has agonizing consequences.

Joyce obviously had some malicious fun in creating Maria, for he eschews sympathetic characterization for what amounts to caricature: she is on one level the proverbial love-starved old maid. A tiny woman with "a very long nose and a very long chin" (*D* 99) that almost touch when she laughs, Maria works in a reform institution run by Protestants and staffed by ex-prostitutes—the *Dublin by Lamplight* laundry (see *D* 483-84). Though she peeks at her body in the mirror for reassurance, she seems totally lacking in self-awareness; one might go further and say that because she cannot see what the mirror reflects, she is essentially a comic figure devoid of the tragic potential of characters like Duffy or Gabriel Conroy. In effect Maria's experience is closer to that of "Araby's" protagonist, but without the epiphany. Her desire for romantic fulfillment is protected and nurtured by an obtuseness that filters out unpleasantness, including mocking allusions to her secret desire.

That which might be a flaw in others in Maria's case permits sanity and the cheerful endurance of a life singularly depressing in its monotonous harshness. Unaware of her slim chances for marital bliss in a land with the world's lowest per-capita marriage rate, she sees nothing odd about a middle-aged ex-nanny employed by an institution for reformed prostitutes in one of Europe's most Catholic countries entertaining ideas of courtship. Her problem is not that she says the mirror lies, but that in her innocence she cannot comprehend the image or its implications. Joyce snickers at Maria, though he seems to admit that her need to love is a normal human desire; still, the only objects of her affections are the seldom-visited men she helped to raise—Alphy and Joe—the first in a series of quarreling brothers in Joyce's works.

It is All Hallow Eve, and the traditional barmbrack cake has been distributed to workers in the laundry: whoever gets the slice with the ring is supposed to be the next to marry. "Lizzie Fleming said Maria was sure to get the ring and, though Fleming had said that for so many Hallow Eves, Maria had to laugh and say she didn't want any ring or any man either . . ." (*D* 101). En route to Joe's house, she takes so much time selecting a piece of cake that the irritated saleswoman "asked her was it wedding-cake she wanted to buy," which makes Maria "blush and smile" (*D* 102). Her next encounter is with a chatty gentleman on a tram, whose attention causes Maria such confusion that she forgets her plumbcake. When at Joe's she is blindfolded and invited to play another Hallow Eve game of divination, her fingers first touch clay, suggesting that death will be her fate in the year to come. Apparently as impervious to symbolism as she is to other threats to her composure, "Maria understood that it was wrong that time and so she had to do it over again: and this time she got the prayerbook" (*D* 105).

Doomed to love from a distance, devoid of self-awareness, at the story's end Maria (probably unconsciously) employs a gnomonic strategy that backfires. Having twice failed to get the ring—thrice counting the barmbrack episode—Maria's ultimate gesture is to sing a song absurdly inappropriate for her. The song, telling of a dream vision about wealth, power, and love, is known to those present, who refuse as one (either out of politeness or because they understand the implications of her omission) to exhibit any awareness that Maria has repeated the first verse twice. The missing second verse (see *D* 484) tells how she

> . . . dreamt that suitors besought my hand,
> That knights upon bended knee,

And with vows no maiden heart could withstand,
That they pledged their faith to me.

The song might be compared to a geometric structure with one part missing—in this case a stanza—which is filled in by the listeners just as other missing pieces in *Dubliners* are by the readers. Maria habitually blocks out what is troublesome, the result here being that her secret and persistent dream is unveiled dramatically. Her obfuscation discloses a secret and ever-present desire to have suitors. Joe, who doubtless cannot express to her his feeling at this moment, finds his eyes full of tears, and unconsciously parodies her displacement in searching about for the missing corkscrew.

In "A Painful Case," James Duffy's attitude toward love is the opposite of Maria's—he abhors it as a danger to the orderly routines that give his life stability. Yet his character is also defined by what he has not, in this case what he consciously excludes from his life. To wall out this basic human need, Duffy (self-aware to a fault) builds a fortress to repel the contact that is Maria's sustenance. It is as if he had read "Clay" from a differing viewpoint, resolving at all cost to avoid entanglements that could wound or make him appear ridiculous or upset his life in any way. Could he have read Robert Frost's "The Mending Wall" as well, he might have considered what he "was walling in or walling out, and to whom he was like to give offense."

As elsewhere in *Dubliners*, the story's prose style reveals through tone, cadence, and word choice a narrative attitude toward the protagonist—Kenner calls it the "Uncle Charles Principle" in *Joyce's Voices*. Here the narrator relates a story with rigid Teutonic precision, amassing a considerable number of facts that describe a Dubliner who seems to take Nietzsche as his guide through life, endeavoring to achieve an invulnerable, tranquil existence worthy of the Übermensch. At the story's center is the question: Could a local bachelor with sufficient self-discipline barricade himself against life's threats to stability and serenity through a dedication to cultural pursuits (music, philosophy, literature, translation) and occasional excursions into political theory (socialist)? Having separated himself from familial entanglements and having compartmentalized his sense of vocation, he is free to pursue his interests unencumbered and alone.

> He had neither companions nor friends, church nor creed. He lived his spiritual life without any communion with others, visiting his relatives at Christmas and escorting them to the cemetery when they died. (*D* 109)

As C. H. Peake has noted, "Mr Duffy is a man who has carefully preserved himself from all the follies which have been the downfall of other Dubliners. . . . [But] in [his] scrupulous avoidance of all the traps—religion, family ties, love, friendship, marriage, politics, art and the rest—he avoids, as well, life itself" (36).

That Duffy's fortress of moral rectitude is vulnerable is first seen in the color pattern of his room, where the splash of scarlet in the rug challenges the predominately somber black-white scheme (*D* 107); so too does the Maynooth Catechism hiding in a notebook seem at odds with the kind of literature and philosophy he reads (*D* 108). What is suggested in these discrepancies is that Duffy pretends an emancipation from bourgeois conventions that has never been tested: for instance, he imagines that he would rob his bank in the right circumstances (*D* 109), but surely he will see to it that such a bold opportunity never occurs. In short, Duffy lacks the courage of his radical convictions.

Duffy's "beast in the jungle" springs in the shape of Mrs. Sinico, whose appearance provides an important key to her character: in the initial description the narrator twice mentions a plainly visible note of defiance about her features (*D* 109), one whose "half-disclosed nature fell . . . under the reign of prudence" (*D* 110). Defiance tempered by prudence is also a feature of Duffy's character, which makes them suited to each other. Mrs. Sinico may well have the defiant courage that Eveline lacks, which would enable her to abandon a family relationship gone dead, and to embark on a perilous journey to some imagined land of fresh air and new beginnings, to a life of uncertainty far from the certain entrapment of Dublin. (It is fruitless to speculate about what these women will find at their rainbow's end; Joyce obviously wished readers to concentrate on the factors that impede embarkation.)[1]

The wife of a sea captain who ignores her, Mrs. Sinico's defiant looks promise a rebellion against life's circumstances—not mere verbal protest, but concrete action. More than just a lover, what she needs is a fellow conspirator, a need with which the lonely Nora Burke of Synge's *The Shadow of the Glen* would surely sympathize.

When it becomes apparent that Duffy is his own cause, enamored of his own voice, Mrs. Sinico acts by taking his hand and pressing it to her cheek. "Mr Duffy was very much surprised. Her interpretation of his words disillusioned him" (*D* 111); he finds safer the abstract world of theory. His revolutionary cant seems incongruous with his timidity of spirit. It is as if he were struggling between two texts, as if the Maynooth Catechism inhibited the moral emancipation urged by Nietzsche. Self-discipline and self-denial come easy, but Duffy lacks the normal responses even of a Bob Doran.[2]

It is irrelevant to suggest that a sordid affair with a married woman would benefit nobody. This is merely one of several possibilities—Molly Bloom would say not an unattractive one for a lonely wife left behind in Ithaca. Elopement and emigration, or an affectionate chaste relationship, are among others. The point is that together there is the potential for growth, happiness, and defiant action against the conventions of Dublin that bind them. (Departure was resolution enough for Synge and Joyce.) When escape fails, Duffy's conventionalism is at fault. The alliance ended, he will revert to his sterile former life, while Mrs. Sinico will turn to alcohol.

The years pass, Duffy's life returns to its dull routines, and nothing is heard of the sea captain's wife until he reads a

[1] See Chapter One here on "Eveline," p. 38.

[2] The *caveat lector* of "The Boarding House," which one such as Duffy could misread, is not against sexual involvement, but against entrapment.

newspaper article concerning her death on the train tracks. The inquest report identifies the cause as "shock" and "sudden failure of the heart's action" (*D* 114), which ironically points not only to Mrs. Sinico's accident but to that earlier scene of Duffy's failed response. On this occasion he does respond, and with devastating self-criticism.

In "Clay," missing objects are important keys to meaning: a ring in a cake, a cake (not for a wedding) left on a tram; a missing verse in a song that mocks the singer. In "A Painful Case," "Clay's" partner, what is present (and should not be) is the splash of scarlet and the Maynooth Catechism; absent in the protagonists's lives are love and meaningful human contact. The counterpoint to this interplay of presence and absence is a newspaper article that serves as a displacement in literary form that mocks its reader. All the facts seem to be present in the article, yet missing is what is present in the story that surrounds it—an account of what is really meant by "the failure of the heart's action." Missing in the article's factual detail are the illogical, unscientific concepts of "broken heart" and incurable loneliness; present is an account of the consequences of Duffy's decision to break with Mrs. Sinico. The story tells of the ultimate cause of the accident described in the article. Each text depends on the other for completion, each frames a missing gnomonic segment.

Even the title of the newspaper article becomes displaced as our awareness of the story's implications grows. Initially it describes the accident victim, later seeming better to fit the survivor James Duffy, or the aborted love affair that causes acute suffering for both victims.

Couched in the heartless tones of factual reporting, the article about the death of Mrs. Sinico divides the story's main body from its ending; it also divides Duffy, attacking his stomach and nerves en route to the source of all this trouble—his heart, thus illustrating by comical example an adage. Mrs. Sinico has supposedly died from "shock and sudden failure of the heart's action" (*D* 114). In response to this news, Duffy leaves his dinner unfinished, the grease congealed on his plate, and thinks, "The shock which had first attacked his stomach was now attacking his nerves" (*D* 116). He retires to a pub where men drink from "huge pint tumblers and [smoke], spitting often on the floor and sometimes dragging the sawdust over their spits with their heavy boots" (*D* 116). Culinary imagery is seen in key phrases: he "gnawed the rectitude of his life; he felt that he had been outcast from life's feast" (*D* 117). If he indeed feels that love is a feast, he must be particulary shocked by his vision of "a goods train winding out of Kingsbridge Station, like a worm with a fiery head winding through the darkness, obstinately and laboriously . . . the engine reiterating the syllables of her name" (*D* 117). One train has killed Mrs. Sinico; now another seems ready to invade his body while chanting her name. No fortress of asceticism can defend him now as his conscience is penetrated by the moral implications of his past failure of the heart's action.

At the story's end James Duffy is punished by a deep longing for the love and human contact he had earlier prided himself on disdaining. His monkish insularity has now been turned inside out to reveal his isolation. Pressing his nose against life's window, "he felt that he was alone" (*D* 117).

The last four stories of *Dubliners* are similarly structured so that meaning emerges out of the same binary opposition of presence and absence, though from this viewpoint only "Ivy Day" and "The Dead" present any complexities. Present in "Ivy Day" are a collection of Dublin party hacks who reveal political vices that are not unique to the Irish: ignorance, treachery, deceit, and a factionalism that historically has made it easy for enemies to divide and conquer. What illuminates the men's character, presumably emblematic of Ireland from 1891 to 1916, is the committee room fire and a memorable day—Ivy Day, the anniversary of Parnell's death. The hacks in the story are no different, it turns out, from the fickle Irish who brought down Parnell, from Joyce's viewpoint the Moses of his time. Yet on the men's lapels are sprigs of ivy that signify loyalty to a memory they betray in word and deed, an absence that defines by the political virtues it represented a corrupt, hypocritical presence that seems to be the Irish condition as Joyce saw it. Memorial torches of perpetual flame are lit to honor great political leaders; yet in the squalid committee room, political hangers-on warm themselves, spit into the fire, or use it to open bottles of stout. Though they wear ivy, they are ignorant of its symbolism, experience no illumination, are incapable of introspection or of understanding the basic truth about Parnell's demise, and are ready on the instant to betray the Irish politicians they serve. By implication, the story asks whether or not a political renewal is possible in Ireland in the century's first decade, whether or not the time is ripe for a new messianic figure; "Ivy Day" answers those questions decisively in the negative. The message here is that of Synge's *Playboy of the Western World*: the Irish enthusiastically embrace heroic figures, then quickly betray them.

If Stephen Dedalus aspires to create his race's conscience, and the characters in "Ivy Day" are representative of that conscience, then he surely has an awesome task before him, one to which Yeats with great frustration and little success was single-mindedly dedicated. Yeats too would have recognized "The Death of Parnell," the poem recited by Joe Hynes, as in that Young Ireland tradition against which he had struggled, where poetry served politics by creating noble sentiment in often ludicrous verse. The unsubtle minds of the men in "Ivy Day" are quick to appreciate sentiment, but slow to distinguish between doggerel and poetry, and slower still to see the disparity between their shabby ideals and the ideals of the political leader whose memory they evoke, whose absence defines their presence.

In "A Mother," Joyce's satirical wit is sharper as he takes aim at the Dublin bourgeoisie with cultural aspirations. The city seems no closer to a cultural renaissance than to a political one, for even here the paudeens rule. Their mentality also predominates in "Grace," where ignorance and conformity stand in the way of clear thinking about issues such as reform, papal infallibility, and alcohol abuse, eventually leading the men to a retreat sermon by one Father Purdon, who seems to say that to serve God or Mammon is really much the same. Though Stanislaus Joyce said "Grace" was patterned on *The Divine Comedy* (228), neither of these stories is structurally complicated in the way of their predecessors; they are slices of Dublin life, satirical stories that hold up art's mirror before grotesque figures who are meant to be representative of the city's whole population, which is unready for a renaissance in culture, politics, or in matters spiritual.

Gabriel Conroy, the isolated protagonist of "The Dead," recalls nobody so much as James Duffy of "A Painful Case," who surrounded himself with barricades against emotional involvement. Though married, Conroy also comes to suffer from a failure of the heart's action, which causes an epiphanic experience through which he will gain more insight than he can bear, leading to a transformation of personality that promises lasting effect. But the wide-angle expansiveness of the Christmas celebration in "The Dead" probably hinders most first-time readers who search for the story's central themes until the last two pages (cf. "Two Gallants"), where Gabriel, having been told of his wife Gretta's infatuation with Michael Furey, experiences profound shock. "He had never felt like that himself towards any woman but he knew that such a feeling must be love" (*D* 223). Recognizing the theme of love's absence, which begins in *Dubliners* as early as "Araby" and "Eveline," we are reminded that "The Dead" is a story integral to the collection rather than an afterthought.

If Conroy reminds us of Duffy, the story's structure parallels that of "Clay," where Maria, repeatedly beset by adversity, keeps a stiff upper lip beneath the nose that nearly meets her chin. The revelation of each unpleasant event brings us closer to an epiphany that she, in her protective myopia, cannot see. Conroy's adversity leads him to understand, suffer, and change in the way Maria in her obtuseness cannot. Isolated by education, temperament, and egotism, Conroy is defeated by forces that conspire against him, and by his ultimate awareness of inadequacy as a man. All his problems seem to spring from a failure of empathy caused by his isolation, but what makes this particular evening disastrous for him is his inability to comprehend time's tricky effects at a moment when Father Time seems determined to trap or defeat him at every turn. When his sensibility is assaulted by his wife's revelation, his consciousness begins to fade out with the waning night and the old year. Though his experience resembles Duffy's, it is at once more devastating and more hopeful for the future, reflecting the end of one cycle and the beginning of another.

If the first line of *Dubliners* suggests Dante's sign over the entrance of the Inferno, the last promises a kind of death and transfiguration quite alien to the sentiment of the earlier stories. Gone is the hardly disguised bitterness of tone, the narrator's desire to score points at the expense of Dublin, the Church, and the ruling powers. Although Joyce's most complicated short story on one level follows the structure of defeat in "Clay," this rather simple pattern is supplemented by an intricate structure of binary opposition which Brewster Ghiselin (316 ff.) and others have discussed.

There are so many dualities in "The Dead" (present-past, east-west, Irish-Continental, male-female, young-old, etc.) that it is perhaps impossible to discuss the story intelligently without touching on at least some of them. As they catch Gabriel Conroy in the vice of their opposition, the common denominator in all these dualities is time. Conroy is a cosmopolitan European who felt as Joyce did that Ireland should look to the Continent; he is a gentleman in touch with the latest books and ideas who chafes under Ireland's provincialism. Like Joyce, he was in some sense ahead of his time or behind it, depending on one's perspective, his time being when Ireland's cultural renaissance emphasized looking westward, learning Irish, assimilating the Celtic past, and getting involved in nationalist politics. Being up-to-date, yet unable to feel the perpetuity of Irish history within him, leads to further estrangement from politically aware Dubliners.

As Tilly Eggers emphasizes, Conroy's most unsettling conflicts are with women, though not as a result merely of male pomposity so much as of his inability to comprehend problems of time and modernity in his dealings with women. For instance, his encounter with Lily the caretaker's daughter is made unpleasant by his inability to see her as the mature young woman she is. In patronizing tones he asks her if she is still in school; stunned to find that he is so far off the mark, he then asks if she is soon to be wed. Lily's answer is, "The men that is now is only all palaver and what they can get out of you" (*D* 178), which could be taken as a rebuke to Conroy as well as to men in general. He is attacked by Miss Ivors for publishing a book review in a pro-British newspaper, which surprises him, but then he seems unaware that a nationalist might object—unaware too that ripening to political maturity in his generation are Maud Gonne and Countess Markievicz, probably the most famous revolutionary women in Irish history. Seemingly unaware of warrior women such as Queen Maeve in Ireland's distant past, he is unprepared to find militancy in a woman (how unladylike!)—and at a Christmas party at that!

Failing to understand these two women, he is sure at least that he has the sisters Morkan pegged right, for they are real ladies of the old school, whose values of hospitality, kindness, and generosity he will later praise in his after-dinner speech. They make one feel so comfortable; they are so unthreatening. These ladies are also lively enough to make one wonder why this story was not named "The Sisters" and the first story of *Dubliners* "The Dead." Though they are really of another time, he seems to share more of their values than he does those of his female contemporaries, which is curiously at odds with his modern preferences for galoshes, sunshades, and Continental travel.

After his minor oratorical triumph, we are prepared for the main event: Gretta Conroy's mental voyage to a nearly forgotten period of her past, launched by Bartell D'Arcy's singing of "The Lass of Aughrim" (*D* 210), a song her girlhood sweetheart Michael Furey sang to her long ago as he stood under a tree getting drenched by a Galway rain. It may well have been the last he sang, since he died soon after. This traditional romantic lover is "very delicate" in health (*D* 219), probably tubercular, and is reminiscent of many pale aesthetes of the nineteenth century from those of Romantic poetry to Jules La Forgue's Hamlet. As Samuel Beckett is reported to have said of the Symbolists, "It was fashionable to die young, and to be pessimistic" (Bair 123). Michael is an image with which the successful, well-fed Conroy, dressed in evening clothes that show his "broad, well-filled shirt-front" (*D* 218), cannot hope to compete. Gretta is transfixed by this memory during moments when her husband has lustful thoughts. Her mind dwells in the past, his in the present; hers on a spiritual, pure love, his on the prospect of a carnal encounter.

The barrier between them is seen in the imagery of "The Dead," which reflects the structure of opposition and tension. In addition to the geographical, temporal, generational, political, male/female, inner-man/outer-man, dead/living dichotomies, we are reminded of the harsh weather conditions and darkness outdoors contrasting with the brightly lit, warm indoor world. As others have noted, Conroy wears galoshes, a newfangled import at the time, advocates green shades for reading, and otherwise shuns nature and the elements that surrounded Michael Furey on that night when he sang to Gretta, and surround him still in the little graveyard of Oughterard. None of these attitudes does Gretta share. Though passion is traditionally associated with warmth, here the equation is reversed, as in Yeats's "The Fisherman": the imagery of cold, wet, and death in *A Portrait*'s first chapter, so negative in its connotations, is a fact of life (or death) in "The Dead."

One of Joyce's notes for *Ulysses* reads, "Dead govern living" (Herring, *Notesheets* 81); in that work, as in most novels, it is commonplace to see the racial, familial, and personal past of the major characters as the primary force molding their consciousnesses. But this note probably has a more specific meaning—that memory resurrects the dead, who exercise considerable influence on the living. Father Flynn seems to attempt coercion in "The Sisters"; Michael Furey in "The Dead"; Stephen's mother and Bloom's father in *Ulysses;* and the dream structure of *Finnegans Wake* at times seems to be about little else.

To say, as Kenner did, that all characters in "The Dead" are dead is to ignore the opposition of the living and the dead, who are fundamentally antagonistic Joycean constituencies (*Dublin's Joyce* 62). The dead are powerful enough in Joyce's works without adding to their number living characters who will soon join them in the usual way. Gretta's memory of Michael, brought back by a song, evokes an image of a shade, never clearly seen in the story, who illuminates through the example of his courage and depth of feeling a glaring inadequacy in her husband. The result is a sort of cuckolding by proxy, a mystical event where the wife's memory of a dead lover dominates the living presence of a lustful husband, who suffers a crisis of consciousness no less profound than that suffered by Richard Rowan of *Exiles*.

At the story's end we find another departure into uncertainty. Florence Walzl calls the ending of "The Dead" "one of the most remarkable ambiguities in literature, a conclusion that offers almost opposite meanings, each of which can be logically argued," and praises its "pattern of ambivalent symbols and . . . great final ambiguity" ("Gabriel and Michael": 29-30). The imagery of annihilation, the prospect of Gabriel Conroy fading out into the snowy landscape is, like the story's title, confusingly ambiguous: Is he drifting off to sleep, or dying, or experiencing a spiritual regeneration that will now allow him to rebuild his marital relationship on love and mutual understanding? The prose rhythm of "His soul swooned slowly as he heard the snow falling faintly through the universe and faintly falling, like the descent of their last end, upon all the living and the dead" looks forward to the ending of Chapter One of *A Portrait*, which also images loneliness, but this passage seems to promise everything at once—death and resurrection, defeat and triumph, paralysis of the will yet a new beginning. Gabriel too is now an outcast at life's feast, his nose pressed against life's window looking outward as the old year wanes, but as in the case of James Duffy, there is no guarantee that correct analysis of this inadequacy of feeling, or the painful experience that accompanies it, will suddenly produce a capacity for love that will fill that gnomonic vacancy and make him whole.

FOUR

Technical Problems in Joyce

We make ourselves a place apart
Behind light words that tease and flout,
But oh, the agitated heart
Till someone really find us out.
Robert Frost, "Revelation"

On Joycean Difficulty

With the publication of *Ulysses*, Joyce established himself as a leading modernist, and thus a difficult writer with whom it was necessary to reckon. This predilection for obfuscation, which manifests itself in his uncertainty principle, spawned what is now widely known as the "Joyce Industry," an activity foreseen by Joyce as the strategy of insuring his immortality. Despite their industriousness, the attention of Joyceans has been engaged more with riddles and textual problems than with precise definitions of the nature of Joycean difficulty, resulting in successive generations of critics addressing the same cruces anew convinced that their answers are either definitive or at least more plausible than those of their predecessors. Their interpretations fail to convince for long, but provide departure points for other commentators to show what they can do.

Defining textual difficulties in such a way as to create opportunities is, in one sense, what literary scholarship and criticism is all about; what makes Joyce more interesting is his desire to add to our problems by creating enigmas, riddles, mysteries to be solved. A cynic might say that it keeps us employed, or that critical relativism is especially justified in such a case, or that Joyce's intention to mystify is irrelevant since authorial intention can seldom or never be established anyway, but most Joyceans are not cynics, just people happy to be sharing their discoveries with others.

AUTHORITY AND INTERPRETATION. This brings us to a consideration of what seem to be problems in advocating the position that Joyce's texts were generally designed to reflect multiple meanings. One problem is that of authority. If interpreters of Joyce are caught up simply in Colin MacCabe's "process of production" (36) reading texts such as we have described from ever differing perspectives, how is it possible to distinguish between more or less plausible interpretations? Is it ever possible to say categorically that a statement in Joyce means *x* or *y*, or must one continually be diffident about meaning?

As early as 1965, in an article entitled, "He Was Too Scrupulous Always," Fritz Senn attached importance to the opening of "The Sisters" as forecasting the experimentalism to come in Joyce's work. Years later, in an important article (now a book chapter), he emphasized the necessity of skepticism in reading Joyce, questioning "how we, as Joyce readers, when we could benefit from such a unique education in applied skepticism [as is found in Joyce's texts], can still be as dogmatic in our own practical performances as we are" (*Joyce's Dislocutions* 97). Senn urges critics to become less assertive, more aware that whatever evidence can be found for one interpretation, equally forceful evidence can always be found to contradict it.

This is useful advice, especially for M'Intosh sleuths and their ilk, but among other things it suggests that Joyce criticism might be a free-for-all. Progress has definitely been made in our understanding of Joyce's texts since their publication; criticism is not just a game where no player really has an advantage; we can hope for more than merely fresh, interesting perspectives. Common sense tells us that we are much more knowledgeable, more sophisticated readers of Joyce than ever before, in large part thanks to the scholarship and rigor of earlier Joyceans, and in part thanks to progress in the editing and publication of manuscripts and corrected texts. No other term but *progress* will do to describe that process by which we are continually able to learn new things about writers such as

Joyce. The more we learn, the greater is our authority as readers; occasionally even our dogmatism may be justified.

Here then is the Scylla and Charybdis of Joycean scholarship: we are caught between an author who devised an uncertainty principle to promote relativism, who teaches skepticism about language, who in *Finnegans Wake* mocked our desire for validity in interpretation ("we must vaunt no idle dubiosity as to its genuine authorship and holusbolus authoritativeness" [118]); opposed to this is the very human need to limit ambiguity, to read Joyce's word world.[1]

Given these opposing forces, authority still must count for something; some readers are better than others, and most would put Fritz Senn at or near the top of any hierarchy of Joyce critics. Too much would seem to depend on our response to the text and too little on the text itself, so that if we are obliged to be skeptical about interpreting Joyce aright, we should be equally skeptical about Joyce's skepticism. We have no recourse but to reject implausibility, to attempt to limit the range of possible meanings, and, more so than with any earlier writer, we are well advised where possible to use an author's implanted keys (there too with skepticism) as the basis for interpretation that should ideally transcend the limits of keyed perspectives.

ON JOYCEAN DIFFICULTY. In the most important Joyce criticism, going back to Robert M. Adams's *Surface and Symbol: The Consistency of James Joyce's "Ulysses"* and further, no very serious attempts to illuminate the nature of Joycean difficulty have been made beyond dealing with allusions and interpreting literary language—in other words, guiding the reader without explaining the special nature of Joycean difficulty. Readers became familiar with the puzzles, enigmas, problems of interpretation, and errors made by various characters that make reading difficult, all as discrete issues of interpretation,

[1] References to *Finnegans Wake* (*FW*) are to the Viking Press edition (New York, 1939).

but usually with no better caveat than that Joyce was a tease.

In his essay "On Difficulty," George Steiner discusses the problem of textual difficulty by subdividing it into four categories that may be useful for getting at the difficulty in Joyce: (1) *Contingent* difficulties, where the obscure word, phrase, or reference may be looked up in a dictionary or other reference work. (2) *Modal* difficulties, where dictionaries won't help because of a system of allusion made difficult by the changing times. Educated readers of the author's historical period and place, because of a shared literary or social heritage, would presumably have encountered no difficulty. (3) *Tactical* difficulties, where obscurity "has its source in the writer's will or in the failure of adequacy between his intention and his performative means" (Steiner 33). Difficulty of this type often occurs as obscurantism in the interest of originality, or in a "rich undecidability" (Steiner 40).

Steiner further distinguishes his first three categories: "Contingent difficulties aim to be looked up; modal difficulties challenge the inevitable parochialism of honest empathy; tactical difficulties endeavor to deepen our apprehension by dislocating and goading to new life the supine energies of word and grammar" (40). The last category is (4) *ontological* difficulties, where the language itself is deemed to be an inadequate vehicle of communication. From Conrad to Derrida, this has been a feature of texts that either cannot or will not "tell us where they are," as in the Frost poem, and where being "found out" seems to be unimportant to the writer. Textual meaning is often private, and the reader is sometimes an intruder on the author's privacy. The writer may be his only common reader, or (and Steiner doesn't say this) there may be important gaps in the text that can never adequately be filled in, such as we have seen in "The Sisters."

Steiner's categories are obviously not the only possible ones for classifying textual difficulty, but they do help us make a beginning with examples from Joyce. We can see, for instance, that as he matures, solving contingent difficulties is Stephen Dedalus's primary means of orientation: "words which he did not understand he said over and over to himself till he had learned them by heart: and through them he had glimpses of the real world about him" (*AP* 62). Presumably he asks what they mean or looks them up before memorizing them, and in *Ulysses* this is also any reader's task who may be uncertain about "parallax" or "metempsychosis." Weldon Thornton's *Allusions in "Ulysses"* and similar reference works (there are now enough to cover bookshelves) provide us with information on many difficult words and ideas. We need not belabor the importance of solving contingent difficulties in Joyce studies; we look up what we can, and puzzle out the rest.

Much of the rest falls into our second category. "*Modal* difficulties," Steiner says, "challenge the inevitable parochialism of honest empathy" (40), so that in many instances we need more specialized commentary, or the will to research the difficulty in question. Educated readers of Milton's day all understood allusions, even quite subtle ones, to the Bible, theology, and classical literature that are incomprehensible to many modern readers.

An obvious context of modal difficulty for most readers of Joyce is Dublin as it existed earlier in the century. At times Joyce seems to be writing primarily for a Dublin audience that will recognize or remember the city market in "Cyclops" and the newspaper columns describing the kinds of produce sold there, or be familiar with the layout of Phoenix Park, or know the streets of "Two Gallants" so well that the circular pattern of Lenehan's walk will become apparent. It is often said that students of Joyce's works are obliged to become his contemporaries.

In *Ulysses*, modal difficulties not only puzzle readers, but often provide humor at the expense of characters. In one instance in "Calypso," Molly Bloom's contingent difficulty becomes modal for the reader. When she asks Bloom the meaning of "metempsychosis" (*U* 4:339), he replies "transmigration of souls," then goes on to explain the word in more detail. Here a subtext emerges to dominate the narrator's metaphorical thinking about change—Ovid's *Metamorphoses*—a work

Bloom is unlikely to have read. Ovid's subject is not precisely metempsychosis, but then, oddly enough, neither is the image pattern.

Why has Ovidian imagery suddenly become relevant? Bloom begins to define "metempsychosis" correctly as "the transmigration of souls" (*U* 4:342), but then metamorphoses the term gradually into "metamorphosis": "Metempsychosis . . . is what the ancient Greeks called it. They used to believe you could be changed into an animal or a tree, for instance" (*U* 4:375-76). This is actually a better definition of human metamorphosis, which usually involves transformation by magic, such as was performed by Circe on Odysseus's crewmen, or as it occurs in Ovid's relevant work. Metempsychosis has more to do with the transmigration of the soul at death into another living form.

As Bloom spins out his hybrid definition, the imagery records what Elliott Gose might call "transformations" parallel to "metamorphosis," transmigrations of living forms to living forms to complement Bloom's explanation. We have seen it before in "Proteus," where Stephen sees a protean dog become "bearish," then stick out "a rag of wolf's tongue," then lope "off at a calf's gallop" (*U* 3:345-48). Immediately after Bloom's definition we read, "The sluggish cream wound curdling spirals through her tea," the cream having become sluglike in Molly's cup, and the color of the liquid having been transformed.

In his mind Bloom compares Molly to a nymph, several nymphs being among the victims of metamorphosis in Ovid. When Molly smells the burning kidney Bloom has earlier bought for breakfast and questions him about it, he descends the stairs "with a flurried stork's legs" and turns the kidney "turtle on its back." By now the organ originally designed to purify some beast's blood, earlier removed from the carcass and displayed as raw meat at the butcher shop, has now become a part of Bloom's breakfast. The transformation process does not end there though, for soon the kidney will become Bloom or waste products, except for the burnt part, which will turn into cat.[2] Here is a modal difficulty of extended allusion that is comprehensible only if the subtext, in this case Ovid's, has been read or read about.

One of the great puzzles of English Renaissance literature is the "two-handed engine" of *Lycidas,* which is to Milton studies generally the sort of enigma that the Man in the Macintosh is to Joyceans, or so John Gordon believes ("M'Intosh": 671). C. A. Patrides says:

> Readers of *Lycidas* will be surprised—and hopefully, amused—by the obsession of scholars and critics with the "two-handed engine" (l. 130). The attempts to interpret the reference and to locate its source continue to proliferate, but, not surprisingly, they only serve to confirm its essential elusiveness. (356)

Patrides then lists parallels, interpretations of the "riddle" (his term), and a checklist on the subject (356-57).

Despite their resemblance as riddles, the "two-handed engine" is clearly a modal difficulty, whereas the M'Intosh mystery is a tactical one, of our third category. Surely very few scholars would seriously contend that Milton intended a puzzle, or that he had no meaning in mind when employing this phrase, but scholars will continue to search in vain for *the* ultimate answer. Presumably the single intended meaning of "two-handed engine" is now lost to posterity, for even if it were discovered (and it may well have been), so much energy has been expended on the subject as to insure against consensus. As we shall see in the following section on "Indeterminacy of Identity," the M'Intosh mystery was clearly *intended* to mystify Bloom and thus the reader.

Steiner's third category, *tactical* difficulty, is the most interesting from the viewpoint of Joyce studies (it is what this book is about), for it allows us to see Joyce as part of the Symbolist

[2] Some of the above paragraphs appeared in somewhat different form in my "Recent Joyceana," a book review for *Contemporary Literature* 24 (1983): 387-94 (p. 388) as part of a discussion of Elliott B. Gose, Jr.'s *The Transformation Process in Joyce's "Ulysses."*

tradition of experimentation, a subject we shall explore in depth in Chapter Five. Steiner briefly discusses Baudelaire, Mallarmé, and Rimbaud as examples of writers who employ a mode of solipsistic integrity that endeavors "to deepen our apprehension by dislocating and goading to new life the supine energies of word and grammar" (40). Poets feel pressured to create original poems, and so invent a "secret tongue" that mystifies. "There is a distinct sense in which we know and do not know, at the same time. This rich undecidability is exactly what the poet aims at" (40). The result may be ambiguity, obscurity, or undecidability. One of Steiner's examples of tactical difficulty is Wallace Stevens's poem, "Anecdote of the Jar."

Steiner's categories address the difficulty of textual language, but they also may cover textual enigmas when the enigmas are set forth in ambiguous language so that no one key will fit. The M'Intosh mystery would therefore be an example of *tactical* difficulty. Another example is the question of how many lovers had Molly Bloom, an enigma that, in following their author's lead, Joyceans have found so troublesome. In these instances, it is not poetic language that is obscure or ambiguous; rather, the rich indeterminacy is in the form of plot puzzles. The effect is the same.

The pseudomystery of how many lovers had Molly need not be rehearsed here (see Adams, *Surface and Symbol* 35 ff., *et passim*) for the same reason that all the answers to the question of M'Intosh's identity need not be given. Where there is no solution, no perspectives avowing solutions need be privileged. For this reason it seems clear that Patrick A. McCarthy's analysis of the Molly's lovers passage is the best to appear hitherto in print; he approaches it as a mathematical problem that was set up so as to have no solution. What I call the uncertainty principle he finds to be Joyce's primary strategy in "Ithaca": "Joyce uses the language of science and mathematics to develop the illusion of objective reliability, then shatters his own smug pose by introducing errors and inconsistencies into the text" ("Unreliable Catechist": 616).

If mathematics was used as the theoretical model for the Molly's lovers passage in "Ithaca," it is close attention to detail in reading that reveals the problem's insolvability. The passage begins with the question, "If [Bloom] had smiled why would he have smiled?" (*U* 17:2126). McCarthy rightly points out that Bloom has not smiled, and consequently does not necessarily have in mind the catalog of lovers attributed to him in the passage that follows ("Unreliable Catechist": 614-15). It begins, "Assuming Mulvey to be the first term of his series . . . ," but this remains an unproven hypothesis. The section on Molly's lovers is so full of contradictions, which in turn give rise to the most implausible lovers, that nothing following the original assumption of Bloom's having smiled can possibly be taken seriously. It is a classic example of the uncertainty principle in operation.

This is also an example of *tactical* difficulty based on a narrator's unsubstantiated assumptions about what Bloom in his own fallibility might have believed. To reveal further muddied waters, McCarthy points out that Bloom is apparently unaware of "Lt. Gardner, the only person, aside from Bloom and Boylan, who might have had sexual intercourse with Molly" (ibid. 615). It is also entirely possible that Molly has forgotten or suppressed the memory of other former lovers.

Whereas in *tactical* difficulty, the writer may in the interest of originality allow us only to glimpse through his smoky glass, *ontological* difficulty brings into question language itself. If there are private meanings here, reference works seldom help; at some level we are not meant to understand, and obfuscation is more clearly an authorial strategy here than in *tactical* difficulty. Rimbaud's "Les Voyelles," which we will discuss later, is a good example, and Lewis Carroll's "Jabberwocky," read without commentary, might fit here as well.

Joseph Conrad's "Heart of Darkness" also belongs in this category, though it is not the story's language that causes obscurity, but rather a dimension of meaning the narrator finds he cannot express. The story's gnomonic gaps remind us of "The Sisters." Marlow's despair of finding the words to communicate the horror he has experienced (or at least sensed) leads him ultimately to what he believes is a failure of narration. F. R. Leavis's objection in *The Great Tradition* (180) that

Conrad makes a virtue out of inarticulateness in the story ignores the power of suggestion on the reader's sensibility.

Another kind of *ontological* difficulty would be found in poems that follow the Symbolist dictum that new languages of poetry must be created. The exoticism of camel caravans and indecipherable language is suggested by Hugo Ball's 1917 Dadaist poem "Karawane" ("Caravan"), which I defy anybody to translate.

jolifanto bambla o falli bambla
grossiga m'pfa habla horem
egiga goramen
higo bloiko russula huju
hollaka hollala
anlogo bung
blago bung blago bung
bosso fataka
ü üü ü
schampa wulla wussa olobo
hej tatta gorem
eschige zunbada
wulubu ssubudu uluwu ssubudu
tumba ba-umf
kusa gauma
  ba-umf

These lovely, exotic words are unspoiled by any encumbrance of denotative meaning.

Much of my final chapter is devoted to the *ontological* difficulty of ALP's letter, and thus of *Finnegans Wake* itself. The subject has been intelligently covered by Wilhelm Füger, who sees the issue as "the central problem of interpretation, namely the unavoidable hermeneutic circle and the fundamental question about the principles and limits of comprehensibility of texts as such" (410). Through an analysis of the letter in question, he sees Joyce's achievement in the *Wake* as combining "his narrative with an implicit analysis of the reading process," stressing Joyce's view of the text's self-referentiality, and the essential mystery of life and art. If this was Joyce's view, he would certainly subscribe to Denis Donoghue's thesis in *The Arts Without Mystery*.

The *ontological* level of difficulty in Joyce provides for Father Boyle the richest of reading experiences. He says, "Then we will experience what literature is, not in the certitude of facts, but in the boundless and fascinating mystery inconclusive of unfacts" (45), and here he is thinking of a passage in *Finnegans Wake:* "Thus the unfacts, did we possess them, are too imprecisely few to warrant our certitude" (*FW* 57:16-22). For Boyle, what binds Shakespeare, Joyce, and Catholic tradition is that these writers' work "builds on mystery, on the void of the suprarational . . . ," a view reflected in Stephen Dedalus's familiar thesis that the world is founded upon the void (Boyle 11; *U* 9:839-42). We shall return to this mystery of *ontological* uncertainty in the *Finnegans Wake* section.

One man's void is another man's plenum.
Robert M. Adams, *Nil*

GNOMONIC DIFFICULTY. The question of incertitude, unlikelihood, brings us by "*commodius vicus*" of recirculation back to our discussion of *gnomon* as Joyce's metaphor for the structural problems or difficulties of his texts. Joyce's gnomonic thinking created a common type of difficulty not covered by Steiner's categories, one that requires the reader to adopt certain strategies in order to discover Joyce's structural design. We have seen that this synecdoche is a geometrical design typically pointing to absence, to the void, to nothing, or to incompletion that the reader is invited to finish. A *gnomon* in the Euclidian sense by definition juxtaposes present form with implied form, and if "The Sisters" is indeed a paradigm story, that implied form supposes variable solutions to indeterminate problems.

Gnomon also reminds us of the theme of "nothing" in literature, discussed by Robert M. Adams in *Nil: Episodes in the Literary Conquest of the Void during the Nineteenth Century*. One can trace the theme of "nothing" in English literature as far back as Rochester's poem and Fielding's essay on the subject. Henry James's *The Turn of the Screw* (1898) and "The Beast in the Jungle" (1903) were written along gnomonic lines, being tales that continually juxtapose presence and absence; the word "nothing" appears at many crucial points. The theme persists in the twentieth century, most notably in existentialism and in the works of Samuel Beckett (*Stories and Texts for Nothing* appeared in 1967), though also in Conrad's *Victory* (1915) and other works. Cynics might immediately see the Joycean connection in terms of plot, since it has been said that nothing of importance happens in his literary works, but Joyce seems to have been interested in "nothing" as a mathematical, spacial, and philosophical concept. More specifically, his gnomonic thinking may well derive from his interest in science, which certainly preceded by many years his writing of "Ithaca," the flowering of that interest.

Space, the void, and nothingness fascinated the young Stephen Dedalus, surnamed after Greece's (the world's) first astronaut, just as it must have fascinated Joyce, for Stephen wonders about it in the first chapter of *A Portrait*: "What was after the universe? Nothing. But was there anything round the universe to show where it stopped before the nothing place began? It could not be a wall but there could be a thin thin line there all round everything" (*AP* 16).

Stephen here echoes the thinking of Archytas of Tarentum, who reasoned:

> If I am at the extremity of the heaven of the fixed stars, can I stretch outwards my hand or staff? It is absurd to suppose that I could not; and if I can, what is outside must be either body or space. We may then in the same way get to the outside of that again, and so on; and if there is always a new place to which the staff may be held out, this clearly involves extension without limit (Čapek 17).

This thinking about infinity Joyce would have encountered in Giordano Bruno's "Concerning the Infinite Universe and Worlds" as a rephrasing of Archytas's statement derived from Lucretius (see Greenburg; Čapek 17). John Locke would later address the same problem.

It is unnecessary to dwell on Leopold Bloom's interest in our subject beyond mentioning that he owns four relevant books: *The Story of the Heavens, A Handbook of Astronomy, In the Track of the Sun,* and *Short but yet Plain Elements of Geometry* (*U* 17:1373-98). As he nods off to sleep, he imagines himself a celestial Odysseus or Wandering Jewish astronaut exiled from his space vehicle: "Ever he would wander, selfcompelled, to the extreme limit of his cometary orbit, beyond the fixed stars and variable suns and telescopic planets . . ." (*U* 17:2013-14). He soon recognizes his land of promise as the "eastern and western terrestrial hemispheres" of his wife's posterior (*U* 17:2229), a kind of fundamental voyeuristic/astronomical thinking to which Joyce's notes on "Ithaca" show him to have been sympathetic. (At his silliest the result was notes such as, "Woman fucked: cries fill space" [Herring, *Notesheets* 434].) As Bloom reclines, their bed becomes a space vehicle that transports them "through everchanging tracks of neverchanging space" (*U* 17:2309-2310).

Joyce's notes for *Ulysses* included references to spacial theories of Nikolai Lobachevsky and Georg Riemann (Herring, *Notesheets* 474; 476), mathematicians whose work led to a fully non-Euclidean geometry, and space/time is, of course, the thematic focal point of the fable of the Mookse and the Gripes in *Finnegans Wake,* which begins, "Eins within a space and a wearywide space it wast ere wohned a Mookse" (*FW* 152). This brief reminder of Joyce's continuing interest in gnomonic space seems sufficient to establish it as a category of Joycean difficulty.

THE JOYCEAN VOID. In the *Tao Te Ching,* Lao Tzu presents the following meditation in which Joyce could have seen the relevance of *gnomon*:

> Thirty spokes
> Share one hub.
> Adapt the nothing therein to the purpose in hand, and
> you will have the use of the cart. Knead clay
> in order to make a vessel. Adapt the nothing
> therein to the purpose in hand, and you will have the

use of the vessel. Cut out doors and windows in order to make a room. Adapt the nothing therein to the purpose in hand, and you will have the use of the room.
Thus what we gain is Something, yet it is by virtue of Nothing that this can be put to use.[3]

Most analytical philosophers believe that the modern interest in vacuity derives largely from verbal confusion and oppose those thinkers who have made it the very center of metaphysical inquiry. A philosopher of this party calls the latter group "know nothings" in the entry on "Nothing" in *The Encyclopedia of Philosophy* (to which I am indebted here), and yet their argument has fascinated thinkers who know much. If matter was created out of nothing, then nothingness preceded matter as nonexistence preceded existence. Such thinking resulted in an objectification of nothing as an actual subject of inquiry. In 1907 Bergson stated it thus: "Existence appears to me like a conquest over nought. . . . If something has always existed, nothing must always have served as its substratum or receptacle, and is therefore eternally prior" (Čapek 13). In 1924 Heidegger restated it: "Warum ist überhaupt Seindes und nicht vielmehr Nichts?" (ibid. 14), which was refined by Paul Valéry in "Le serpent" to read, "Que l'univers n'est qu'un défaut / Dans la pureté du Non-Être!" (ibid.). Heidegger lectured on nothing in Freiburg in 1928. Sartre's *Being and Nothingness* appeared in 1943.[4]

Generally coincident with Heidegger's interest in *Nichts* is the uncertainty principal of Werner Heisenberg (1930), whence this present book takes its title, which further undermined traditional notions of space and time. Čapek says, "According to the principle of uncertainty both the concept of precise position and that of sharply defined velocity [of any elementary particle] lose their meanings; consequently, the

[3] Thanks to Michael Uebel for this passage.

[4] The best work on vacuity in Joyce has been done by John Bishop in *Joyce's Book of the Dark*. See the chapter entitled "Nothing in Particular: On English Obliterature" (40-63), to which I am indebted here.

concept of the 'state of the world at an instant' loses its definiteness too" (290).[5]

In the same year, 1930, Gödel noted a similar theorem in mathematics, that "in any formal system adequate for number theory there exists an undecidable formula—that is, a formula that is not provable and whose negation is not provable" (*The Encyclopedia of Philosophy* 3:348).

Related to this mode of inquiry is Alexius Meinong's earlier theory of objects, first explained in his article "Über Gegenstandstheorie" (1904), which says that nonexisting objects have properties just as existing objects do, that the property of objects does not imply existence, which allows us to discuss the legitimate properties of square circles, married bachelors, and the like.

Meinong was rather ineffectually rebutted by Bertrand Russell in *The Introduction to Mathematical Philosophy* (169), a work from which Joyce copied extensive notes for the "Ithaca" episode of *Ulysses* (see Herring, *Joyce's Notes* 49-52; 103-111). Joyce seems to have been more interested in vacuity's power of suggestion than in any metaphysical implications, though his interest in zero and infinity did at times lead to existentialist thought patterns. I quote a passage from my introduction to notebook V.A.2 to illustrate the connection between Joyce's interest in nullity, zero in mathematical terms, and its philosophical implications.

> In Russell's chapter on rational, real, and complex numbers we find, "It will be observed that zero and infinity, alone among ratios, are not one-one. Zero is one-many, and infinity is many-one" (p. 65). Joyce has "0 = 1/many, ∞ = many/one, 1 = 1/1." . . . In the text what began as mathematics becomes metaphysics: "From inexistence to existence [Bloom] came to many and was as one received: existence with existence he was with any as any with any:

[5] See Heisenberg's *The Physical Principles of Quantum Theory*, trans. Carl Eckart and Frank C. Hoyt (University of Chicago Press, 1930), chapters 2 and 3.

from existence to nonexistence gone he would be by all as none perceived" (*U* 17:67-69; *Joyce's Notes* 50).

Most of the scientific and mathematical theorizing about nullity, uncertainty, and the void came decades after Joyce's use of the Euclidian term *gnomon,* so there is no direct connection to be made between, say, Heisenberg and *gnomon*. Nevertheless, the term is a perfect private symbol of Joyce's lifelong interest in matters such as the juxtapositions of presence and absence, matter and the void, existence and nonexistence, an interest he mentioned to his son Giorgio in 1935: "My eyes are tired. For over half a century, they have gazed into nullity where they have found a lovely nothing" (*Letters* 3:361n.; quoted in Bishop 61).

On Joycean Error

In *The Silent Years,* J. F. Byrne said that Joyce's "definitely favorite mirth rouser was when anyone pulled a boner. Always he sat in an elfin crouch waiting and hoping for a blunder." The example Byrne gives is when a classmate defined a "pedestrian" as "a Roman footsoldier," which evoked in Joyce a "spontaneous shout" of hilarity (147). As a writer, from first to last, Joyce delighted in strewing the pathways of his fiction with error and confusion. The first tenet of Joyce's uncertainty principle may have been that his own amusement varied in direct proportion to the reader's consternation.

Scholars have not been unaware of errata as humor in Joyce's works, but for the most part they have generally avoided error as a topic with theoretical implications. Then, too, from Adams's *Surface and Symbol* to Bernard Benstock's "On the Nature of Evidence in *Ulysses,*" to McCarthy's "Joyce's Unreliable Catechist," all exceptionally fine works within their province, one receives the impression that error first appears as a theme in *Ulysses*. James Maddox, for instance, indicated that error is a major motif in "Ithaca" (Maddox 189). Undeniably so, but in fact error is a constant theme throughout Joyce's works, though when found by readers it is generally treated as an aspect of the individual text. But an error in Joyce is not merely a misstated fact requiring correction; as a subject of inquiry it leads us to matters of thematic importance. In the following section I am not interested in cataloging all the errors in Joyce, but rather in making sense of error as a Joycean strategy.

As in the dramatic monologue, *Dubliners* characters often reveal their ignorance or vulgarity through errors. Eliza of "The Sisters" mentions the *Freeman's General* (surely few Dubliners were unaware that the newspaper was the *Freeman's Journal*) and later "rheumatic" wheels (*D* 16-17), the newfangled inflatable kind, so that we are less surprised when she violates wake decorum by revealing embarrassing details about her dead brother, Father Flynn. She speaks easily of his body being washed and of the night he was found laughing in the confessional late at night, details we can accept as true while remaining suspicious about her common sense in revealing them. On the other hand, it is precisely because Eliza is a foolish person that we see the priest's dirty linen aired; other adults in the story are extremely reticent about Father Flynn, and it is only with her that the boy makes any headway toward solving the mystery that puzzles him. Eliza is no genius, but her errors are the portals of discovery.

Maria of "Clay" is also error-prone and foolish, similarly lacking in self-awareness, so that displacement becomes the primary technique of illumination in the story. Imagining herself to be flirting, she forgets her cake on the tram, which nearly causes a row at Joe's. When blindfolded she chooses the clay that mischievous children had placed among other objects of divination, she understands this to have been a mistake, and she chooses again. It is her error in singing the first verse of "I Dreamt that I Dwelt" twice that illuminates her frustrated longing for romance (*D* 106).

As the story's notes attest, the general discussion toward the end of "Grace" is a veritable catalog of amusing historical errors. As in the other *Dubliners* stories, error functions to stress the backward provincialism of characters (here they are men) who by class, education, and nationality represent the masses whose collective conscience Stephen Dedalus will imagine himself capable of creating through his art. That art will be created out of words and facts of which Dubliners, through irreverent misuse, show themselves to be contemptuous. But at least in "Grace" the friends gathered at Tom Kernan's bedside have done enough reading to get their facts mixed up, which is more than can be said for all but a few of the characters in *Dubliners*.

Garrett Deasy, in the "Nestor" episode of *Ulysses* (2:185 ff.), is a fool in the *Dubliners* tradition, closest to the men in "Grace," but with a new twist. Unlike them, being a schoolmaster, he is supposed to be wise, as his antecedent in *The Odyssey* is. He also resembles Polonius in Shakespeare's *Hamlet*. Deasy's subject, on this day at least, seems to be Irish history, and, though one might make allowances for his Ulster viewpoint, he is astonishingly consistent in getting his facts wrong. (This has been pointed out by Adams and many others.) By implication, this makes his lecture to Stephen on the value of money seem wrong as well, and the anti-Semitism he shares with the Englishman Haines all the more disturbing. The coins that dance on his shoulders as he tells his anti-Semitic joke (*U* 2:448-49) belie the sincerity of his position.

It is well known that Joyce introduced errors in a calculated way into *Ulysses*, usually to undermine the authority of some character for comic effect. For instance, in his notesheets for *Ulysses*, Joyce accumulated enough material on palmistry to demonstrate a thorough knowledge of the subject, yet he allowed Zoe to make mistakes while reading Stephen's hand (*U* 15:3677-93; Herring, *Notesheets* 43-47). One note for "Penelope" reads "MB mistakes her age" (Herring, *Notesheets* 499), which yields a chuckle at Molly's expense (*U* 18:475; cf. 17:2275-76). A careful study of the notesheets reveals other instances in which the facts are correct, only to appear as errors in *Ulysses*. This is error in the *Dubliners* tradition.

Many errors in *Ulysses* were introduced by printers and went uncorrected until the Garland edition (1984); these have been well documented by Adams, Benstock, McCarthy, and others, as have the many errors of Leopold Bloom, which also are generally of the *Dubliners* kind. Others are of the narration, such as the absurd measurements of Bloom's physique (*U* 17:1817-19); the notesheets indicate that Bloom's tiny chest was not a printer's error (469). Others we classify at our peril, because they may or may not be intentional on Joyce's part, such as the age calculation on *U* 17:446-61, where at one point somebody multiplied Stephen's age not by 17, the difference between his age and Bloom's, but by 70. Adams is far more certain than I am that the mistake is Joyce's, that "this is not a parodic error" (183), but he is certainly right that it may not matter since "Joyce was less concerned with intellectual precision than with the machinery of precision, with the click and glitter of accuracy" (*Surface and Symbol* 182).

At this point we might entertain some speculations. Joyce admittedly made mistakes, and, in a novel of the length and complexity of *Ulysses*, he surely knew that he would make a good many and that the printers would introduce more. This may have bothered him, and the bother could have expressed itself in a strategy of obfuscation, so that readers would find it difficult to distinguish his errors from Bloom's. But then, he also must have delighted in the confusion all this would cause posterity. Confusion was surely a part of his uncertainty principle, for more often than not in Joyce's works error is a source of humor.

Riddles should hence be considered in this context, since Joyce's intention in introducing them is not merely to give readers a puzzle to chew on, but also to proliferate error. There are many ways to be wrong in deciphering Stephen's riddle of the fox burying his grandmother under a holly bush (*U* 2:94-115), or in speculating about how many lovers Molly has embraced carnally in her lifetime (*U* 17:2133-42), or who M'Intosh is, or what is the meaning of U.P.: up (see Adams, *Surface and Symbol* 192-93), but it is surely impossible to prove one answer right in any of these instances. The whole point of the riddles is to encourage readers to speculate, to argue, to disagree, to amass more evidence, to shout "Eureka!" while the author chuckles. This was precisely the point of Joyce's leading his friends on to guess the permanent title he had decided to give "Work in Progress."

So far we have discussed characters who make humorous errors, and riddles that tease us. When our viewpoint is shifted slightly, we see that there are characters in Joyce's work who live in error, or have mistaken viewpoints that cause them great unhappiness. At some point they either have epiphanies that enable them to see clearly, or they do not, and it is precisely this quality that makes them interesting as characters. The boy in "Araby" blinds himself to the implications of romantic love, and refuses until the story's end to see that his pilgrimage to buy a love trophy is ludicrous. He then sees the error of his ways (not just his mistake about the bazaar), and is presumably transformed. In "Two Gallants," it is the reader who is led into error about the intentions of Corley and Lenehan until the end, when a gold coin eliminates any ambiguity about their motives. "A Little Cloud" is about a Dubliner who lives in error about his vocation; whatever he is destined to become, it is not a poet. "A Painful Case" shows us a man who mistakenly believes that he can, through rigid self-discipline and orderly living, insulate himself against life's uncertainties. The erroneous nature of his rigid lifestyle is finally revealed, much to his cost.

In his maturation Stephen Dedalus has to make his way through a maze of antagonistic viewpoints expressed by Church, State, friends, and family. Since we know that his development in *A Portrait* is on one level measured by vocabulary acquisition, reflected in the maturing style, it is amusing to find error tossed into his path, as when Dante "made that noise after dinner and then put up her hand to her mouth: that was heartburn" (11). Since presumably ladies do not belch, Stephen has been taught a euphemism before he is prepared to understand it. The noise he will later think of as heartburn.

Wells asks Stephen whether or not he kisses his mother before he goes to bed. When it is reported that he does, gathered classmates laugh. The affirmative answer is then quickly denied, which Wells duly reports to the others.

> They all laughed again. Stephen tried to laugh with them. He felt his whole body hot and confused in a moment. What was the right answer to the question? He had given two and still Wells laughed. But Wells must know the right answer for he was in third of grammar. (*AP* 14)

In his naiveté, Stephen believes in the probable existence of universally understood rules of conduct in matters such as the curious custom of kissing. The initiates are older, and so have learned the right answers. At the moment, correct answers to ritual questions seem more important than correct conduct, and truth seems to count for very little: i.e., whether or not one actually kisses one's mother. Stephen's confusion is the quandary of uncertainty and error, and his frustrated reading of the world, like that of the boys in the first three stories of *Dubliners*, parallels at many points our reading of Joyce.

Like the above-mentioned Dubliners, Stephen also begins consciously to live in error, which in *A Portrait* is specifically equated with sin. As he reflects upon the hell-fire sermons, Stephen imagines Emma and himself in a holy landscape, standing as "children that had erred. Their error had offended deeply God's majesty though it was the error of two children" (116). Fires of lust have led Stephen into brothels, so that he has become an "erring sinner" (135). When later he has his vision of the bird-girl, he consciously decides to walk among the snares of the world, to fall as Lucifer fell, into error, and to take the consequences of rebellion as an artist must: "To live, to err, to fall, to triumph, to recreate life out of life!" (172). To this extent, like Satan, Stephen remains a believer in God and His righteousness, because he refuses to blur the distinction between erroneous and right conduct. Rather, Stephen chooses error as the artist's way of knowing the corruption of a world that has chosen to turn its back upon a Judeo-Christian God whose existence he does not deny. It is no accident that he is cited for heresy in his school essay, or that he is bullied for defending Byron against charges of heresy and immorality (79-81). Heresy must be defined in terms of an orthodox belief that Stephen chooses to oppose, but not blaspheme against or ignore as irrelevant, which would be the position of Buck Mulligan in *Ulysses*. In *A Portrait*, Stephen's rebellion never ceases to be defined in conventional Catholic terms.

At the beginning of *Ulysses*, Stephen is degraded and demoralized by his rebellion, though vowing to fight on. He at first refuses Haines's invitation to affirm his apostasy (1:605 ff.), though when pushed we read, "You behold in me, Stephen said with grim displeasure, a horrible example of free thought" (1:625-26). This statement contains a curious paradox: if he does indeed think freely, then why should he view his apostasy as horrible, and reflect such grim displeasure with his position? The answer must be that he is not as free to disbelieve as he imagines, that he feels guilty, is uncomfortable with the paths of error and the directions in which they lead him—that with Rimbaud, one of his role-models, he recognizes the horrible loss in personal terms of waging war against convention in his native land. This, then, must be one of the basic truths about Stephen: that he is torn asunder by his religious rebellion, that he finds himself unfree to evolve toward an easy, guilt-free apostasy.

As a rebel, perhaps Stephen's most important model is Satan, especially Milton's, who as God's enemy never falls into the error of agnosticism or atheism, and who feels an ever-deepening sense of degradation at each triumph in the battle for influence over God's new creature. Joyce may have turned his back on Stephen in *Ulysses* because his character was too fixed, as he said, but more precisely because Stephen is programmed for defeat in life, as in art.

Stephen's rebellion against convention is meant to insure artistic and theoretical originality, without which there is no life as an artist. As one of numerous half-truths and errors he later peddles as part of a Shakespearean theory that he eventually says he doesn't believe, in the library scene of *Ulysses* Stephen says that "a man of genius makes no mistakes. His errors are volitional and are the portals of discovery" (*U* 9:228-29). This often-quoted viewpoint seems to make little sense, for how could all the errors of genius be intentional? Some errors of literary geniuses are doubtless portals of discovery that yield insight into author or character, but others are indeed mistakes that show only that a genius may be as error-prone as ordinary people. Concerning the common, garden variety of errors, Stephen doesn't enlighten us.

What is more enlightening is to consider through the Steppe-Gabler *Handlist* the usage patterns in *Ulysses* for *erred, erring, error,* and *errors* (*err* is uninteresting). Here again we find support for the thesis that Joyce frequently associated error with sin. *Erred* and *erring* in each case refer to sin, usually with the implication of sexual licentiousness (*U* 13:375; 13:749; 15:2226; 15:906; 15:940; 16:1537). In "Nestor," where historical error is emphasized, Deasy erases a typing error (*U* 2:298) and mentions *errors* twice in conjunction with female sin and promiscuity (*U* 2:389; 2:394). The terms *error* and *errors* are used to mean something like *mistake* or *folly* or *heresy* in six more instances (*U* 15:2642; 15:3078; 17:702; 17:1138; 9:867; 15:2100), though in "Eumaeus" Bloom reflects "about the errors of notorieties and crowned heads running counter to morality" (*U* 16:1201).

In "Circe," however, Stephen's comment to The Cap, "You remember fairly accurately all my errors, boasts, mistakes" (*U* 15:2100), unless he is simply redundant, suggests that for him *errors* and *mistakes* are not the same. If we return to Stephen's point that "a man of genius makes no mistakes. His errors are volitional and are the portals of discovery," we see the probability of his distinction between *mistakes,* which are more petty, and *errors,* which should mean moral indiscretions willfully indulged in by one who spurns higher authority to follow the dictates of nature. On the other hand, if there is a distinction, it is often blurred, for Stephen tells Cranley, "I am not afraid to make a mistake, even a great mistake, a lifelong mistake and perhaps as long as eternity too" (*AP* 247). Even here, though, both *mistake* and *error* are associated with sinful habits that eventually may bring damnation.

Stephen's romantic theory of Shakespeare, which says in effect that the bard's biography is implicit in his plays, runs parallel to his theory of the errors of genius. One discovers the nature of genius through genius's intentional errors and sinful ways, just as the playwright's life and personal obsessions are discovered in the plays. In fathering this illegitimate theory that he privately disowns, Stephen feels compelled to persevere in order to impress upon his audience the quality of his mind—his genius—even at the cost of his self-respect. They are to recognize in his error a rare ingenuity, careless of truth. "They list. And in the porches of their ears I pour" (*U* 9:465) not a poison, but a theory that is meant to cause them to sit up and take notice. Yet he fails to convince, and fails to gain any satisfaction from the erroneous theory he peddles. His audience will mock or forget or take little notice.

If Stephen recognizes that he requires the freedom to err in matters of literary theory, moral conduct, or belief, he seems unaware that he is seriously in error in pursuing his aesthetic philosophy, though admittedly this may be a necessary stage through which he must pass to attain originality. On the one hand, as we shall see below in Chapter Five, his poetic technique and outlook have been shaped by the French Symbolists and Shelley, and on the other his aesthetic theories, as expressed in Chapter Five of *A Portrait*, are derived from Aquinas. In both cases there is the odor of embalming fluid. The poets he admired, the aesthetic theory he hones before Lynch, lead him inward, into realms of the imagination, to the contemplation of art rather than life.

None of this leads him to develop further the social conscience that would seem to be emerging as a result of his struggle with poverty, or from his clashes with the authority of family, state, and church. His poem, "Are You Not Weary of Ardent Ways" (*AP* 223-24), which reeks of the 1890s, is not the poem of a young man who is set on forging in the smithy of his soul the uncreated conscience of his race (*AP* 253). Neither is there any evidence that he could write a book like *Dubliners;* in fact he seems far more suited to write another "Wanderings of Oisin." Here is perhaps the central paradox of Stephen, that he wishes to be a heretic, a revolutionary in art, to live in error and poke about in Dublin's alleyways, and yet his artistic and aesthetic consciousnesses lead him only deeper into the imagination.

In *Ulysses* we see Stephen's inevitable entrapment within the self. As we leave claustrophobic "Proteus," we turn with relief, as Joyce must have done, to the felt life of Leopold Bloom's world. Like a *Dubliners* character, Bloom makes many ludicrous errors, especially in matters of scientific fact, but unlike Stephen, he does not live guiltily in opposition to moral convention. It is a commonplace of Joycean criticism to point out that, though they both must deal with anxiety, guilt, isolation, and bondage of sorts, Bloom is the generally well-adjusted survivor Stephen must learn to become if he is to live happily in the world. Up to this point in his life, Stephen seems to have found no better role model than Bloom, which provides an appropriately Homeric twist to the novel.

James Card has shown that Molly Bloom's monologue is a tapestry of contradictions (*Anatomy* 38-55). He says, for instance, that Molly is "quite contrary since virtually everything that passes through her mind is contradicted by something else that passes through" (ibid. 38). The effect is to make her a comical character and, perhaps, to reinforce the stereotype of attractive women who are illogical. In addition, as we shall see, error is relevant to Molly's character not merely because she mistakes her facts, or contradicts herself, or because she lives in error as an unfaithful wife who secretly prefers her husband, but, more interestingly, because as a woman of Gibraltar she is an absurdity. In tarting her up with an exotic heritage, Joyce stretched the social and historical fabric of her parentage and early life well beyond credibility, something he could hardly have done to a Dubliner. The first sixteen years of Molly's life cannot so easily be dismissed, as we shall see in Chapter Five.

In 1976 I spent a week working in Gibraltar's Garrison Library on Joyce's sourcebooks for "Penelope." My leisure time was spent interviewing Gibraltarians about their impressions of Molly's story as Joyce has it in *Ulysses*. My approach with local people was to ask them to pretend for the moment that Molly's story was historical—that she was the daughter of Lunita Laredo and an Irish-Catholic drum major or officer of the garrison. Such a match, they said, would have been impossible, for there would have been nobody to marry them, and from both the garrison and the influential Jewish community they would have received intolerable pressure. Jewish women did not date men from the garrison, and none ever became prostitutes. If the mother had been gypsy, Molly's story would have made sense, but the locals knew everything about the Laredo family going back at least two centuries, and there were no gypsies among them. In short, they considered the story to be wildly romantic, and if the match had ever taken place, it would still be vividly remembered as local folklore, especially since no rabbi, priest, or minister would have tied the nuptial bonds of Molly's parents.

Molly is thus a sociological error whose memories of Gibraltar are made almost entirely of guidebook material, but whose memories do not include the Laredo family, who continued to reside in Gibraltar throughout her girlhood, or more than the barest Spanish vocabulary. But for these dubious memories, one could scarcely guess by accent, appearance, and attitude that she has ever been out of Dublin. What is of interest is not that she makes so many mistakes, or that in some sense she lives in error as Stephen does, but that the psychological makeup of her character consists of mismatched parts covered with a thin overlay of exoticism. Molly is a sociological error presumably deriving from Joyce's increasing tendency to create absurdities in the latter part of *Ulysses;* but in part she may derive from Joyce's knowledge that he knew too little about Gibraltar ever to paint an accurate portrait. To this subject we shall return later.

FIVE

Indeterminacies of Identity

Late-nineteenth-century fiction contains many examples of mysteries or indeterminacies of identity, due largely to novelists' increasing concern with psychology. For example, Melville's *Billy Budd* and Hawthorne's *The Scarlet Letter* raise doubts about our capacity to understand human motivation sufficiently well to make moral judgments. Famous examples are Conrad's *Lord Jim*, where Jim's failure to live up to a code of honor brings into question his essence as a gentleman, and Kurtz of *Heart of Darkness*, whose flirtation with evil so intrigues Marlow that he forms a mystifying loyalty to the trader and, faced with the inscrutable darkness of the human heart (not to mention Africa), plunges finally into epistemological skepticism. Ambiguity, inscrutability, obscure motivation—these qualities lie at the center of Henry James's most interesting characters as well.

Marlow's fascination with Kurtz is in many ways a paradigm of discovery in this literary period; though he imagines himself to be prying into the secrets of the human heart, as does Roger Chillingworth in *The Scarlet Letter*, the secrets of the mind and its motivation are really the focal points of discovery. So too with these earlier writers. What is interesting too is how their baffled realization of the mind's complexity easily leads to the range of epistemological skepticism experienced by Marlow, who may have understood more than he can successfully relate, which is still only a fraction of the whole truth. The tension between a narrator's need to penetrate apparently inscrutable minds and the obligation to tell a story is, of course, a common condition of twentieth-century fiction too.

This rehearsal of what is common knowledge helps us begin a definition of indeterminacy of character in fiction. I use the term in a specific sense: such a character embodies an unsolvable mystery of identity.[1] Five observers (or critics) peering

[1] On coincidence as the source of indeterminacy of identity, see Hannay, especially 343-47.

from different angles at a subject will, of course, receive varying impressions; so to this extent all characters have an indeterminate dimension. Of interest to me, however, are those who embody an intriguing mystery at the center that cannot finally be understood. An ambiguous character makes sense on more than one level; an indeterminate one remains mysterious while obliging the serious reader to formulate meaningful statements. In fiction of this century, indeterminate characters often dwell in unrealistic or surrealistic circumstances, so that an air of mystery pervades.

This is typical of Harold Pinter's plays. Following the example of Beckett, who has successfully made comedy out of our preoccupation with inscrutability, Pinter infuses mystery into the commonplace for maximum shock effect. He does this in part by making character identity indeterminate. The following exchange of letters, which supposedly took place early in Pinter's career, reveals much about his attitude on this subject: "Dear Sir, I would be obliged if you would kindly explain to me the meaning of your play *The Birthday Party*. These are the points which I do not understand: 1. Who are the two men? 2. Where did Stanley come from? 3. Were they all supposed to be normal? You will appreciate that without the answers to my questions I cannot fully understand your play." Pinter's answer was "Dear Madam, I would be obliged if you would kindly explain to me the meaning of your letter. These are the points which I do not understand: 1. Who are you? 2. Where do you come from? 3. Are you supposed to be normal? You will appreciate that without the answers to your questions I cannot fully understand your letter."[2]

In his letter Pinter tries to plant seeds of doubt about the possibility of certitude in understanding the identity, origin, or motivation of his dramatic characters. At first glance the questions seem straightforward, but Pinter would say, as Samuel Beckett has before him, that these are the basic metaphysical questions of our age. Identity, motivation, and origins in a typical Pinter play are quite obviously indeterminate by design; nobody communicates well with anybody

[2] *The Daily Mail*, London, 28 November 1967, in Esslin (30).

else; there is a dreamlike atmosphere; the setting is slightly surreal; action is unpredictable. Playgoers cannot know more than the simple dialogue, which teases them with possibilities, tells them.

There is considerably more evidence on which to judge literary character in Joyce than in Pinter, but when we find his uncertainty principle operative, the more the evidence the greater the complexity. Mystery lies at the center of Pinter's characters because what was discovery in *Heart of Darkness* has become a rather tired truism, the search into the human heart by now a familiar, though often shocking, game. In our paradigm story, "The Sisters," the boy sees his task as serious and compelling. But we have noted there how indeterminacy in Joycean character in the case of Father Flynn is designed to lead readers to inquire into insoluble problems. In *Ulysses* the most basic questions are often unanswerable because few readers could agree on the definition of terms. Is or is not Bloom a Jew? (What is a Jew?) How faithful is Molly?[3] (How does one define fidelity? Does being faithful in spirit count?) Will Stephen become a successful writer? (What are the signs of success?) The more central the question about Joycean character, the more impenetrable the mystery, despite thousands of details that can be used as evidence.

As illustrations of this thesis, in this chapter I ask a few questions that should allow us to see distinctions between mysteries of identity and problems of character where genuine insights are possible. These questions have intrigued many Joyce commentators for decades. Using varying approaches, and with varying results, I try to answer them. 1)Who, after reams of commentary has been published, is the Man in the Macintosh really? 2)Why has Stephen Dedalus made so little progress in fulfilling his artistic vocation between *Stephen Hero* and the end of *Ulysses*? 3)How central is Molly's Gibraltarian background as it defines her identity?

[3] Although, these two questions will remain indeterminate as long as there is no agreement on definitions, this has never stopped commentators, who often attack problems of identity as if literary characters were historical figures. This has been a serious fault in Joyce studies.

The Man in the Macintosh is a good starting point because it is generally assumed that he actually has an identity if one could only find it; my thesis is that he has none, that he is merely a teasing construct of words. If we ask who Stephen Dedalus is, the best answer may be that he is an artist as a young man; more specifically, he promises to be a poet. But he makes so little progress in this direction that we seem obliged to rephrase the question: Does who he thinks he is have anything to do with his inability to fulfill his vocation? I presume to answer the question from a vantage point that makes sense to me, and assume that self-definition and identity are linked. Stephen, apparently so implacably opposed to authority in whatever form, is paralyzed to artistic stasis by a literary forebear—not by Aristotle or Aquinas, whose theories he successfully assimilates, but by a single poem of Arthur Rimbaud that he cannot make his own and that blocks his path to originality. Since this issue never surfaces as a problem in the works where Stephen appears, I perceive an indeterminate gap in characterization of major importance that could explain why his vocation is so elusive.

Later I intend to explore an important mystery in Molly Bloom's background that leads us to an indeterminate gap in her identity—the significance of her early life in Gibraltar and the implications thereof, which never surface in *Ulysses.* On the most basic level, when we ask who Molly is, we must focus on where she is from. She is a woman of mixed Irish-Catholic and Jewish background who was born and raised in Gibraltar, and who came to Dublin when she was sixteen. Just as Stephen's struggle with Rimbaud is never an issue, neither is the fact that on her mother's side Molly is descended from the Laredo family of Gibraltar and Tangier, a well-known Jewish family that still inhabits those places. (A kinsman, Leopoldo Laredo of Tangier, once wrote me a letter.) Courtship between Jew and nonJew was extremely rare on the Rock in Molly's day, and the prevalent idea that her mother might have been a prostitute is far-fetched given the sociological context of Molly's childhood. In fiction a character may be anything the author likes, but Joyce's inclusion of precise historical details about Molly's life in Gibraltar presents curious theoretical problems. Being strict Jews, neither the Laredos nor the rabbis would ever have tolerated the marriage of one of their girls to an Irish Catholic or remained quiet while Molly (legally Jewish) was raised to maturity as a daughter of the regiment. With irreconcilable, incongruous literary and sociological identities, her background seems as indeterminate as that of M'Intosh, certainly as unlikely as that of her eventual husband, the son of a Hungarian Jewish convert to Protestantism, Rudolf Virag (Bloom), and an Irish-Catholic (?) mother, Ellen Higgins.[4] Bloom turns out to be a Protestant-Catholic Jew, and yet none of these. Indeterminacy of character in the Joycean sense means that in some important way a character cannot be what he/she is.

The contours of indeterminate character in Joyce emerge more distinctly if we remind ourselves, for a moment, of where this experimentation was to lead. *Finnegans Wake* was to contain the most radical notion of characterization to be found in any literary work. In *The Sigla of "Finnegans Wake,"* Roland McHugh writes of the inhabitants as

> fluid composites, involving an unconfined blur of historical, mythical and fictitious characters, as well as nonhuman elements. Joyce's technique of personality condensation is ultimately inseparable from his linguistic condensation. Coincidences of orthography and pronunciation are enforced with indifference to the ostensible logic of their past. That which is not coincidence is pared away, and the greater the similarity of two persons' names, the more usefully their personalities conjugate. (10)

In his manuscripts, Joyce found it easier to refer to these shadowy figures by using symbols, or sigla, rather than proper names. This subject will be considered briefly below.

We begin with our first example in *Ulysses*, a shadowy fig-

[4] Shari and Bernard Benstock, in *Who's He When He's at Home*, explore many problems of character identity in Joyce's work.

ure, quite a minor personage, who is curious because he seems all lacuna and no substance. He is the famous Man in the Macintosh whom Bloom sees in "Hades," a popular subject of inquiry.

Joyce's Raincoat Phantom

Being of autodidactical mind, curious about scientific and mathematical problems, but deficient in the training required to do more than make a muddle of things, Leopold Bloom, we are told, has spent four years of his leisure time in the attempt to square the circle (*U* 17:1072; 17:1696), a tantalizing problem that for generations had puzzled more gifted mathematicians.[5] McCarthy has shown that in the year of Joyce's birth, Ferdinand Lindemann proved the problem to be insolvable ("Unreliable Catechist": 611). McCarthy is surely correct in assuming that Joyce knew as much. The author of *Ulysses* must have been greatly amused at the idea of poor Bloom spending so much time on a problem with no solution. Not content merely to torment characters, Joyce constructed problems analogous to the quadrature of the circle for his readers, who have often bit the bait with the ferocity of starving game fish. We will consider two examples from *Ulysses*, one where a nonexistent mystery of character was created by a reader, and, in another category, two attempts to solve the famous M'Intosh mystery, which was created by Joyce.[6]

[5] A few pages of the M'Intosh section appeared under the title "Joyce y el fantasma de la gabardina" in Spanish in *Quimera* (Barcelona), no. 6 (April 1981): 34-37; it was then translated into French and published as "Joyce et le fantôme à la gabardine," *Europe: revue littéraire mensuelle* 62 (janv.-fév. 1984): 25-30.

[6] Considerations of space prevent me from discussing in detail here another category of problem that arises from a reader's inability to spot aspects of indeterminate character: the attempt to solve an unsolvable problem with historical evidence and rigorous scholarship, as if literary characters had an historical past. In my "Molly" section I follow historical leads with, I hope, an awareness that this leads us into indeterminacy. Without any such apparent awareness, Erwin R. Steinberg sifted evidence in "The Religion of Ellen Higgins Bloom" that might indicate whether Bloom's mother was Protestant or

Precedents in *Ulysses* give us some idea of the slippery ground rules for playing such games. Quite early (*U* 2:94-115), Stephen Dedalus teases his young pupils with a riddle:

> The cock crew
> The sky was blue:
> The bells in heaven
> Were striking eleven.
> Tis time for this poor soul
> To go to heaven.

No question seems to have been asked, but a nonsense solution is given by Stephen that suggests more about his sense of guilt over his mother's death than it does about the riddle: "The fox burying his grandmother under a hollybush." Nonsensical answers and epistemological skepticism begin early and continue late in Joyce's works.

Joyce would have been delighted no end with Michael H. Begnal's detective article, "The Unveiling of Martha Clifford," a classic study of its type. Begnal pointedly rejected Robert M. Adams's caveat about mystery identities in *Surface and Symbol* and assumed without reliable evidence that Martha Clifford, Bloom's flirtatious correspondent in *Ulysses*, must be somebody other than Martha Clifford. Now the charade begins. Is she Miss Dunne of "Wandering Rocks?" Nooo. Is she Gerty MacDowell? Nooo. Is she perhaps Molly Bloom herself? "The idea is enticing, but again the evidence will not support it" (403). How about Lydia Douce and Mina Kennedy? Still not enough evidence. It could not be Mrs. Breen or Milly Bloom or Cissy Caffrey or the society women of "Circe."

Are we getting warmer? Well, let's do a bit of algebra. Let Henry Flower (HF) = Leopold Bloom (LB), and Martha Clifford (MC) = X.

> The interval from H to L, and from F to B, is four; applying this to MC, we get QG (impossible), or IZ (impossible), or perhaps, working first backward and then forward, IG

Catholic. I suggest that this question be tabled until we have decided whether Bloom is Protestant, Catholic, Jew, or none of these (i.e., indefinitely).

> (eureka!). As bizarre as it seems on first examination, Martha Clifford's true identity is Ignatius Gallaher, and we should look closely at the evidence before recoiling in derision or horror. (404)

It seems Leopold Bloom, using the name Henry Flower, has been exchanging love letters with the famous London journalist Ignatius Gallaher (see the *Dubliners* story "A Little Cloud"), who has answered an ad in a Dublin newspaper reading, "Wanted, smart lady typist to aid gentleman in literary work" (*U* 8:326-27), it seems, in order to engage in a legpull. Begnal calls him a "female impersonator" (405). Letters of protest arrived at the *James Joyce Quarterly,* and several were printed in the Spring 1977 issue.

After considerable speculation about the possibility of a hoax being perpetrated on *JJQ* by Ignatius Gallaher, by now well known for literary hoaxes, inquiries were subsequently made, and it turns out that Begnal was not Gallaher in disguise, but a person in his own right who went on to publish other work on Joyce. In some quarters it was felt that Begnal had it backwards, that it was really Martha Clifford who was the impostor, Clifford in reality being an accomplished male impersonator who disguised herself as Gallaher in order to fool not only Chandler, but also the readers of "A Little Cloud," who themselves may not be all the people they seem to be. If his article was intended as a hoax, then Begnal is an ally and I am unjust.

Joycean sleuths, apparently unaware that some problems have no solutions, especially when they are created either by Joyce to keep us busy, or by ourselves to keep us busy, have for long been captivated by one of the most tantalizing enigmas (Martha Clifford is neither tantalizing nor an enigma) in modern literature—the Man in the Macintosh, who first appears at a funeral in the "Hades" section. Noticed by Leopold Bloom and a reporter, his mistaken name M'Intosh (we never learn his real one) is included in a list of mourners intended for a Dublin evening newspaper. Asked by the reporter to identify the stranger, Bloom completes his question, "Do you know that fellow in the . . ." with "Macintosh" (*U* 6:891-94), referring to the stranger's raincoat. The reporter moves on, and before Bloom can correct this misunderstanding the name M'Intosh has stuck.

Critics seem to congregate in two opposing camps on this issue: one believes that the mystery is solvable, and the evidence reliable if difficult; the other believes that the M'Intosh mystery is a hoax. Nobody in the novel seems to know precisely who M'Intosh is, or why he is at the cemetery, but for no apparent reason this identity problem often returns to tease the curious mind (in two senses) of Bloom and thus the reader. Just when M'Intosh begins to fade from memory, Joyce supplies fresh sightings and beguiling hints as to his identity. "In Lower Mount street a pedestrian in a brown macintosh, eating dry bread, passed swiftly . . ." (*U* 10:1271-72); later a phantom voice says, "The man in the brown macintosh loves a lady who is dead" (*U* 12:1497-98). That night he is spotted by Stephen Dedalus and his drunken companions (*U* 14:1546) and more confusing hints are given. In one of Bloom's fantasies in the bordello, M'Intosh rises to point an accusing finger at him before a mob (*U* 15:1560-64); later Bloom imagines his grandfather wearing a brown macintosh (*U* 15:2307), and remembers M'Intosh again when the obituary article appears in the *Evening Telegraph* (*U* 16:1261-65). Preparing for bed, Bloom repeats the incessant question that disturbs him throughout the day—"Who was M'Intosh" (*U* 17:2066).

Possible answers to this not-very-interesting question have been devised with more earnestness than cleverness by scholars who feel that in not following in the footsteps of Sherlock Holmes they have missed their calling. With few exceptions, each is sure that M'Intosh must be somebody other than M'Intosh, that he is a symbolic character, that there is, in short, an answer to Bloom's question and that they have finally (we hear a sigh of relief) solved the mystery once and for all. Since M'Intosh was the thirteenth mourner at the funeral he must be Death, but he could be the Risen Christ, and if he "loves a lady who is dead" he is surely James Duffy of Joyce's story "A Painful Case" or possibly Hades, who loved Persephone. More than one has suggested that M'Intosh is Joyce, who could not resist inserting his face into the corner of his painting; but he could also be Theoclymenos, an outlaw acquaintance of Telemachus. Others are convinced he was one Dusty Rhodes, or a friend of Joyce's father named Wetherup, or perhaps simply Bloom's *Doppelgänger* or maybe the Irish poet James Clarence Mangan, a poor literary outcast admired by Joyce.

If few agree on precisely who M'Intosh is, many believe that he must be somebody, that literary enigmas are really no different from historical ones, and that mysteries in *Ulysses* can eventually be solved by analyzing the hints Joyce gave us in the text. They are similar to mathematical problems that require a different approach, or more ingenuity. M'Intosh sleuths assume that Joycean riddles must have answers.

It is thus pointless to examine all the attempts to discover the identity of M'Intosh, but we will consider two in some depth. One of the latest and most intensely argued of the commentaries on M'Intosh is by John Gordon, who in "The M'Intosh Mystery" judges this case to be perhaps second only to Milton's "two-handed engine" as "the most famous enigma of our literature."[7] He acknowledges that many attempts to solve the mystery have appeared in print, that skepticism now seems to be the orthodox position, that the evidence is "pretty flimsy," but he examines it nonetheless. His startling conclusion is that M'Intosh is the ghost of Rudolph Bloom, come from his grave in the west of Ireland to be with his dead wife. He walks around the cemetery in a raincoat, seen by Bloom and others in "Hades" and "Oxen of the Sun," where somebody actually seems to know him, but we are presumably asked to believe that Bloom, who has a conversation with an imaginary Rudolph Bloom in "Circe," repeatedly fails to recognize the ghost of his father. This curious ghost, who eats dry bread and mopes about, is visible, in human form, and yet father and son do not speak or recognize each other.

Gordon combs the evidence with all the ingenuity of a Ste-

[7] Readers may remember the chapter "In the Arms of Murphy" in Gordon's *James Joyce's Metamorphoses*, where the thesis is that the sailor W. B. Murphy of "Eumaeus" is Molly's old flame Mulvey.

phen Dedalus arguing his theory of Shakespeare (the difference being that Gordon seems to believe his theory). The case for Rudolph Bloom is argued with a quality of desperation that attests to his presumed belief that all Joycean mysteries have definitive solutions if one only reads the evidence right.

When someone calls M'Intosh a "seedy cuss," we are not told that the meaning of this bit of American dialect is transparently clear, but that "seedy" is an apt term for a Jewish father, who is a "cuss" or cursed because he is a suicide. "Where the deuce did he pop out of?" says someone else, and we are told that "pop" is a term for father. Bloom's striking down of poppies in "Circe" is an Oedipal act. That M'Intosh is called "Dusty Rhodes" cannot be mere nonsense; it must be a clue, and obviously refers to Rudolph Bloom's having been a traveling salesman. He died of poison like Hamlet's father, and so all this is tied into the Hamlet motif of *Ulysses*. (That Hamlet's father was not a suicide is apparently not a problem.) The argument goes that the M'Intosh mystery either can or cannot be solved, and if it can be, then the identity is clearly Rudolph Bloom. No provision is made for authorial mystification, nonsense, humor, or any lack of double entendre—every word is a potential clue if it fits, though not if it doesn't.

A second assault on the citadel was recently made by Brook Thomas, who revealed that he knew precisely the indeterminacy he faced when he quoted Joyce's famous line in the Ellmann biography: "I've put in so many enigmas and puzzles that it will keep the professors busy for centuries arguing over what I meant, and that's the only way of insuring one's immortality" (Thomas 69; Ellmann, *James Joyce* 521), but he nevertheless devotes some twenty pages to M'Intosh.

What Thomas makes of M'Intosh is a virtual free-for-all. Whereas most would have it one way, as Gordon does, Thomas is open to presumably every possibility. He finds no incompatibility in the idea that M'Intosh may be Joyce presiding "over the death of one of his own characters" (70) and, at the same time, the risen Christ. In Zurich Joyce wore a brown overcoat, which if not precisely a macintosh could still be evidence that Joyce is our man (Thomas does not speculate about whether or not Christ wore one). And then, of course, there are the parallels with King Hamlet, and even Virag gets into the act by wearing a macintosh at one point in "Circe" (*U* 15:2307). "M'Intosh is truly 'all in all' " (Thomas 74), but later Thomas says "perhaps there is nothing behind the macintosh to grasp" (114), which seems odd considering all the grasping.

Aha, now we are getting somewhere. M'Intosh "would be someone conspicuous by his absence from a list we could compile from characters in *Ulysses*" (116), which narrows down the field considerably. That list might include Mr. Duffy of "A Painful Case," but a more conspicuous absence is James Joyce. On the other hand, "M'Intosh is Joyce and he is not Joyce" (123). I propose that we assemble all the M'Intoshes together for a family reunion, give them each in turn Odysseus's bow, and the ones who do not shoot themselves or each other in stringing the bow we shall henceforth call M'Intosh presences, and those who become fatally impaled on the arrows absences.

Robert M. Adams has responded with appropriate skepticism to Joyce's practice of attempting to ensure his immortality by creating textual enigmas: "We may be excused for feeling that the fewer answers we have for the novel's riddles, the better off we are," and "the meaningless is deeply interwoven with the meaningful" so that "the book loses as much as it gains by being read closely" (*Surface and Symbol* 218; 245-46). Adams is quoted in Frank Kermode's *The Genesis of Secrecy*, where half a chapter is devoted to the M'Intosh enigma (49-73). Kermode poses questions that probe not the mystery itself, nor Joyce's motivation or intention, but the reader's inability to resist the games of interpretation.

> Why does the view of Adams commend itself to us not at once, not as intuitively right, but as somehow more surprising and recondite than the attempts to make sense of MacIntosh? Why, in fact, does it require a more strenuous effort to believe that a narrative lacks coherence than to believe that somehow, if we could only find out, it doesn't? (53)

Though the right questions are certainly being asked, Kermode's answers to the problem of reader motivation will not satisfy commentators who like puzzles and don't mind Joyce leading them up the garden path to endless pitfalls, or who, suspecting this is the case, insist on leading themselves into error and thus turning the tables on Joyce. It would seem that one either elects to play literary sleuth, or one refuses and creates, as Adams and Kermode have, a secondary realm of inquiry.

Happily, there is a third alternative. Faced with the dilemma of trying to solve a hopeless enigma or probing the equally enigmatic mystery of reader motivation, we may choose to ask, "How did Joyce get the idea to create the M'Intosh enigma?" Here we move to the more solid ground of manuscript evidence.

As I have mentioned elsewhere, there is a word in Joyce's notebook numbered VIII.A.5 in the Buffalo manuscript collection that provides the only reliable key we have to the M'Intosh mystery (Herring, *Joyce's Notes* 8; 27). (None of the evidence in *Ulysses* seems reliable.) Compiled during 1918 in Zurich, this notebook contains borrowings from books that Joyce found useful in the earlier stages of his composition of *Ulysses*. One of these was a German encyclopedia of Greek and Roman mythology by W. H. Roscher. (It has been often remarked that Joyce had an encyclopedic mind, but little noted that he used encyclopedias.) Turn to "H" and under *Hades* there is more than anybody not writing a book like *Ulysses* would probably care to know about the king of the underworld (1:1779). In Section 2 one learns that with the aid of his *Tarnkappe*, a cap granting the wearer invisibility, Hades helped his elder brother Zeus in the War of the Titans. This cap, an old symbol of the power of gods to render themselves invisible, enabled the wearer to hide himself as in an impenetrable cloud.[8] The discussion in Roscher continues, but Joyce wrote

[8] In a letter to me, Cóilin Owens notes that in Joyce's story "Clay," Maria wears an old brown raincoat and seems invisible to the young men on the tram. On Hallowe'en Irish fairies "are normally concealed by a *fé-fiada* (magi-

Tarnkappe in his notebook among other notes about Hades and then presumably considered possible modern-day equivalents. What he decided upon was a brown raincoat called a macintosh, quite an appropriate choice for Ireland's climate; and then, as was his practice when he used his notes in the novel, he carefully marked through the word with coloring pencil. Though it is not known to grant invisibility, in *Ulysses* at least the wearer and the cloak somehow become indistinguishable from each other. We never see through the macintosh to the wearer's identity.

In German *tarnen* means "to camouflage," "mask," "screen," or "disguise." We have no evidence that M'Intosh wishes to hide, or knows he is a mystery to others, but in *Ulysses* he is effectively disguised from Bloom's scrutiny and ours. Then, too, one is reminded that Odysseus was the grandson of Autolycus, the cunning thief who had the power to disguise stolen cattle; Joyce played Autolycus when he called his novel *Ulysses* and took elements of Homer's story, disguising them for his own modern purposes. After his return to Ithaca, and thus during most of *The Odyssey*, Odysseus is disguised to all but his son Telemachus and his patroness Pallas Athene. Joyce's notesheets for the "Eumaeus" section carefully distinguish between the real Odysseus and Pseudangelos, meaning "false messenger," his disguised self. So much is Odysseus his grandfather's grandson that he cannot help fooling his own father Laertes, whom he has not seen in many years, before revealing his true identity.

If Joyce seems to be saying that it is fun or necessary to play roles at times, acting out our part so as to deceive others, paradoxically enough an exception must be made for M'Intosh. Stephen Dedalus deceives his library companions with a theory of Shakespeare he admits he doesn't believe; Leopold Bloom enacts fantasy roles in "Circe," but fools nobody; his Penelope's thoughts often consist of speculations about possible roles she will play with her husband or lover. But M'Intosh does not intentionally deceive. He literally has nothing to

---

cal mist or cloak), but can be seen occasionally when this appurtenance is lifted." See P. W. Joyce, *A Social History of Ancient Ireland*, 1:245 ff.; 264-65.

hide under his raincoat because he exists only as his author's deceitful ploy to keep us guessing. In this Joyce is closer to the Autolycus tradition than are any of his characters, because he accepts as given that the artist is a forger of meaning and of identity, *forger* being one meaning of the word *artist* in his native city.

Even if M'Intosh's intentions in all this can never be known, remaining forever hidden in the cloak of invisibility provided by Joyce to characters without substance or dimension, like the ghost of Hamlet's father, Joyce's own intentions, his own visibility, are betrayed by that one piece of manuscript evidence—the word *Tarnkappe*, which in "Hades" gave him the idea for a shade to haunt Bloom and future Joyce scholars.

Toward an Historical Molly Bloom

In *Conversations with James Joyce*, Arthur Power reported Joyce as saying, "In realism you are down to facts on which the world is based: that sudden reality which smashes romanticism into a pulp. . . . In *Ulysses* I tried to keep close to fact" (98).[9] This is a familiar Joycean attitude that, like all received opinions, must periodically be reexamined. Joyce's dedication to factual accuracy has seldom been challenged since Robert M. Adam's *Surface and Symbol* helped readers distinguish between surface detail and symbolic meaning in *Ulysses*. Not only did Adams document Joyce's near-compulsive dedication to factual authenticity, he also examined the now-familiar pattern of intentional errata in *Ulysses* (not to be confused with textual corruption), which provided readers with curious humor and Joyce with camouflage for those inevitable errors he hadn't intended. It is precisely here that one sees his dedication to factual accuracy in conflict with his uncertainty principle.

Keeping in mind Joyce's remarks to Power, and presuming to apply Stephen Dedalus's petulant observation that "a man of genius makes no mistakes. His errors are volitional and are

[9] An earlier version of this section appeared as "Toward an Historical Molly Bloom" in *ELH* 45 (1978): 501-521.

"The Jewish Woman of Gibraltar," John Frederick Lewis, *Lewis' Sketches of Spain and Spanish Character, made during his tour of that country in 1833-1834, drawn on stone from his original sketches* (London, 1836).

the portals of discovery" (*U* 9:228-29), I propose to test the verisimilitude of Molly Bloom, who is today nearly as much a puzzle as she was when *Ulysses* was published in 1922. Although the "eternal feminine" qualities she is meant to embody have frequently been challenged, scant attention has been focused on her realistic dimension. Yet we know little about the relationship of Molly's past to her present, of Gibraltar to Dublin, or why for the first time in his literary career Joyce tried in "Penelope" to create a setting extraneous to his native city. Since her monologue can be read as a catalogue of Irishisms and Dublin expressions, we usually ignore a central fact of her characterization—that she is a woman of Gibraltar, thus springing from an historical and sociological background unknown to Joyce except from guidebooks.

HISTORIES AND GUIDEBOOKS OF GIBRALTAR. Since Molly's Gibraltar was created out of books, let us first turn to these for a fuller description of the environment that molded her character.[10] Gibraltar's one ineluctable historical fact of life is, of course, the British conquest. On 24 July 1704, Sir George Rooke seized it from Spain, aided by British and Dutch troops under the command of Prince George of Hesse-Darmstadt. Since then Gibraltar has been an outpost of Empire, where military prerogatives tend to predominate. The Spaniards attempted to recapture their lost peninsula in 1727, and sporadic efforts continued throughout most of the century, highlighted by the Great Siege, which lasted from July 1779 until February 1783. Despite the great destruction and loss of life, Britain's determination to keep its fortress did not waver. If the nineteenth century was a calmer time, the garrison still continued in a state of readiness, tunnelling new gun emplacements, installing ever more powerful ordnance. By Molly's eighth birthday in 1878, roughly one-third of the 18,000 inhabitants were of the garrison; uniforms were everywhere, big guns rattled

[10] Joyce's use of Gibraltar guidebooks is a familiar subject now that nearly all of his sources have been uncovered. In addition to Adams, see Card, "A Gibraltar Sourcebook"; Herring, *Notesheets* 69-73; Herring, *Joyce's Notes, passim.*

china and windows, in gun practice and also to signal the opening and closing of frontier gates at dawn and sunset. Only residents and visitors bearing special passes were allowed to stay the night; all others-mostly Spanish workers and servants like Molly's Mrs. Rubio—scurried across to La Línea at night, loaded with contraband goods that helped ease a life of abject poverty. At night smugglers went to work loading tobacco into boats destined for Spanish ports.

British commentators of the last century ignored Gibraltar's people, who were generally seen as undeserving colonials, slightly more evolved, but less interesting, than the Barbary apes upon whose symbolic presence continued British rule depended. The Rock was a tourist attraction, a free port, a sign of British strength (Spanish weakness). Typical in attitude, though unusually abrasive, is Richard Ford in *A Hand-Book for Travellers in Spain*, a book that Joyce seems to have read. Despite an unusually thorough, detailed description of Gibraltar in the 1840s, Ford's prejudice against all that is un-British and un-Protestant was so blatant that subsequent editors had to blunt his barbs.

Here is a typical view: approaching Gibraltar by ship, the traveller would be met offshore by small boats filled with men haranguing the passengers in several languages to put up at local inns. If approaching by land, one would bisect the ugly squalor of La Línea, noted for whores and wineshops, pass by the sullen, shabby Spanish sentries and enter Gibraltar, whose relative prosperity rested on smuggling and military spending. Walking through passport control (easy for British, more complicated for foreigners), one might imagine in the Rock a British lion, reclining, head toward Spain, as if to say "disturb me ye who dare."

British by conquest, and now by choice, Gibraltar is international in every other way: geologically it is African; linguistically and geographically Spanish; in population it is all of these, plus Genoese, Maltese, Jewish, Moroccan, and more remote strains. Main Street (Waterport Street) and Irishtown were in continual motion in Molly's time, with merchants dressed in costumes hawking their wares. Samuel Clemens, visiting Gibraltar in 1867, was struck by the local color:

> The soft-eyed Spanish girls from San Roque, and veiled Moorish beauties (I suppose they are beauties) from Tarifa and turbaned, sashed, and trousered Moorish merchants from Fez, and long-robed, bare-legged Mohammedan vagabonds from Tetouan and Tangier, some brown, some yellow, and some as black as virgin ink—and Jews from all around, in gaberdine, skull-cap, and slippers, just as they are in pictures and theatres, and just as they were three thousand years ago, no doubt. (*Innocents Abroad* 50)

A visitor might ride a pony up to the galleries (permit required) and to the ruins of the Moorish Castle, the grounds of which have become the local prison. No itinerary could omit the Barbary apes and the celebrated views of the Straits, Morocco, and Spain. After a strenuous day one could relax in the Alameda, where Molly listened to concerts and mingled glances with potential suitors. The Alameda was admired by W. H. Thackeray, who described it in 1844 as

> always beautiful, especially at evening, when the people are sauntering along the walks, and the moon is shining on the waters of the bay and the hills and twinkling white houses on the opposite shore. Then the place becomes quite romantic; it is too dark to see the dust on the dry leaves. (35)[11]

Joyce could have read this, but more likely Molly's memory of Alameda concerts as occasions for flirtation is indebted to the *Gibraltar Directories* and the 1878 edition of Ford (351).

When the Alameda was too hot, one could retire to the Garrison Library, where Tweedy borrowed (and never returned) Hozier's *History of the Russo-Turkish War* (*U* 17:1416), and Molly would have found novels to her dubious taste. Outside there are benches shaded by palm trees; inside a waiter brought (brings) teas, beer—even whiskey—to afternoon bridge players or officers reading last week's *Sunday Times*. All things considered, Gibraltar may have the world's most civi-

[11] M. A. Titmarsh was the pseudonym of Thackeray in *Notes of a Journey from Cornhill to Grand Cairo*.

lized library, though surely little research is ever done there.

In Molly's day the Theatre Royale presented operas in autumn, plays in winter and spring; sometimes there was a concert or ball. Since Tweedy decided not to send Molly to school in Britain, as was most often done with officers' children, she could have attended the garrison school during weekdays, and after school gone in for voice lessons with Signor Labocetta, in anticipation of her singing debut in Dublin at the age of sixteen (*U* 16:1443-44). La Línea offered occasional bullfights, but one ventured into the hills beyond at considerable risk due to the robber bands and various discomforts. Gibraltar was so much a man's world that Molly's desire to flee her boring existence there is easily understood (*U* 18:676-77).

Molly's reminiscences of her last year in Gibraltar, 1886, might have included reference to the hanging of a Spaniard, who was convicted of burgling an old sapper's house, killing the owner in the process. He attributed his crime to drink, and was hanged by a pardoned criminal, who was then spirited out by boat that same night. This happened in May, the month Lieutenant Mulvey left the Rock and within two months of Molly's departure. Earlier in 1886 she would have remembered the visit of the Duke of Edinburgh, who presented a concert by a "toy symphony" aboard his flagship *The Minotaur*. The next day the *Gibraltar Chronicle* noted that "His Royal Highness's toy symphony was received with rupturous applause," to which the Duke replied that he hoped no serious harm was done.

Life in nineteenth-century Gibraltar was considerably less romantic than a reader would guess from books such as Henry Field's *Gibraltar*, a major influence on "Penelope."[12] Six thousand bored soldiers, plus visiting sailors, spent much of their time in wineshops, their thirst presumably reaching a crescendo in the notorious summer heat. Summer is also the season for levanters (*U* 18:607), when an east wind settles a black cloud over the Rock, sending humidity up into the warmer air above. This stifling atmosphere produces general discomfort.

[12] See Card, "A Gibraltar Sourcebook."

At the same time health conditions were bad: many children died during dentition; yellow fever killed 5,000 people in 1805; another 899 in 1813, still 1,667 more in 1828—and this out of a population estimated at 10,000 in 1811.

Two causes of epidemics were contaminated water and the custom of washing houses to combat disease. Stagnant pools, of course, bred mosquitos. In April 1869, two wells were sunk, and for the first time Gibraltar had a dependable supply of fresh water. (Now water catchments on the eastern side normally insure against drought.) On 8 December 1869, about the time of Molly's conception (on this day in 1868 Gibraltar had an earthquake), Lady Airey, the Governor's wife, presided over the inauguration of Gibraltar's first public fountain.[13]

H. W. Howes says that in 1871, the year after Molly's birth, Gibraltar had "a native population of 10,116 souls, of which number there [were] 7,877 without employment," a condition caused in part by the opening of the Suez Canal in 1869 (182). In 1885, the year before Molly's romance with Mulvey, Howes says, "There was so much poverty that large sums of money raised by subscriptions had to be granted for relief. 4,038 persons were in receipt of relief daily from 10 September to 7 November. As if to fill to the brim the local cup of sorrow, on 10 December a terrific storm occurred causing widespread damage" (183). This was also the year of a cholera epidemic that closed the border for a time. The guidebooks Joyce read ignore Gibraltar's poverty and sufferings, and so does Molly Bloom.

Molly gives us a tourist-eye view, one nearly devoid of information about the lives of her parents or other Gibraltarians, a view composed of a few historical details, the usual places of interest, with occasional asides of lesser-known facts from the *Gibraltar Directories*. Consider, for instance, *The Traveller's*

[13] J. T. and D. M. Ellicott unconsciously describe this celebration in prose worthy of the fantasies of "Circe" and "Cyclops": "In the evening a Te Deum was sung in the Roman Catholic Church, and later the Italian Opera company gave a performance dedicated to the Sanitary Commissioners, with a hymn composed especially for the occasion. In spite of heavy rain the new 'Airey Fountain' was illuminated, as were the buildings around the square, where two bands played" (47).

Hand-Book for Gibraltar by An Old Inhabitant. At some time in 1921 Joyce read the *Hand-Book*, or had it read, and notes were copied into notebook V.A.2 (now at Buffalo), which was compiled to supplement the late typescripts and galleys for *Ulysses*.[14] Reading this book, we see the origins of Molly's references to the galleries, Ince's Farm, the Rock Gun, Catalan Bay, St. Michael's Cave, and the Jewish burial ground overlooking Europa Point. Up on the Rock she could see Marbella, the snow-covered Atlas Mountains, and the Bay of Tangier. The Old Inhabitant describes these views and every other place of interest in Gibraltar, but—typical of such guides—he leaves us ignorant about people's lives.

Joyce is hardly to blame here: there were no books about daily life in Gibraltar, and he was admirably conscientious to read the many books his notes reveal he consulted. There are, nevertheless, the expected inaccuracies and distortions. Molly twice calls Fig Tree Cave Firtree Cove (*U* 18:790; 18:824); and she tells Mulvey how O'Hara's Tower was struck by lightning (*U* 18:783-84; Herring, *Joyce's Notes* 60). Joyce, easily frightened by lightning, which may indeed have struck the tower, could have managed more interesting observations with a bit more reading. Although the *Hand-Book* says the theory "deserves little attention" (48), local people knew that in the 1790s General O'Hara, then Governor, had the tower built without authorization to spy on the Spanish naval base at Cadiz, but since the distance is some fifty-eight miles it would have needed to be one of the world's tallest structures. "O'Hara's Folly," as it was sometimes called, was never completed, and its inventor had to pay the construction costs. The *Hand-Book* says it lay in ruins in 1844. Either it was destroyed by lightning or, as one of my informants believes, rather than tolerate a monument to slow wit the government allowed the HMS Wasp to blast it to pieces. Mulvey, at any rate, would have seen little but scattered stones.

Molly combines fact with fiction when remembering the

[14] See Herring, *Joyce's Notes* 59-64. All of Joyce's notes from *The Traveller's Hand-Book* are from pages 39-70; they enriched Molly's memories roughly at *U* 18:282-390. The single exception is Molly's reference to "the statue of the fish" in the Alameda gardens (*U* 18:546).

tailless Barbary apes (*U* 18:784 ff.), who remain one of the Rock's attractions. The *Hand-Book* (62-66) is correct in noting their occasional raids on chicken coops and vegetable patches, but is also responsible for Molly's belief in the ape's unlikely dexterity in throwing stones. Our Old Inhabitant says that these creatures were originally brought to Gibraltar (62); Molly, on the other hand, subscribes to the old myth of a secret interconnecting passage under the Straits, by means of which apes travel to and from Africa.[15] The *Hand-Book* does, however, support the myth by making them seem mysterious: "their habits, their retreats, and their modes of life, are alike unknown. Neither their bones, their skins, nor their skeletons have ever been discovered" (63). Joyce copied this down, later having Molly speculate that the secret passage is reached through Saint Michael's Cave, by which means "the monkeys go under the sea to Africa when they die" (*U* 18:794). Less credulous ape-watchers know that scavenger birds quickly dispose of animal remains on the Rock. The Barbary ape's instinctive fear of darkness has also made it unlikely that any observer has seen an ape voluntarily entering the recesses of a cave. It is by shibboleths such as these that the native spots an alien presence in his midst.

Because Molly Bloom shares a birthday with the Blessed Virgin Mary, and because her thinking is recognizably Irish and Catholic, we tend to forget that by birth she is also Jewish. Indeed, since this identification depends on the mother, it is one she could claim with greater authority than Bloom, who is the victim of anti-Semitism and a troublesome identity problem.[16] With such a psychological disposition, it is curious that Bloom makes much of his wife's nonexistent Spanish back-

[15] A recent *Gibraltar Guide* says, "More recent discoveries of bones of this species at various places in Europe suggest that our apes are the last survivors outside Africa of animals which travelled widely when Europe and Africa were connected by a land bridge" (n.p.).

[16] At least there is no evidence that Lunita Laredo is not Jewish (cf. *U* 18:1184), while there is considerable reason to believe that Ellen Higgins (born Hegarty [*U* 17:537]) is Catholic. While scolding her son Poldy in "Circe," Ellen Bloom evokes both the "blessed Redeemer" and "the Sacred Heart of Mary" (*U* 15:287-90). But of course she is as much a stereotype as her husband.

ground and temperament (*U* 16:876-80), but nothing of her Jewishness, though it is partly the magnetism of this that triggers his subservience to Bella Cohen (perhaps even Zoe Higgins) in "Circe" (*U* 15:1336; 15:2742 ff.). Molly does say that Bloom was initially attracted to her "on account of my being jewess looking after my mother" (*U* 18:1184-85), but in *Ulysses* any Jewish qualities Molly might have are swamped by the Spanish-Moorish-Irish emphases and her husband's role as Wandering Jew *cum* Odysseus. During Joyce's flirtation with Marthe Fleischmann in Zurich, he insisted on a Jewish exoticism that was not there (Ellmann, *James Joyce* 448); in *Ulysses* he neglects to include in Molly's thoughts any awareness of her Jewish heritage or her mother's family, and this is a principal lacuna in her character.

Molly's ignorance is not necessarily Joyce's, whose reading of the "Gibraltar" entry in the *Jewish Encyclopedia* indicates that he gave more thought to this problem than appears in either novel or manuscripts.[17] He certainly knew enough to associate her sensuousness with Morocco and the Orient. Bloom says, "That's where Molly can knock spots off them. It's the blood of the south. Moorish" (*U* 13:968-69), and a few pages later he remembers her "Moorish eyes" (*U* 13:1114-15). In "Circe," Molly appears in Turkish costume and scolds him in Moorish (*U* 15:317); *Ulysses* ends with one of Molly's fondest memories—being kissed under the Moorish wall in Gibraltar. Few students of *Ulysses* are aware that such imagery has its legitimate basis, as Joyce knew, in historical accounts of the migration of Jews to Molly's birthplace.

Lunita Laredo, Molly's mother (*U* 18:848), was supposedly a Spanish Jewess, but to be more precise the Laredos, like nearly all the Jews of Gibraltar, were Sephardim (Spanish Jews) originally from Morocco. Here a distinction should be made. Jewish tribes have maintained a primitive existence in the interior, mostly in the Atlas Mountains, for some two thousand years, long before the Sephardim arrived. Some of

[17] See Herring, *Joyce's Notes* 73, where Joyce copied the names of three prominent Jewish families of Gibraltar—Benoliel, Elmaleh, and Abudarham. For information on Gibraltar's Jews, I have consulted A.B.M. Serfaty; *The Jewish Encyclopedia; The Encyclopaedia Judaica*; and Budgett Meakin, Chapter 23.

these were converted to Islam and became assimilated Berbers, while others stayed Jewish and fled to the towns of the interior, where they lived into the twentieth century as semi-slaves in ghettos. These original Jews were to some extent protected by local authorities, but lived in great poverty and filth, performing humiliating tasks in constant danger from Moslems, against whom they were never allowed to defend themselves. Bloom hardly exaggerates when he tells the Citizen that Jews were "at this very moment . . . sold by auction in Morocco like slaves or cattle" (*U* 12:1471-72). It is little wonder that in this century so many Moroccan Jews have emigrated to Israel.

A second group of Jews, Sephardim fleeing Spanish persecution, settled in the coastal area of Morocco, mostly in the years 1391, 1414, 1492, and 1610 (Meakin 453). In 1473 some of these refugees persuaded the Governor of Andalucia to let them settle in Gibraltar, but when they approached the Rock local people, fearing a Jewish-Moorish alliance, attacked them, killing some and driving the others away. Morocco was little safer than Spain, but during the Moorish invasions many Jews had welcomed the Moors as deliverers from Christian oppression, hence the belief that persecution there would be less severe. The 1492 edict of Ferdinand and Isabella obliged Jews to choose between exile, baptism, and death; the Moors allowed them to settle and keep their religion, but the price they exacted in return was high. The Sephardim experienced occasional pogroms and felt unsafe even during the best of times. A few became the advisors of sultans, even ambassadors; others profited from handicrafts, usury, or salesmanship. The highest position to which they could normally aspire was that of interpreter to a foreign consul, or even consul itself, which involved the protection of a foreign government and access to lucrative dealings. In any event, the coastal Sephardim lived far better than their country cousins.[18]

After 1704, when Gibraltar became British, many Moroccan

[18] According to Martin Gilbert, between 1864 and 1880, "More than five hundred [Moroccan] Jews were murdered in sixteen years, often in broad daylight in the main streets" (4). Between 1948 and 1972, some 260,000 Jews left Morocco for Israel (6; 13).

Sephardim sought refuge there, attracted by the tolerant atmosphere and the business climate. One hitch to settlement was the Treaty of Utrecht in 1713, in which Spain conceded the legal jurisdiction of Gibraltar to Britain. The spirit of the Inquisition is evident in Article 10, which states that "Her Britannic Majesty, at the request of the Catholic King, does consent and agree, that no leave shall be given under any pretense whatsoever, either to Jews or Moors to reside or have their dwellings in the said town of Gibraltar" (Hertslet 2:202).

As conqueror of Gibraltar, Britain could afford to make a few diplomatic concessions: anti-Semites in Spain were appeased with Article 10; the Sultan of Morocco, who might be relied on for supplies (especially important because of potential Spanish embargoes), was assured by an agreement of 1729 that his traders (mostly Jews) would encounter no discrimination. As for the Jews, they would find Article 10 no obstacle to settlement if they contributed generously to the Governor's coffers, whose revenue sometimes depended on irregular forms of taxation. When the Foreign Office protested Jewish settlement, proper assurances were given that either (a) no Jews lived on Gibraltar permanently, or (b) they were just now being discovered and expelled (which could mean that they were put aboard some ship for a few days), or (c) those who remained would be shipped out when they had paid their substantial debts to non-Jewish merchants. Despite these uncertainties, Jews stayed and gradually prospered in an atmosphere of respect and tolerance.

Their relative prosperity did not mean that the Jewish community of Gibraltar developed without class distinctions. Of the 1,533 Jews there in 1878,[19] many were lowly porters or street vendors, wearing distinctive costumes described variously as "loose bagging breeches reaching below the knee, a tunic, and a haik or capote of cloth or bedticking . . . shaven crowns [covered] with a close skull cap" (MacKenzie 2:258-59) or "Fez caps, and fearfully dirty brown and black bernouses, without undergarments of any sort besides dirty 'pyjamas' " (Calpensis 14) or "fur caps, Zouave jackets, and baggy trou-

[19] The "Gibraltar" entry of *The Jewish Encyclopedia*.

sers" (Stoddard 189). Refugees arrived in dribbles and spurts. Eleven years before Molly Bloom's birth, in 1858, over 3,000 Moroccan Jews fleeing the impending Spanish-Moroccan War arrived in Gibraltar, where they camped in tents on the North Front, and were supported in large part by local Jews, whom the refugees outnumbered (Serfaty 30). In the decade that followed, a period of hardship for Gibraltar, Lunita Laredo began a romance with Brian Tweedy.

THE LAREDO FAMILY. The best source of information on Molly Bloom's maternal lineage, the Laredo family, is *Memorias de un viejo Tangerino*, by Isaac Laredo. Laredo was about a year younger than Molly Bloom, having been born in Tangier in 1871. In his prologue he says he has been a journalist since the age of fourteen, working on newspapers in Gibraltar, various Spanish cities, and Tangier. In Tangier he helped found two Spanish language newspapers, and, according to the *Gibraltar Directory and Guidebook* for 1902, he was Secretary of Gibraltar's New Hebrew School in that year. (It was probably in this guidebook that Joyce found the surname for Molly's mother.) Old in years, rich in memories, Laredo decided to write a book on Tangier. (Actually, *Memorias* is more an anthology of short biographies and photos of friends, relatives, and officials.)

Chapter Fourteen of *Memorias* is about the Laredo family, which takes its name from the seaport town of Laredo, near Santander. There are both Christian and Jewish Laredos, but those in Morocco and Gibraltar are Jewish. These Sephardim trace their lineage back more than ten generations and count among their ancestors many pious rabbis. In Tangier the family is especially known for its work in the Jewish community and its schools: Rabbi Joseph Laredo opened a synagogue there, Abraham Laredo ran the *Hebrâh* (Society of Good Works), which ministered to the dying; Jacob Laredo helped manage the Israelite Hospital; Abramo Laredo worked for the Italian consulate, was president of the Community, and published a book collating the Moslem, Julian, and Gregorian calendars (1887); Moses J. Laredo died at thirty-one, having contracted a terrible disease while reinterring the corpse of a Jew who had been dragged from his grave in the countryside near

Tangier. Isaac's son, Abraham I. Laredo, wrote *Berebes y Hebreos en Marruecos* and *Les noms des juifs du maroc.*

The first Laredo to settle in Gibraltar was one Solomon Laredo, a licensed porter from Tetuan, Morocco, who came in 1757. He had two sons, David and Abraham, and so the family took root. They were there in the year of Molly's birth, when Judah Laredo was Secretary of the Hebrew School, and they remain there today.

Because of their historical fear of expulsion, Spanish invasion, and persecution, Gibraltar was for the Sephardim an island refuge in a troubled sea. Denied their ancestral home, they spoke its language—Ladino, a Spanish dialect of Inquisition days—viewed Spain daily from their windows, and were treated to the sound of guns, which seemed a daily reminder that the terrible sieges of the past century could be renewed at any time. Living as a minority group in a small town where everybody knew everyone else, it would have been hard to find a closer knit Jewish community in the nineteenth century. Courtship with gentiles was an anathema, marriage with them an unforgivable act resulting (figuratively speaking) in the transgressor being cast into the outer darkness. If acceptance by non-Jews was uncertain, the condemnation of one's erstwhile family and friends was not. The Laredos could scarcely have borne the shame of Lunita's giving birth to the daughter of an Irish Catholic from Gibraltar's garrison.

THE ROMANCE OF MOLLY'S PARENTS: A LITERARY SOURCE. Molly Bloom is a startling example of the uncertainty principle extended to character, for in shaping her exotic background, Joyce must have known that the social realities of Gibraltar in 1869-70 all but excluded the possibility of serious courtship and marriage between a couple such as Molly's parents. Precisely this topic was explored by Vicente Blasco-Ibáñez (1867-1928) in a novella entitled *Luna Benamor* (1909), which was published in an English translation while Joyce was drafting the later chapters of *Ulysses* (1919).[20] Chances are good that

[20] Vicente Blasco-Ibáñez, *Luna Benamor* (Valencia and Madrid: 1909), trans. Isaac Goldberg (Boston: 1919). I quote from the Goldberg translation. The no-

Joyce read *Luna Benamor* or knew about it, because he places the name Benamor in the begats of "Circe" (*U* 15:1865). The novella itself seems to have no connection with *Ulysses*, but it may well have suggested the gnomonic romance of Molly's parents that Joyce implied and never wrote. I shall incorporate here the clear summary of *Luna Benamor* by Day and Knowlton:

> Luis Aguirre is a young Spanish member of the foreign service, awaiting a ship at Gibraltar after having received an appointment as consul to Australia. The cosmopolitan scene at Gibraltar is described through his eyes. He falls in love with a young Jewess, Luna Benamor, granddaughter of an old and successful money changer, whose ancestors were Spanish Jews. Luna's father was an exporter of Moroccan tapestries in Rabat. . . . At the time the events at Gibraltar take place, Luna, now bereft of parents as well as sister, is with her grandfather and her uncle. . . . She has been betrothed since the age of twelve to Isaac Nuñez, a Jew whose family lived in Tangier and who had become successful in Buenos Aires. . . . Aguirre wins Luna's heart, but her family and traditions oppose the union. Isaac comes to Gibraltar at this time, and Luna bids farewell to Luis, saying that she would always remember this episode as a beautiful dream. . . . Luna says that Aguirre's God is not hers, and [so she] turns her back on love. (115-16)

Although the novella takes place in the first decade of this century, as does *Ulysses*, the fabric of Gibraltar society was little changed from the time of Molly's childhood. Probably no other novel reveals more about the daily lives of ordinary peo-

---

vella is just over a hundred pages in length. "Benamor" is a common enough Sephardic or Moslem name with "romantic" connotations ("the son of love"). Luna is often called "Lunita" in the novella (Goldberg 23; 50), and the way she got her name is of some importance to her (48-50). "Lunita," of course, means "little moon." "Molly," curiously enough, is a nickname for "Gimol." These given names are common in Gibraltar only among Jewish women. Cf. "Luna Benady" in Herring, *Notesheets* 509.

ple on the Rock, especially those of the Jewish community. Since it is the central issue of *Luna Benamor*, religious barriers are continually emphasized: "Religion filled the existence of these people, to the point of suppressing nationality. Aguirre knew that in Gibraltar he was not a Spaniard; he was a Catholic" (15). Imbued with conscious anti-Semitism since childhood, he at first refuses to believe that such a beautiful girl could be Jewish, imagining her to be "a creole from the colonies, perhaps, born of some Oriental beauty and a British soldier" (22). When Aguirre proposes to Luna, she wonders, "How can this be arranged? Are you going to become a convert to my religion?" To which he replies, "Man alive! I, turn Jew?" (58). Yet it is precisely their differences that attract them to each other.

Luna's fiancé arrives in Gibraltar just in time to add his voice to those of relatives and friends who urge her to renounce Aguirre. Torn between love and duty, Luna chooses duty. The parting scene takes place in Cathedral Square amid a cacophonous symphony of the bells of Saint Mary's, the evening gun that sounds the closing of the gate to Spain, and issuing forth from the choir of the Protestant Cathedral is the hymn Molly recalls Bloom saying he would set to music—Newman's "Lead Kindly Light" (*U* 18:381). Unintimidated by all this, Luna Benamor insists that "she was a Jewess and would remain faithful to her race" (92).

Luna Benamor is altogether a more believable story of Gibraltar than the one Molly tells us about her girlhood. Both Lunas must choose between religion, family, community, and tradition on the one hand, and a love that would bring exile and suffering on the other. Luna Benamor chooses wisely; Luna Laredo does not.

MOLLY IN GIBRALTAR. Robert Adams, describing Joyce's use of the *Gibraltar Directory and Guidebook* as a source for Molly Bloom's memories of the Rock, minimizes the inaccuracies and anachronisms he discovered as the "merest trifles" (*Surface and Symbol* 233). True, perhaps, of isolated details, but taken together these reveal Joyce actively and consciously undermining social reality in order to hint at a mysterious dimension of Molly's past that has scarcely been glimpsed by critics of *Ulysses*. Significant demands are placed on our credulity. In effect, we are asked to believe that this daughter of an Irish officer, Brian Tweedy, and a Spanish Jewess, Lunita Laredo, born on 8 September 1870 in Gibraltar, had a typical girlhood, growing to maturity in a carefree atmosphere of warm nights, lazy summer days, free of worries or obligations, living with a hard-drinking Irish officer, cared for by a Spanish maid, reading novels in her endless spare time, flirting with young lieutenants as she ripened, free of parental guidance or social censure.

Beneath the surface of Molly's girlhood reveries, however, is a subcurrent of troubled complexity that never rises to the conscious level of her monologue. In reality, as the daughter of an Irish officer and a local Jewess, living contiguous with a formidable Jewish community that considered mixed marriage an anathema, Molly would have had a curious relationship to all social groups. Indeed, this would have been an important key to her character. Today her background would elicit considerable comment but no discrimination; during the 1880s her social situation would have made Bloom's enviable by comparison. Molly could well have been rejected by all but the most tolerant in Gibraltar: by the Jews as an outcast (though legally Jewish) like her mother; by local society as a daughter of the regiment (*U* 11:507); by the garrison as the product of a scandalous union. Even though civil marriages had been allowed since 21 February, 1862, a mixed marriage such as the Tweedys' would have been so rare as to insure them a place in Gibraltar's folklore down to the present day.

To balance the scandal of Molly's affair with Blazes Boylan in 1904 is the scandal of her birth in 1870, hinted at when she remembers Bloom "hadnt an idea about my mother till we were engaged otherwise hed never have got me so cheap as he did he was 10 times worse himself anyhow" (*U* 18:282-84). Despite the obfuscation, it seems clear that she only told Bloom about her mother after their engagement, hoping that by this time his love would override any thoughts of rejection; that if it weren't for her mother she would have made a better match.[21] He "hadnt an idea about my mother" refers not to Luna's Jewishness, which Molly would have used to lure Bloom, but to some dark secret that he must not learn about too soon. Lunita, of suppressed memory, may even be to blame for Molly's crises of self-confidence during courtship, which cause her to undervalue herself and, perhaps, to be more sexually available than prudence would allow or competition would demand. Molly should have been in many ways desirable: she had beauty, a good voice, and an exotic background, and is the daughter of a major (or drum major) in the Fusiliers; yet she recalls only two suitors before Bloom—Mulvey and Gardner, whom she has attempted to conquer by all means short of sexual intercourse, and this despite evidence of her strong Catholic belief and a respect for wagging tongues. Instead of lingering in Gibraltar, where eligible officers were plentiful, but where her background was presumably known, she allows herself to be transported by her father at the age of fifteen to a less promising environment where, barely eighteen, she marries a man of similarly dubious origins—the son of a Catholic mother (Irish-Hungarian) and a Hungarian-Jewish father who was a former peddler and a suicide.[22]

If Molly's circumstances and actions strongly hint that she is illegitimate, Joyce for once would have been on solid historical ground. An illegitimate Molly would be all the more likely to plead "for a morality of indulgence," in Joseph Voelker's words (148). Even if Gibraltar's tolerance in the 1860s had ex-

[21] Gifford and Seidman annotate this passage badly: "Molly's mother, Lunita Laredo, a Spanish Jewess, who died early in Molly's life; i.e., Bloom did not know that Molly's mother was Jewish" (500). This is pure nonsense; however, the statement can be read (and is so read by John Henry Raleigh, who has suggested improvements in this essay) to mean that Bloom would never have gotten her cheap if she had told him initially about her mother. But one must account for Molly's silence on this subject, what she revealed about her mother, and "he was 10 times worse himself."

[22] The respective heredities of Leopold and Molly Bloom are curiously symmetrical: both are of mixed Jewish-Irish blood, one being Hungarian in the same obscure way that the other is Gibraltarian.

tended to intermarriage between Jews and Christians, officers would not have thought local girls their equals unless they were British. Or at least they would have typically considered Spanish and Jewish girls to be unsuitable for honest courtship. Most single officers had Spanish mistresses, who also bore their children, but any talk of marriage would have caused serious concern at Headquarters, probably resulting in an immediate transfer for the officer in question. As a Roman-Catholic Irishman, possibly attached to Headquarters, Tweedy would have needed to walk a narrow line, yet we are asked to believe an historical absurdity: that he fathered a child on a local girl and raised her as his daughter as if this were perfectly customary in military society.

Indeed, Molly's parents seem to have been designed to challenge our credulity. Brian Tweedy is the product of such fantastically loose historical manipulation that at no point can he be taken seriously. Both battalions of his regiment, the Royal Dublin Fusiliers, served on Gibraltar for short periods during Tweedy's reputed stay there (Adams, *Surface and Symbol* 233), but his tenure seems independent of regiment. There is also some doubt about his rank. Bloom believes him to have been a major, a view that is supported by Molly's memories of Tweedy's officer friends, but in "Sirens" he is remembered as a drum major (*U* 11:508).[23] By far the strangest thing we know about him is his battle record. He leaves Molly alone to fight in Bulgaria at the Battle of Plevna, where drum majors were not in great demand (cf. *U* 17:1419-25; 18:690).[24] Having survived the 143-day siege of Plevna, which fell to the Russians on 10 December 1877, Tweedy is next in South Africa, where in January 1879 he fights for Britain at Rorke's Drift in the Zulu

[23] Although I maintain that Molly's parents could not have been married in Gibraltar, and that Jewish opposition to their liaison would have been almost insurmountable, it must be admitted that the possibility of an illegitimate child's being reared and tolerated in the garrison increases if Tweedy had been a Sergeant Major. The view that this was indeed his rank is currently growing in popularity, but the text is quite ambiguous.

[24] Presumably either Joyce, or Bloom, or Tweedy has taken liberties with Hozier's *History of the Russo-Turkish War* (*U* 17:1385).

War (*U* 15:781; 15:4618; 18:690). Joyce carefully excluded him from the Franco-Prussian War (1870-71), perhaps to avoid the suggestion that Molly's conception was immaculate.

All we know about Lunita Laredo is that Molly resembles her in eyes and figure (*U* 18:890-91), for she has simply disappeared after giving birth to Molly, as if she had existed merely to add spice to her daughter's lineage, like a gypsy ancestor or a skeleton in grandpa's closet. It is perhaps as well that her character suffers from invisibility, given Molly's happy memories of Gibraltar, because in reality she would have either died in childbirth or fled Gibraltar and an impossible situation. As an unwed mother, Lunita could hardly have stayed without going on the streets, something Tweedy and the Jewish community would have sought to prevent. Had Brian and Luna somehow resolved their religious differences and married, then her reception at garrison tea parties could only have been equalled in frigidity by his reception in the shops of Main Street.

Ultimately Gibraltar is a dash of local color in the drab landscape of Dublin that was never meant to be examined closely, one of the many qualities in a composition that is Molly Bloom; still, since heredity and environment do determine character, and Joyce has confidently given us the essential details about her early life, his expressed dedication to factual authenticity encourages us to examine them for accuracy. The weaknesses are there: regardless of what Molly is, or knows, she does not in "Penelope" reveal a native's knowledge of her birthplace, or any understanding of her mixed heritage or the society that has produced her. But beyond these unresolved problems of her background, and her ignorance of their necessary impact on her developing psychology, Molly is simply unconvincing as a woman from Gibraltar—even one who has lived twenty years in Dublin.

One problem is Molly's language, and the linguistic constructions expressed in her thoughts. If Bloom is right that Molly has "forgotten any little Spanish she knew" (*U* 4:60-61), then she is surprisingly forgetful, since fifteen years on the Rock would ordinarily have insured a fluency in the local dialect of Andalucian Spanish that the next eighteen could hardly have erased. Molly's undiluted Irish brogue, a gift from her father (*U* 18:889-90) is thus a bit unrealistic. However, at least twice, probably unconsciously, she does use Spanish words as if they were English: "the vague fellows in the cloaks asleep" (*U* 18:1591) (*vago* = loiterer, vagabond) and "the watchman going about serene with his lamp" (*U* 18:1597) (*sereno* = night watchman). A better knowledge of Spanish, or further traces of Spanish accent in her English, would have been better evidence of a Gibraltar childhood.[25]

Like Joyce, Molly chooses exile, and like him she turns memories into memoirs, the facts of the past into the fiction of the present. In trying to get at those facts we, in turn, are tempted to invent alternate fictions to supply missing pieces to the puzzle of her early life that Joyce created. To envision an historical Molly living in the Gibraltar of her period is, ironically, to create a fiction to rival Joyce's, but if this sets in relief the indeterminacy of Molly in *Ulysses*, we may perhaps be excused for taking such liberties.

My fictions revolve around the premise that the most important problem of Molly's youth was one of identity, which, in turn, must have led to a decision of whether to sail with her father to Dublin or stay on the Rock. There have always been two separate communities in British Gibraltar—the garrison and the town—and in the nineteenth century segregation was nearly total except in commerce. In making Molly's mother a Jewess from the town and her father an officer of the garrison, Joyce seems to have disregarded the social tension that would have been a daily worry for a girl like Molly. Her ignorance of town society and its dialect is a sign of her total commitment to garrison life, even though this militates against her memory of near total freedom of activity. Deprived of all relatives but her father, acquainted only with military families, growing up in a tiny enclave segregated from a small community in an isolated military fortress several thousand miles from the British

[25] Let this not be taken to mean that I would have urged Siobhan McKenna to read "Penelope" with Spanish intonations.

Isles—this would have been an unusually confining experience for an independent girl like Molly with a healthy curiosity about life. A choice of garrison would inevitably have led to emigration.

But what if Joyce had possessed the intimate knowledge of Gibraltar that he had of Dublin—would he not have seen that Molly's social isolation could easily have led her to choose town over garrison? If she had, the result might have been a scenario like the following: At an early age Molly recognizes her isolation, using the freedom her father gives her to rebel against the snobbery and confinement of garrison life. Eventually she makes friends with Gibraltarians, seeking to overcome suspicion through assimilation. The doors of the Laredo family are opened to her, which means grandparents, cousins, the security and responsibility of blood ties, perhaps even a place in the Jewish community. Spanish is now preferred to English for daily use. Having chosen town over garrison, the Laredos over Tweedy, the natural warmth of the people convinces her that at last she belongs. Molly marries a local man, stays in Gibraltar, and *Ulysses* as we know it never takes place.[26]

Molly's leaving Gibraltar may be seen as a voyage into exile and uncertainty, a rejection of assimilation, and her life with Leopold Bloom the unhappy consequence of this early decision. Barely eighteen, her unrequited need for love and domestic warmth leads her into an unsuccessful marriage. In 1904 she finds herself without affection, understanding, or a normal sex life, her continuing nostalgia for Gibraltar being a sign that she has sunk roots into the rocky soil that can never be nourished by Liffey water. Molly's afternoon in Boylan's arms is little more than a protest against the callous neglect of Brian Tweedy and Leopold Bloom; her monologue now emerges as a *cancion de soledad*, a sad song of home.

CONCLUSION. In the final chapter of *Ulysses* Joyce was faced with an artistic problem that, given his publishing deadlines, he hadn't the time or space to resolve very effectively: how to

[26] Cf. Herring, *Notesheets* 492: "Better for Penelope stay at home."

create in some fifty pages a believable, appealing, perhaps immortal female character of the stature of Leopold Bloom and Stephen Dedalus. The solution was straight interior monologue consisting of frequent nostalgic memories of Molly's girlhood in order to provide that indispensable dimension of her past, but never before in his works had Joyce depended so heavily on a semblance of truth that rested on so thin a veneer of substance as in the case of Gibraltar. There were, however, important reasons why Molly had to come from there and no other place: (1) Epic topography: Gibraltar is at the mouth of a great womb, the end of the known world for ancient mariners, part of the Pillars of Hercules through which, as Richard Ellmann has noted, Dante's Ulysses was obliged to sail (*Consciousness* 29).[27] Thus, according to Michael Seidel, "Gibraltar appears at the end of *Ulysses* to provide Dublin a connecting, Mediterranean axis" (246). (2) It was there that Willie Mulvey, an old flame of Joyce's wife Nora Barnacle, was stationed.[28] (3) Molly's character is based in part on that of Nora, who came from Galway, a city known for its Spanish connections. In Joyce's curious logic, therefore, Nora could be Spanish in the way that Joyce was Scandinavian, Dublin being a city founded by Danes. Molly could thus be Spanish, Moorish, and Irish, Jewish and Catholic, an adulterous Penelope yet faithful in her fashion.

Composition of character and place were further complicated by Joyce's obvious abandonment of any steadfast principle of creating "that sudden reality which smashes romanticism into a pulp" (Power 98), signs of which can be seen as early as the "Aeolus" episode. Exigencies of time plus his growing preoccupation with stylistic experimentation perhaps increased Joyce's intolerance of whatever rules of verisimilitude he might earlier have followed. This was reinforced by the strongly absurdist mood that created many of the undecidable critical problems that have kept us so busy unravelling the denouement of *Ulysses*.

As a defense against the charge that in making his Penelope

[27] Cf. Ellmann's *Ulysses on the Liffey* 172.

[28] See Garvin 104-105.

a woman of Gibraltar he had abandoned his earlier dedication to factual authenticity, Joyce might well have quoted his Trieste lecture of 1912 on Daniel Defoe:

> Pedants strained to expose the paltry errors into which the great precursor of the realist movement had fallen. How could Crusoe stuff his pockets with biscuits if he had stripped before swimming from the beach to the stranded vessel? How could he see the goat's eyes in the pitch-dark cave? How could the Spaniards give Friday's father an agreement in writing when they had neither ink nor pen? Are there any bears or not on the West Indian islands? And so on. The pedants are right: the errors are there; but the broad river of the new realism carries them off majestically like bushes and reeds uprooted by the flood. ("Daniel Defoe": 13)

A Portrait of the Artist As Rimbaud

In *The Poetics of Indeterminacy,* Marjorie Perloff discovers an anti-Symbolist line of descent beginning with Rimbaud and extending down through Gertrude Stein, William Carlos Williams, Ezra Pound, Samuel Beckett, John Ashbery, John Cage, and David Antin.[29] The overall design is beautifully coherent for showing the tradition of indeterminacy in modern poetry. On the other hand, if we start again with Rimbaud and examine his influence on Stephen Dedalus through Joyce, we see something different. Rimbaud was himself part of a tradition—the Romantic visionary tradition—and for him as for Stephen, indeterminacy is a function of vision. For the writers in Perloff's line of descent, indeterminacy was mostly a feature of poetic language.

In formulating an uncertainty principle, Joyce was building on the tradition of Rimbaud, and he applied the principle not merely to language, but to structure and character as well. Neither he nor Stephen rejects symbolism; many studies have

[29] An earlier version of this section appeared as "Joyce and Rimbaud" in Bushrui and Benstock.

shown their debt to Symbolist poets, and Joyce's success in combining Symbolist and Naturalist techniques in his early works is beyond dispute.

In this section I wish to explore an indeterminacy of character in Stephen Dedalus that is related to Rimbaud, and that is central to our understanding of the growth of Joyce's artist figure and of why he cannot reach full maturity in the fictional structures Joyce creates. (In Chapter Six, "How Joyce Ends," we shall see how the form of *A Portrait*, and especially its ending, makes impossible Stephen's artistic maturation.) Also to be explored is a separate issue, Joyce's debt to the French poet, which is most apparent in his view of himself as an artist.

It is common knowledge that Joyce could recite Verlaine and Baudelaire by the hour, that he derived much from the Symbolist aesthetic, and that the mind of Stephen Dedalus in *Ulysses* is steeped in French culture, but as yet no sustained effort to connect Joyce and Stephen specifically with Rimbaud has appeared in print. What has been written is sometimes contradictory or confusing. While Hugh Kenner calls Stephen a "Dublin Rimbaud" (*Dublin's Joyce* 24), David Weir disputes this notion, calling the resemblance "external and general" and choosing Baudelaire over Rimbaud as the more important influence on Joyce ("Stephen Dedalus": 87).[30]

At least two of Joyce's Dublin friends would have agreed with Kenner: C. P. Curran wrote a few paragraphs about Joyce's interest in Rimbaud during their University College days, specifically about the French poet's theories of linguistic experimentation, and his mysteriously enigmatic manner. He also mentioned Joyce's ability to recite Rimbaud's "Voyelles" from memory (30-32). Oliver St. John Gogarty, on the other hand, wrote venomously of how reading Rimbaud changed Joyce for the worse, making him an antisocial ingrate who rejected all that was conventional and decent. Eventually, he suggests, this led to a loss of mental balance and the hopelessly obscure *Finnegans Wake*:

[30] Two articles on Joyce's debt to Baudelaire and the French Symbolists, by Morse and Kronegger, fail to mention Rimbaud.

> From Flushing I received a postcard with a photograph of Joyce dressed to resemble Arthur Rimbaud. Rimbaud's revolution against established canons made him a god to Joyce. We must not leave Rimbaud out of the reckoning; if we do, we fail to understand the influence that fashioned Joyce. Rimbaud, disgusted with mankind, had withdrawn from the world. The logical end was for him to withdraw from all authorship because his kind of private writing would lead only to talking to himself. Joyce did not withdraw, so he ended by listening to himself talking in his sleep—"Finnegans Wake." (9)

Gogarty was, of course, woefully biased in his analysis of the important processes that shaped Joyce's literary development. Gogarty's biographer, Ulick O'Connor, echoes the half-truths gleaned from his subject: "When Joyce started to adopt Rimbaud's custom of deliberately reviling those who helped him, Gogarty found himself unable any longer to stomach his friend's Latin posturing" (86). The waters have been considerably muddied.

BAUDELAIRE, RIMBAUD, AND THE ROMANTIC TRADITION. Joyce would have rebelled against the conventional order had he never read Arthur Rimbaud, but it is hard to imagine any avid reader of literature at the end of the nineteenth century not being fascinated with Rimbaud's life and work, especially a reader who so valued originality and the dramatic gesture of defiance. Rimbaud lived what was probably the most adventurous life of any poet of the modern age. Although Joyce was by nature unadventuresome, he certainly sensed a strong affinity in other ways, and we know that affinity was a matter of great importance to him. Rimbaud was a stunningly authentic genius while still in his teens, a quintessential artist-rebel whose proto-Surrealist poems, daring lifestyle, and striking aesthetic theories dazzled a generation of writers. At University College, Joyce would have been about the age at which Rimbaud gave up poetry to become a wanderer and student of languages. After a stint in Paris, Rimbaud's favorite city, Joyce would give up medical school and the prospect of a conventional career to elope with a chambermaid for Pola and Trieste, a school of languages and a life of uncertainty and penury.

Although Joyce knew about Rimbaud long before, the only two published letters in which he mentions him are from September 1905 and October 1906, not long after his flight to the Continent with Nora; in the earlier letter he clearly sees Rimbaud as a kindred spirit.

> It is possible that the delusion I have with regard to my power to write will be killed by adverse circumstances. But the delusion which will never leave me is that I am an artist by temperament. Newman and Renan, for example, are excellent writers but they seem to have very little of the temperament I mean. Whereas Rimbaud, who is hardly a writer at all, has it. (*Letters* 2:110; cf. 173)

The second letter, from Joyce to his brother Stanislaus, Richard Ellmann cites as proof that Joyce read Arthur Symons's *The Symbolist Movement in Literature,* a book dedicated to W. B. Yeats (Ellmann, *James Joyce* 235n).[31] C. P. Curran (31) says that Joyce read Symons in 1900 or 1901, and that his copy of Verlaine's *Les Poètes Maudits* (Paris, 1884), which also has a section on Rimbaud, is dated 1902. Although Joyce may have read Verlaine first, Symons's book had the greater impact on him, as it did on writers and students of literature in the English-speaking world generally. Curran describes the effect on his fellow Dublin students:

> Huysmans's symbolism of colours fitted in, too, with the Rimbaud sonnet, *Voyelles,* which Joyce would repeat to me. Imitating Rimbaud and *À Rebours,* we would push these *fin-de-siècle* fancies, as I imagine students were doing in every university town, to the correspondence of

[31] Joyce says of Gerhart Hauptmann that "his temperament has a little of Rimbaud in it. Like him, too, I suppose somebody else will be his future" (*Letters* II: 173), referring to Symons's often misunderstood statement of Rimbaud that "even in literature he had his future; but his future was Verlaine" (295). The most important work done on Joyce, Symons, Verlaine, and the Symbolists has been done by David Hayman in *Joyce et Mallarmé.* See also Tindall, *James Joyce: His Way of Interpreting the Modern World.*

> colours with the sounds of musical instruments and with the sense of taste, compiling, for example, monochrome meals, tables d'hôte in black puddings and caviare, black sole with Guinness and black coffee. (29)

Although Symons's book was hailed as the first real introduction of the French Symbolists in English, the first mention of Rimbaud in print probably came in a newspaper article by George Moore, where he was lumped together with LaForgue, which in 1891 was reprinted in a volume of Moore's essays entitled *Impressions and Opinions*. Since Joyce knew of Moore quite early, either his article or *Les Poètes Maudits* was perhaps his first source of information on Rimbaud. If the source was Moore, the introduction could hardly have been more misleading. The impression it gives is of a frail, ethereal boy dragged across Europe by a lecherous old Verlaine, who supposedly stabbed the boy in a drunken frenzy (actually he shot him in the wrist). Rimbaud is said to have lain "hovering between life and death" for several weeks in a Brussels hospital. Joyce's interest in the French poet can be documented as late as the publication of Edgell Rickword's *Rimbaud, the Boy and the Poet* (London, 1924), which was in his library.[32] Into Buffalo notebook VIII.B, which Hans Walter Gabler dates 1919-1920, Joyce copied "Voyelles."[33] That Rimbaud was a model for Shem the Penman is a matter of speculation, since there is some blurring of distinction with Baudelaire and other artist-pariah figures.

Symons's *The Symbolist Movement in Literature* remains the single most important source for the young Joyce's understanding of the "enfant terrible" of French poetry, because it contains the essential Rimbaud to which he responded. It recounts his life, emphasizes the rebellion, his visionary nature, the originality, and it quotes only one poem—"Voyelles," the

[32] See Connolly, ed., *The Personal Library of James Joyce*, item 252.

[33] A facsimile copy of VIII.B appears in *The James Joyce Archive*, ed. Michael Groden et al. in the volume entitled *Notes, Criticism, Translations, and Miscellaneous Writings* 2:381. Also in Joyce's hand appear poems by Albert Samain, Stéphane Mallarmé, and Leon Bloy, and prose selections from Walter Pater.

one Rimbaud poem that we know Joyce could recite from memory.

Later Joyce must have read the *"lettres du voyant"* on sense disorientation. These famous letters of May 1871 contain Rimbaud's discourse on the history of poetry from the aspiring visionary poet's viewpoint and, more importantly, reveal his theory of sense disorientation.

> Now, I am degrading myself as much as possible. Why? I want to be a poet, and I am working to make myself a *seer*: you will not understand this, and I don't know how to explain it to you. It is a question of reaching the unknown by the derangement of *all the senses*. The sufferings are enormous, but one has to be strong, one has to be born a poet, and I know I am a poet. This is not at all my fault (Rimbaud 303).[34]

> I say one must be a *seer*, make oneself a *seer*.
>
> The Poet makes himself a *seer* by a long, gigantic and rational *derangement* of *all the senses*. All forms of love, suffering, and madness. He searches himself. He exhausts all poisons in himself and keeps only their quintessences. Unspeakable torture where he needs all his faith, all his superhuman strength, where he becomes among all men the great patient, the great criminal, the one accursed—and the supreme Scholar!—Because he reaches the *unknown*! Since he cultivated his soul, rich already, more than any man! He reaches the unknown, and when, bewildered, he ends by losing the intelligence of his visions, he has seen them. Let him die as he leaps through unheard of and unnamable things: other horrible workers will come; they will begin from the horizons where the other one collapsed! (Rimbaud 307)

In the second letter the Romantics are judged according to their success as visionaries. "Lamartine is at times a seer.

[34] Fowlie's edition contains both the original French and an English translation. Some readers might prefer the *Oeuvres Completes d'Arthur Rimbaud*, (Paris: Éditions Gallimard, 1963).

Hugo . . . in his last volumes. Musset is . . . loathsome. . . . [But] the second Romantics are very much seers: Théophile Gautier, Leconte de Lisle, Théodore de Banville. But, since inspecting the invisible and hearing the unheard is different from recovering the spirit of dead things, Baudelaire is the first seer, king of poets, a *real God!* . . . The new school, called Parnassian, has two seers, Albert Mérat and Paul Verlaine, a real poet" (Rimbaud 309-311). Rimbaud became a visionary poet in this French Romantic tradition. He was especially indebted to Baudelaire, and through him to Boehme, Swedenborg, Poe, Blake, and De Quincey.

"*Voyant*," or "seer," needs some definition if we are to understand the word as Rimbaud used it. An appropriate context is given in M. H. Abrams's *Natural Supernaturalism*, Chapters 7 and 8, on visionary experience. Abrams emphasizes that the constant themes of Wordsworth and other English Romantics contain this imperative: that the poet must learn to experience freshness of sensation while viewing the common, everyday scenes in nature. Rimbaud shared this aim in part, but preferred to achieve originality through artificially induced sensations, or visionary distortions of perception. Romantics wish to see afresh as a child might see in order "to make the old world new not by distorting it, but by defamiliarizing the familiar . . . " (Abrams 379). Wordsworth wished "to liberate the vision of his readers from bondage to the physical eye, habitual categories, social custom, and caste prejudice, so that they may see the world that he has come to see (Abrams 406-407). Rimbaud goes the Romantics one better and shows us sights unseen before or since by his readers; freshness of sensation, defamiliarization, originality of vision have become the final goal rather than a means of liberating readers, the result being poems calculated to startle and amaze.

Abrams (414) places Baudelaire in the visionary tradition by citing his advocacy of freshness of sensation and childlike seeing—"the child sees everything *new*; he is always *intoxicated*"—but the emphasis has shifted to the agony of vision, the *voyant* poet's fixation, possession, and obsession in the act of contemplation. Vision has become a malady. From here it is but a step to Rimbaud's "artist as sick man" who feeds on the distilled poisons of his own system.

Where Rimbaud parted ways with Baudelaire was on the subject of addiction, which, for a poet willing to risk insanity in his quest for freshness of sensation, was a rather small matter. Edgell Rickword says that while in Paris, Rimbaud ". . . moved among . . . men of letters like a drunkard or a visionary. He intoxicated himself, systematically, with alcohol, hashish, and tobacco. He relished the impressions of insomnia, and lived like a somnambulist . . ." (47). The result of this *voyant* regimen was the sort of violent, surrealistic, sensational vision of corruption seen in the following stanza from "Le Bateau ivre." The translation is by Samuel Beckett, as quoted by Perloff (222).

Iridescent waters, glaciers, suns of silver, flagrant skies,
And dark creeks' secret ledges, horror-strewn,
Where giant reptiles, pullulant with lice,
Lapse with dark perfumes from the writhing trees.

Here we see the *voyant* posing as a madman journeying through a strange, beautiful, and rather horrifying land of the imagination totally different from the Charleville he detested.

From Rimbaud's *dérèglement de tous les sens* to synaesthesia, or the reverse, is but another step; for Stephen Dedalus, as for Rimbaud, Huysmans and other writers, the step was an important one. Synaesthetic experience promised uniqueness of sensation that could lead to originality of expression—perhaps even the new language to which many poets aspire. (All the "indeterminate" poets described by Perloff aspired to a new language.) For our purposes the line of descent is principally from Poe to Baudelaire (especially "Correspondances") to Rimbaud's "Voyelles" to Joyce's epiphanies, the "Proteus" episode and beyond in *Ulysses*.[35]

"Correspondances" speaks of nature as a temple, of man reaching it "through symbols dense as trees that watch him

[35] See articles by Kronegger, Weir ("Stephen Dedalus"), and Loss (152-54).

with a gaze familiar." "Some perfumes are, like children, innocent, / As sweet as oboes, green as meadow sward, / —And others, complex, rich and jubilant, / The vastness of infinity afford, / Like musk and amber, incense, bergamot, / Which sing the senses' and the soul's delight."[36] Odors, sounds, feelings mingle—not quite synaesthetically perhaps, but close; here the similes are unmixed; there is the conventional "green as meadow sward" and the stranger, more evocative similes "perfumes innocent as children"; "as sweet as oboes." But the overall effect, of suggestion, of sensual evocation, is one many poets of the nineteenth and twentieth centuries, from Mallarmé to Wallace Stevens (cf. "Peter Quince at the Clavier"), sought to emulate.

"Voyelles" is a direct descendant of "Correspondances"; like Baudelaire, Rimbaud compiles images for telling effect, but here the strange metaphor has become monstrous, the ethereal suggestion a violent assault on the sensibility, the sense indeterminate. The Fowlie translation (121) reads:

"Vowels"

A black, E white, I red, U green, O blue: vowels,
One day I will tell your latent birth:
A, black hairy corset of shining flies
Which buzz around cruel stench,

Gulfs of darkness; E, whiteness of vapors and tents,
Lances of proud glaciers, white kings, quivering of
flowers;
I, purples, spit blood, laughter of beautiful lips
In anger or penitent drunkenness;

U, cycles, divine vibrations of green seas,
Peace of pastures scattered with animals, peace of the
wrinkles
Which alchemy prints on heavy studious brows;

[36] The complete works of Charles Baudelaire in French are to be found in *Oeuvre Completes*, ed. Marcel Ruff (Paris: Éditions du Seuil, 1968). A good English translation, and one that I have used here, is *Baudelaire: Selected Poems*, trans. Joanna Richardson, 42-43.

O, supreme Clarion full of strange stridor,
Silences crossed by worlds and angels:
—O, the Omega, violet beam from His Eyes!

Mallarmé meditated on the shapes and sounds of letters, but Rimbaud seems to be the first to associate them with colors. The logic of this particular linking escapes us, and, though critics have used considerable violence in yoking the sonnet's vowels and colors together, the logic is surely a private, indeterminate one. We can do little more than speculate about the seriousness with which this synaesthetic linking is to be taken, but an entirely new dimension seems to have been brought to poetry. If a reader could assimilate the system, a virtual kaleidoscope of flashing colors would strike the mind's eye as the words are read. The visual arts would seem to have merged with the literary, so that in addition to rhythm, sound, sense, allusion, and the other common properties of poetry, there would be color. Rimbaud said in "Alchimie du verbe," "I invented the color of the vowels!—*A* black, *E* white, *I* red, *O* blue, *U* green. —I regulated the form and movement of each consonant, and, with instinctive rhythms, I prided myself on inventing a poetic language accessible some day to all the senses. I reserved translation rights" (Rimbaud 193). Obviously the idea turned out to be a matter more for aesthetic speculation than for reader response, but "Voyelles" certainly stimulated the imaginations of Joyce and his generation.

RIMBAUD, JOYCE, DEDALUS. Though Blake is a model for the young Stephen Dedalus in his budding visionary stage, Rimbaud embodied more of the particular kind of revolutionary qualities that Joyce admired. He was an apostate, a vagabond, a pariah who rejected religion, family, country and every kind of convention. He struck the Luciferian pose, inspired the Decadents, and in all things seemed to surpass others in rebellion. In this even Baudelaire seemed to take second place. Rimbaud's exile, his experiments in synaesthesia, his search for a new language, the violence of his imagery, surpassed only by the violence of his disgust—all this would have been enormously appealing to a writer like Joyce.

As a result Stephen Dedalus indeed seems destined to become the Dublin Rimbaud, at least until he struggles free of his model. We often forget that Stephen wishes to become a poet, not the master of prose Joyce was to become; his bitterness matches Rimbaud's, and so does his desire to create radical experimentation in poetic technique. Though Joyce himself overshadows all of Stephen's models, the biographical parallels with the French poet are striking. They reject country, family, religion for a revolutionary aestheticism and see exile as their inevitable destiny. The young poets are fervently religious boys, brilliant though erratic students who become caught up in social rebellion. Enid Starkie says Rimbaud "was a religious nature looking for spiritual certainty" (17). Henry Miller affirms that, at the age of twelve, "Rimbaud's piety was so exalted that he longed for martyrdom" (87). Stephen's faith is a major theme of the works in which he appears. The rebellious Rimbaud cried, "Death to God," while cunning Stephen refuses to kneel at his dying mother's bedside. Their religious revolt became an all-out battle against matriarchy. The son of an absent father (cf. Simon Dedalus in *Ulysses*), Rimbaud's battles for freedom of movement, conduct, and expression were frantically waged against a domineering mother. Attempting to coerce him into a return to the fold in "Circe," the ghost of Stephen's mother *"raises her blackened withered right arm slowly towards Stephen's breast with outstretched finger"* (*U* 15:4218-19).

If mothers are an anathema to artists, father figures (as opposed to real fathers) are consciously sought. Harold Bloom quotes Nietzsche as saying, "When one hasn't had a good father, it is necessary to invent one" (56). Rimbaud's name must be added to those of Telemachus, Icarus, and Hamlet as archetypal figures whose most memorable acts are determined by the authority of present or absent fathers. Stephen's discussion of paternity indicates that the subject is of some importance to him (*U* 9:828-45), and *Ulysses's* Homeric structure is a promise that father-son relations will be crucial. Rimbaud's father, an army captain, abandoned the family; in Georges Izambard, Rimbaud's teacher, and later in Verlaine, the poet sought a father figure intelligent enough to direct his development as a poet while, at the same time, capable of the love and understanding he had lacked at home.

The disgust that Stephen and Rimbaud feel at the national coalition of Church and bourgeoisie becomes a revolutionary philosophy. Since Ireland suffered from British domination, and France from its recent defeat in the Prussian War, each artist (like Baudelaire) feels a sense of racial inferiority. This is the subject of "Mauvais Sang," in *Une Saison en Enfer* (Rimbaud 174-83), and of several of Stephen's comments in *A Portrait* and *Ulysses* (cf. *AP* 203; *U* 16:1171).

In *Stephen Hero,* we find some justification for Kenner's christening Stephen the "Dublin Rimbaud." We read that Stephen

> sought in his verses to fix the most elusive of his moods and he put his lines together not word by word but letter by letter. He read Blake and Rimbaud on the values of letters and even permuted and combined the five vowels to construct cries for primitive emotions. To none of his former fervours had he given himself with such a whole heart as to this fervour. (32)[37]

In Joyce's *A Portrait of the Artist as a Young Man,* it is through words, language, that Stephen Dedalus comes to know the world around him, his reality being continually shaped by vocabulary acquisition (62). Instinctively, he grasps the mystical power of words, a sure sign of the artistic temperament. In this he resembles the boy in "The Sisters," who has embroidered for *paralysis, gnomon,* and *simony* private meanings. Stephen follows in the footsteps of writers who have sought a new language for poetic expression; in *A Portrait* the language he comes to use is obviously derivative of Newman, Pater, and the *fin-de-siècle* writers, especially in his villanelle, but like Rimbaud, who echoed Baudelaire until he found his own voice, he is gradually moving closer to originality of expres-

[37] See Hunting, who was apparently unaware that she was anticipated by Stephen. Her point is that more important than the configuration of the letters in "Voyelles" is their function as "cries for primitive emotions."

sion. The discovery of new literary languages and forms, a feature of *fin-de-siècle* writing generally, was a major concern of Joyce as well, from the evolutionary prose of *A Portrait* to the linguistic experimentalism of *Finnegans Wake*.

From *Stephen Hero* through *Ulysses*, synaesthesia is often the subject of Stephen's thoughts when he is alone, evaluating his perceptions, honing his verbal skills, exploring the freshness of his sensations. This seems to be an extension of his earlier onomatopoeic definitions ("suck" [*AP* 11]; "kiss" [*AP* 15]) and private associations ("wine" = "dark purple" [*AP* 46-47]). In a climactic scene of Chapter Two of *A Portrait*, the disgusted Stephen leaves the school play to walk rapidly down the hill. "Pride and hope and desire like crushed herbs in his heart sent up vapours of maddening incense before the eyes of his mind" (*AP* 86). His agony of despair is calmed by the odor of horse piss and rotted straw. Herbs in the heart, eyes in the mind, the reassuring smell of corruption, these are the terms of a kind of metaphorical thinking highly unusual in a schoolboy—unless, of course, he or the narrator has been reading Symbolist poetry. In Chapter Four, having just rejected with finality the priestly vocation, sure now that he was meant to be an artist, Stephen turns for guidance in his thinking to "Voyelles," "Correspondances," and Symbolist theory, which will now shape his development.

> He drew forth a phrase from his treasure and spoke it softly to himself:
>
> —A day of dappled seaborne clouds.
>
> The phrase and the day and the scene harmonized in a chord. Words. Was it their colours? He allowed them to glow and fade, hue after hue: sunrise gold, the russet and green of apple orchards, azure of waves, the greyfringed fleece of clouds. No, it was not their colours: it was the poise and balance of the period itself. Did he then love the rhythmic rise and fall of words better than their associations of legend and colour? Or was it that, being as weak of sight as he was shy of mind, he drew less pleasure from the reflection of the glowing sensible world through the prism of a language manycoloured and richly storied than

> from the contemplation of an inner world of individual emotions mirrored perfectly in a lucid supple periodic prose? (*AP* 166)

In gauging the appeal of word rhythms to be greater than word hues, Stephen strains at the bonds of apprenticeship. Later he listens to the cries of circling birds: "like the squeak of mice behind the wainscot: a shrill twofold note. But the notes were long and shrill and whirring, unlike the cry of vermin, falling a third or a fourth and trilled as the flying beaks clove the air. Their cry was shrill and clear and fine and falling like threads of silken light unwound from whirring spools" (*AP* 224). Still later, Stephen thinks, "A trembling joy, lambent as a faint light, played like a fairy host around him. But why? Her passage through the darkening air or the verse with its black vowels [*A* = *noir*] and its opening sound, rich and lutelike?" (*AP* 232-33). In such moments of intense aesthetic reflection, Stephen is to Rimbaud as Rimbaud was to Baudelaire; the apprentice stage was a necessary stop on the road to a new language of poetic expression. The vehicle was synaesthetic thinking.

In the Martello Tower, where, Oliver Gogarty said, Joyce talked of little but Rimbaud, Buck Mulligan stands on the parapet at the beginning of *Ulysses*, wipes his razor clean of shaving soap with Stephen's handkerchief, and says: "—The bard's noserag! A new art colour for our Irish poets: snotgreen. You can almost taste it, can't you?" A few lines later he also calls the sea "snotgreen" (*U* 1:73-78). The handkerchief is obviously the main point of reference, but there are other allusive ones. Mulligan's quip comes after a decade in which there appeared seemingly countless slim, green volumes of Irish Revival poetry such as Chandler of Joyce's story "A Little Cloud" envisions publishing. Green is Ireland's color, and "snotgreen" is an appropriate, if disgusting, color for decadent art (if it must have one). But what makes the color still more apt is that both Mulligan and Dedalus know that *morves d'azur* (snotgreen) comes from Rimbaud's "Le Bateau ivre" (line 76). In a parody of creative activity, Stephen will lay "dry snot picked from his nostril on a ledge of rock, carefully"

(*U* 3:500-501). In a comical way, Mulligan is signaling his disgust with Stephen and Rimbaud, who, Gogarty said, taught Joyce ingratitude. The francophile standing before Mulligan, possibly Ireland's first decadent poet, will not soon forget his biting wit.

It is hardly an accident that "Proteus," the art of which Joyce said was philology, is also the most colorful episode of *Ulysses*, or that Rimbaud's color "snotgreen" appears in the episode's third line (*U* 3:3). In *Ulysses*, as in *A Portrait*, the French poet is most in Stephen's thoughts when walking alone, reading the book of himself, measuring his progress as an artist against the certain loss of vocation (priest in *A Portrait*, teacher in "Nestor"). The difficult opening of "Proteus" is most often interpreted in terms of its internal references to Aristotle's *De Anima* (Books 2 and 3) and Jacob Boehme's *Signatura Rerum*, but while Stephen is in a sense learning to read God's signature in nature, as Wordsworth did, he is more precisely learning to be a seer in the visionary sense. He closes his eyes to perceive, an act his aesthetic principles and his theory of epiphany, as discussed in *Stephen Hero* and *A Portrait*, show to be essential to his growth as an artist. Stephen, like his French predecessor, has assimilated a literary tradition he can use. In flux in the opening of "Proteus" are nature, thought, literary and philosophical references, language, and identity, the entire effect being quite definitely synaesthetic.

> Ineluctable modality of the visible: at least that if no more, thought through my eyes. Signatures of all things I am here to read, seaspawn and seawrack, the nearing tide, that rusty boot. Snotgreen, bluesilver, rust: coloured signs. Limits of the diaphane. But he adds: in bodies. Then he was aware of them bodies before of them coloured. . . . Shut your eyes and see.
>
> Stephen closed his eyes to hear his boots crush crackling wrack and shells. . . . I am getting on nicely in the dark. My ash sword hangs at my side. Tap with it: they do. . . .
>
> Rhythm begins, you see. I hear. . . .
>
> Open your eyes now. I will. One moment. Has all van-

ished since? If I open and am for ever in the black adiaphane. *Basta!* I will see if I can see.

See now. There all the time without you: and ever shall be, world without end. (*U* 3:1-27)

Stephen reads nature, shuts his eyes to see, says, "Rhythm begins, you see, I hear," and finally opens his eyes to see if he can see. Having seen so much already, he then sees time. The perceptual exercises are complete, the command by Rimbaud that the artist make himself a seer has been obeyed. Once the mood has become set, Stephen is more prepared to see, think, evaluate, and experiment with words that will express his vision.

Like Wordsworth, Stephen will see and describe the most common things and occurrences in nature, but unlike Wordsworth this will give him no pleasure, for he is deeply embittered by life, haunted by the past and fearful of the future. In "Telemachus" he scorns the usurper; in "Nestor" he scorns the oppressor; in "Proteus" he scorns himself. His self-hatred derives from his sense of failure as a writer—that he is still honing the tools of his art, and as yet has produced only a few derivative poems. Like Yeats and Rimbaud, Stephen knows that artistic skill is cultivated, that artists make themselves artists; being born with artistic temperament is hardly enough. Though he concentrates on these matters in "Proteus," dumps file cabinets of relevant material into his consciousness as he walks on the beach, Stephen is obviously the artist as a young man, impatient that he is still apprenticed to the singing masters of his soul. Readers see his metempsychotic affinities with Icarus, Dedalus, Telemachus, Hamlet, and Christ and accept them, but Stephen seems to share Mulligan's view that he is nothing but a *poseur*, an imposter freshly returned from Paris in his "Latin quarter hat," flaunting the newly acquired veneer of French culture. "God, we simply must dress the character" (*U* 3:174). Gogarty spoke of receiving a photo of Joyce wearing the complete Rimbaud costume; in *Ulysses* Stephen wears Mulligan's trousers and distinctly foreign headgear, a sign that he is not yet his own man.

Though Stephen might not agree, apprenticeship is, of

course, a commonly accepted means of attaining mastery. In "Proteus," Stephen is apprenticed to no writer more consciously than Rimbaud, where the idea is to forge out of his personality a new being who will see anew, express anew. Rimbaud was thinking along these lines when he wrote: "I is someone else. It is too bad for the wood which finds itself a violin. . . . For I is someone else. If brass wakes up a trumpet, it is not its fault . . ." (Rimbaud 305). The phrase "*Je est un autre*" has struck a chord in Stephen's mind during this hour on the beach, where he feels his identity as much in flux as language, tide, and sea. "Yes, used to carry punched tickets [in Paris] to prove an alibi if they arrested you for murder somewhere. . . . Other fellow did it: other me. Hat, tie, overcoat, nose. *Lui, c'est moi*" (*U* 3:182-83). Later, he thinks, "My soul walks with me, form of forms" (*U* 3:279-80). He imagines himself among his Viking ancestors "on the frozen Liffey, that I, a changeling" (*U* 3:307-308). Still later he thinks, "Me sits there with his augur's rod of ash, in borrowed sandals" (*U* 3:410-11). Remembering a borrowed pound while in the library, he will use a theory of molecular change to release himself from the debt: "Wait. Five months. Molecules all change. I am other I now. Other I got pound" (*U* 9:205-206). Stephen walks, thinks almost continually about Paris, listens to the "fourworded wavespeech: seesoo, hrss, rsseeiss, ooos" (*U* 3:456-57), and feels thoroughly uncomfortable with himselves. Wherever he walks, Rimbaud's footprints seem already imprinted on the sand.

Feeling unfortunate, perhaps, not to have written "Voyelles," and perhaps remembering the theory of the children's book as the poem's source, Stephen ridicules himself in unconscious anticipation of Thomas Pynchon: "Books you were going to write with letters for titles. Have you read his F? O yes, but I prefer Q. Yes, but W is wonderful. O yes, W" (*U* 3:139-40). "The virgin at Hodges Figgis' window on Monday looking in for one of the alphabet books you were going to write" (*U* 3:426-27).

Still captivated by "Voyelles" in "Eumaeus," Stephen sits in the cabmen's shelter watching either the words of Leopold Bloom's discourse on life change color or some unspoken ones in his mind:

> Over his untastable apology for a cup of coffee, listening to this synopsis of things in general, Stephen stared at nothing in particular. He could hear, of course, all kinds of words changing colour like those crabs about Ringsend in the morning burrowing quickly into all colours of different sorts of the same sand where they had a home somewhere beneath or seemed to. (*U* 16:1141-46)

In *Finnegans Wake*, the character of Shem, especially in "Shem, the Penman" (*FW* 169 ff.), is a caricature of the artistic temperament (so offensive to Gogarty) that Joyce associated with Rimbaud and himself in his letter of September 1905 (*voir supra*). There is little need to catalogue the antisocial traits of Shem, or his persona Glugg "the bold bad bleak boy of the storybooks" (*FW* 219). He is the quintessential artist as *voyant*, poet, outcast, rebel, and threat to all decent people; he is a "stinksome inkenstink" (*FW* 183), the "first till last alshemist [who] wrote over every square inch of the only foolscap available, his own body" (*FW* 185). Rimbaud, of course, wrote "Alchimie du verbe" (which contains Shem's name), where he discussed "Voyelles" (Rimbaud 192-95).

In *A Portrait*, Stephen's body is lice-ridden, even "his mind bred vermin" (*AP* 174; 234), and though one remembers Donne's poem "The Flea," vermin remained an unlikely subject for literature until Rimbaud wrote "Les Chercheuses de poux" (Rimbaud 92-93); Shem, as seen by Shaun, is far more disgusting: "a condemned fool, anarch, egoarch, hiresiarch, [who has] reared [his] disunited kingdom on the vacuum of [his] own intensely doubtful soul" (*FW* 188), a "seeker of the nest of evil in the bosom of a good word" (*FW* 189)—a *voyant*, the son of a *voyeur*—in short, a madman.

Though by implication Rimbaud seems present in Shem's character, he is there as part of a visionary tradition extending back to the biblical prophets and forward through Boehme,

Swedenborg, Blake, Baudelaire, de Nerval, and others who lived lives of the imagination, who risked persecution for heresy, and whose cultivated eccentricity seemed a sign of their incontrovertible dedication to truth. In using himself as the chief model for Shem, Joyce showed that he felt he belonged in that visionary company; it was with a sense of pride that he scrupulously exposed his vices and faults, imaginary or real, in a manner parodic of Rousseau, cataloging them with a satirist's pen to make of his own hide, so to speak, a tapestry.

BLOOM AND STEPHEN. Gogarty was quite right. The influence is there, from *Stephen Hero* to *A Portrait* to *Ulysses,* on the mind of Stephen Dedalus as it must have been on that of the young Joyce, being most apparent in reveries where aesthetics is the subject; but we know that Joyce broke the mold and went beyond Rimbaud, whereas when Stephen tries to push on toward truly original theories of experimentation and expression, his thoughts weave synaesthetic patterns in colors and vowels. Stephen is thus paralyzed by a classical case of the anxiety of influence as defined by Harold Bloom, though in a curious way: he does not misread his predecessor, or wrestle with his poems, but rather he exhibits a fixation on "Voyelles" as the great imaginative poem of the past, a great poetic/linguistic breakthrough that will allow further breakthroughs by younger poets like Stephen, who will extend the new tradition of indeterminacy seen by Perloff. The promise held out is a means to originality of expression through startling experimentation, perhaps a secular re-visionism, to state it punningly. But if "Voyelles" is the future, it is also the past. Stephen is so burdened by this knowledge that he suffers from the "disease of self-consciousness" that often affects the unsure apprentice (Harold Bloom 29). That Stephen's is not simply a temporary condition is seen in the allusions to "Voyelles" in all the works in which Stephen appears, which take place over a period of years.

Stephen's problem with Rimbaud is all the more intriguing because it is never discussed or even alluded to as a problem; hence it is the central indeterminacy of his character. The story of Stephen is the story of the artist's growth, but the harder he struggles to fulfill his vocation the more resistance he meets, the goal being continually just beyond his reach. The nature of this opposition is the subject of the final chapter of *A Portrait*—Church, State, family, history, language—all discussed in outraged tones, but the poet who offers to guide him is, like Leopold Bloom, the figure who stands in his path. Here too is resistance. The French poet has to be either vanquished or assimilated in the mind, but in any case he must be gone beyond for Stephen to be able to write. Since Stephen must overcome self-doubts, gaining mastery over his masters in order to blossom in his vocation (and his story is essentially about this struggle), he shares with Rimbaud a dimension of intercourse that sheds a greater light on his character than do the shadowy forebears most often evoked by critics—Telemachus, Hamlet, Icarus, Daedalus—none of whom was known for his experiments with language or literary form. Yet this enervating fixation is largely hidden from the reader's view, only to emerge in the image patterns of Stephen's reveries. Though the struggle takes place offstage and is of lengthy duration, it is apparent that Stephen must emerge victorious if he is to create original art.[38]

By *Finnegans Wake*, Rimbaud had about served Joyce's purpose; although his interest doubtless remained, his use of the French poet, as with so many other writers, had become more ornamental than essential.[39] The experimentalism of Rimbaud

[38] David Weir argues in "Moore's Young Man" that Stephen is part of a tradition of aesthetic young men common in the 1890s, "of aristocratic pretensions and artistic sensibilities" (4), who aren't expected actually to become artists. While incontestably true on the level of literary history, this view ignores the sincerity and uniqueness of Stephen's struggle with his literary forebears. Wrong in a different way is William Empson, who in *Using Biography* rejects the skeptical view of Stephen expressed by Hugh Kenner in *Dublin's Joyce*. Empson says, "Now, Joyce was an extremely self-centred man, fiercely determined to become a great novelist; he is wildly unlikely to have presented himself, without any warning or explanation, as incapable of becoming one" (204). This is an autobiographical fallacy.

[39] For an example of ornament, see William York Tindall, *James Joyce* (109). He cites "Mithyphallic" (*FW* 481.4) as "a distortion of Rimbaud's 'Ithyphalliques' ('Le Coeur Volé')." Some would disagree that Rimbaud was used in a

and "Voyelles" was a blockage through which Stephen had to pass to attain mastery; *Ulysses* reflects in plot and form Joyce's own successful struggle with his literary forebears. *Finnegans Wake* proclaims on every page the virtuosity to which Stephen aspires, one surpassing anything of which Rimbaud could have dreamed. Hence he is little celebrated in Joyce's final work. Stephen's struggle for mastery was no longer the author's subject, which had now become literary virtuosity itself. Still, those with unusual perceptual abilities may occasionally glimpse the young French master on the Wakean Parnassus, in rather reduced circumstances, detached from the work itself, paring his fingernails as if he bore no responsibility for the babulous funferall below.

---

way more ornamental than essential in *Finnegans Wake*. Both David Hayman and Adaline Glasheen see an important connection there between colors, rainbows (evoking Rimbaud's name), and "Voyelles." Perhaps they are right, but this would seem to be the subject of another essay. See also Raynaud (306).

SIX

How Joyce Ends

After Kafka it becomes hard to believe not only in answers but even in endings. . . .
Irving Howe (30)

In Lewis Carroll's *Alice's Adventures in Wonderland,* the King says gravely to the White Rabbit, who is preparing to read some incriminating verses, "Begin at the beginning, and go on till you come to the end: then stop" (94).[1] A true Aristotelian, the King preaches the orthodoxy of literary form that persisted well into the nineteenth century. Though Aristotle wrote of plays in the *Poetics,* for long his generic views governed literary discourse: any narrative was supposed to have a beginning, a middle, and an end. An epic, like a modern novel, could begin in the middle, but this merely reordered the narrative sequence without omitting any of its three elements.

Alexander Welsh has defined beginnings and endings as "arbitrary disjunctions in a sequence of events that is presumed continuous" (10) by which he meant that fictional time does not begin or end with the events that are the subject of narration; but if they are arbitrary they are also especially significant points in time that often reveal a writer's basic concept of order. Plots do not typically begin at any moment in the life of a character; they begin in ways that provide orientation. Endings may function to clarify or cause the reader to ponder some lack of clarity, either to impose order or to show the necessity of disorder. An ending may come at a logical stopping place, or in mid-sentence, as in *Finnegans Wake,* but whatever the particular ending there can be no doubt about its significance. All things that stop, end—a trip, a noise, a shower of rain—but the process by which literary texts end is called *closure;* and a literary ending, I would say, is the ultimate narrative unit in a text that is the culminating created achievement of the process of closure.

[1] A few pages of this chapter appeared in my "Comment Joyce finit ses chapitres et ses livres."

Historically, a writer dependent on royalties or favor had little freedom to buck the rules of formal orthodoxy—especially in closure—prior to the twentieth century. Reader expectations were too compelling. The reason for this lies not only in Aristotle and literary tradition, but in human psychology. There is a close correlation between intelligible order and our sense of what ought to be. A normal human gestation period is nine months-neither eight nor ten. No good restaurant would tamper with the order of our meal—first offering us the bill, then a liqueur, then a fruit course, the main dish, to be followed by coffee and soup. In literature, structure and order are far more apparent than in life. Most things in our experience end by simply stopping, without resolution or denouement. Most of us were born, and will die, at inconvenient moments. Since literary texts normally embody the intelligible structural order that we need and often miss in our daily lives, the writing or reading of literature is often more satisfying than the study of history or contemporary events, which are a good deal more enigmatic. Reader expectations reflect this.

So it is that the beginnings of narratives came to have a set function—to capture our interest and to provide orientation. Middles provide plot complications to sustain that interest, and to rouse our curiosity about the eventual resolution of entanglements. This resolution traditionally satisfies us that an appropriate reordering has taken place.

Now for the countertradition. Although closed endings are satisfying, increasingly modern writers have had other ideas about beginnings and endings, and have pointedly resisted opportunities to provide orientation and resolution. In *The Art of the Novel,* Henry James was one of the first to see that the orthodoxy of literary form had become a straitjacket. He said, "Really, universally, relations stop nowhere, and the exquisite problem of the artist is eternally but to draw, by a geometry of his own, the circle within which they shall happily *appear* to do so" (5).[2] He looked back upon the nineteenth-century

[2] Quoted in Marianna Torgovnick (5), as was the passage from *Alice's Adventures in Wonderland*. I am generally indebted in this chapter to Torgovnick.

novel, and especially Dickens, and remarked how often novels end with "a distribution at the last of prizes, pensions, husbands, wives, babies, millions, appended paragraphs, and cheerful remarks."[3] In disparaging Dickens, he was surely thinking in part of *Great Expectations* (1861), the ending of which Dickens was persuaded to change after its publication. Convinced by Edward Bulwer-Lytton that readers wanted an ending where love is requited, Dickens revised the chapter accordingly. Such easy acquiescence to popular taste offended the early moderns, who began to dismiss opportunities for resolution and orientation in favor of ambiguity. James saw in his lifetime the emphasis in fiction gradually shift from the closed to the open ending, from traditional orderings of events to fractured form. Partly in response to a widespread interest in psychology, writers began increasingly to view familiar surroundings as Marlow does the Congo in Conrad's *Heart of Darkness*, as confusingly enigmatic.

Robert M. Adams, in *Strains of Discord*, was probably the first to define the open ending in widely accepted terms: "The open form is literary form (a structure of meanings, intents, and emphasis, i.e. verbal gestures) which includes a major unresolved conflict with the intent of displaying its unresolvedness" (13). The lack of resolution cannot be inadvertent; it must be an authorial strategy to delay or deny us our reward as readers.

Alan Friedman, in his book *The Turn of the Novel*, equated open endings with "an expanding, unresolved moral consciousness" and thus wrongly, in my opinion, emphasized them as a more honest representation of modern consciousness than closed endings. He says: "Earlier fiction attests chiefly and eloquently to the difficult necessity, the coherence and the dignity, of achieving a closed ethical experience in the course of life. Modern fiction attests chiefly and as eloquently to the reverse: an open experience" (xv). I doubt that fictional endings are a true test of the consciousness of an age; furthermore, open and closed endings have always coexisted.

[3] Torgovnick (11), from James's "The Art of Fiction."

While it is true that there is one dominant tradition of form in the English novel, and generally true that in the earlier periods novels end in resolution, whereas modern ones most often do not, one gets the impression from Friedman that at some point there was a radical disjuncture in the novel, a general rebellion against the orthodoxy of form. Actually, self-conscious and parodic literary forms go back a long way in history. Friedman mentions *Tristram Shandy* as if it were a puzzling anomaly, when in fact Sterne was aware of the conventions of form, which he turned topsy-turvy, from his reading in Rabelais and Burton's *The Anatomy of Melancholy*. One remembers too that Samuel Johnson, while granting us closure, entitled the last chapter of *Rasselas* "The Conclusion in Which Nothing is Concluded."

A most fascinating book on endings is still Frank Kermode's *The Sense of an Ending*, a treatment of the way fiction and especially fictional endings reflect our philosophical or religious needs as human beings, living in a perturbing temporal framework that, unlike the novel, seems to have neither beginning nor end. Kermode is interested in what fictional closure says about us.

Whereas Friedman's bias is modernism, that of Marianna Torgovnick is the nineteenth-century novel; even though her title is general, *Closure in the Novel* does for the novel of the last century what Barbara Herrnstein Smith's *Poetic Closure* does for poetry. She is right to say that "by the nineteen-sixties and nineteen-seventies, the 'open' ending had become too trite and expected to have great imaginative force. 'Open' endings [she says] can be as 'merely conventional' as the older techniques for ending they replaced" (206). Torgovnick has also rightly seen the concepts of open and closed endings as in themselves simplistic; she provides us with a list of more specialized terms: the epilogue ending, the scenic ending, endings that emphasize circularity, parallelism, incompletion, tangentiality, linkage, an overview, a close-up, or confrontation.

In her conclusion Torgovnick prefers practical criticism to

theory: "A theoretical framework for the discussion of closure can help us define particular contents and effects, but cannot, in itself, substitute for practical critical analyses, and for the kinds of fine distinctions called for by a given text" (198). In other words, we must be prepared to work hard to justify an ending in terms of the novel's beginning and middle rather than any external structure we might wish to impose. Though it is true that we must apply terms in such a way as to illuminate fictional structures rather than distorting them to fit preconceived notions, we do need terms of classification such as Torgovnick herself has given us. On the other hand, she refuses to look ahead to the problems of indeterminacy or disjuncture in literary form that are a feature of some of the most important literature of our century. Since she pretends to treat the entire tradition of the novel, Torgovnick's major weakness is thus the twentieth-century novel. She seems never to doubt that endings make perfect, unambiguous sense if only we can discover it, but frequently modernist and contemporary texts are too self-reflexive or otherwise strange to be neatly categorized. A reader would find little in her book to help decipher the endings of, say, Samuel Beckett.

Of the major twentieth-century novelists in English, there is one whose endings have proved especially interesting—D. H. Lawrence. His strategies for closure provide a useful contrast to those of Joyce, and they resist easy categorization. Lawrence has been called the leading antimodernist of his day because of his dislike of art for art's sake, and his interest in preaching the gospel of love to a decadent industrial society (Beebe 175); yet like typical modernist endings, his are also usually open, although they seem to derive more from pessimism than structural design. The impediments to a final ordering in Lawrence's novels and stories are signs that he felt that things seldom work out the way we plan them.

Whereas modernist endings call attention to themselves as verbal structures, Lawrence's direct his readers' attention outward into the world or toward a higher world in which some sort of vision of the future is evoked. I would call his open endings "visionary" and place him in a tradition that goes back through Wordsworth, Blake, and Milton.[4] Lawrence dreamed of a higher world of possibility but wrote about this one; his subject was human beings (especially couples) in a natural context transformed by the vision of a symbolic landscape that speaks of regeneration to those who are attuned to its voice. His endings serve this strategy.

Lawrence's endings are seldom puzzling, but the implications of his strategies for ending are. I have always sensed that this was a difficult structural problem for him, if not an emotional one. Afflicted with tuberculosis, he hated to admit the possibility of his demise; at the same time he ardently wished for the collapse of industrial society, and hoped that he would play a part in the reconstruction to follow. His attitude toward those two envisioned endings—personal and societal—must have influenced his fictional endings. He seemed always to be looking ahead. In *Mysteries of Identity*, Robert Langbaum says that Lawrence "always negates his last step in order to take the next one" (289). If excessive anticipation was a problem, so too was despair. In *The Fox* Lawrence said, "You pluck flower after flower—it is never *the* flower. . . . That is the whole history of the search for happiness, whether it be your own or somebody else's that you want to win. It ends, and it always ends, in the ghastly sense of the bottomless nothingness into which you will inevitably fall if you strain any further" (177).

Lawrence's visionary ending is a "threshold ending"—where characters, now safely past some major crisis, stand at the beginning of uncertain but challenging futures, looking toward another place that promises to be better than this one. Lawrence asserts, but seldom demonstrates, that a proper orientation has been achieved, and that protagonists are now moving in the right direction. One of his books of poetry is entitled *Look! We Have Come Through!*, which would be an excellent title for a study of his endings.[5]

[4] For more on the visionary in Lawrence, see Jay Clayton's *Romantic Vision in the Novel*.

[5] Maria DiBattista views the problem of closure in *Women in Love* as associ-

Lawrence emerged out of the mainstream of the English novel (F. R. Leavis was right about this) to bend the genre to his visionary purpose; following in the footsteps of Laurence Sterne and *Tristram Shandy*, Joyce immersed himself in and then parodied the conventions of the novel, sending it in a new direction. These two writers were antithetical in nearly every way, but they both resisted neat orderly closures.

Joyce, the very measure of all that is modernist, began with the didactic zeal of Lawrence (see *D* 269 *et passim*), but for him the world was considerably more complex, and though in temperament he remained a revolutionary, his interest gradually shifted more to revolutionary literary form, style, and structure that reflected the complexity of his vision. Whether or not he foresaw the industry his works would inevitably create, or whether he devised his strategy of obfuscation because he imagined his message to be revolutionary, Joyce, like Sterne, was a writer who consciously sought to train literary critics to read his works, and to do so within the artifice itself. The reader thus becomes co-creator of the meaning of a literary work written by an author who believed his task was to give us only part of the text's meaning—perhaps even believed that this was all any author *could* do given his view of language.

Joyce's desire to veil while revealing meaning may derive from the French Symbolists, but he merged the idea with modernist technique to produce self-reflexive endings that bear his gnomonic stamp of incompletion.[6] With some exceptions, *Dubliners* stories are calculated to puzzle, but they do so in a variety of ways that prepare us for the experiments of the later works, and they are, oddly enough, more sophisticated than the endings of *Finnegans Wake* in my view.

---

ated with Lawrence's ambivalence about modern apocalypse: "*Women in Love* begins but cannot conclude Lawrence's own struggle with the memory of classical narrative, which trusted, not naively, but livingly, in a final day of historical reckoning. *Women in Love* is the Judgment Book that publishes the decrees of a Providence that Lawrence could neither ignore nor accept" (90).

[6] Here my position owes much to Father Robert Boyle, who in *James Joyce's Pauline Vision* emphasizes Joyce's view as antirational and perspectivist, his fictional world as essentially mysterious.

By endings in the Joycean context I refer to endings of narrative units such as stories, chapters, episodes, set-pieces, as well as larger structures. Worthy of consideration are thus the chapters of *A Portrait*, the episodes of *Ulysses*, the chapters and books of *Finnegans Wake*, and even smaller units or set pieces such as the sections of "Wandering Rocks," or the Christmas Dinner scene of *A Portrait*. However, this is a much larger study than I have envisioned for myself here.

Joyce's endings range between two poles: those that are clear in meaning, strong in closure, or simply unremarkable, to endings of an indeterminate nature. Some are like riddles—enigmatic until one discovers the hidden irony or tricky meaning; others are ironic, or ironic and circular. Still others are enigmatic but heuristic. Here a curious pattern is discernible: the heuristic ending, most commonly found in such *Dubliners* stories as "Araby," is a didactic strategy for sending the reader back into the story for clarification. The heuristic ending is the structural forebear of the ending for which Joyce is most famous. As he became more interested in form than didacticism, he began to employ the ironic strategy of circularity: the first and last words of "Penelope" are "yes," and the last sentence of *Finnegans Wake* is widely thought to flow into the first. At this point Joyce simply refuses to let the reader go; regardless of the text's difficulty, the reward of a cyclical return now seems to be not so much clarification as the pleasure of reexperiencing the text.

In this circularity one may perhaps discern a Viconian influence, but that of his Catholic education seems stronger. Death and resurrection—either in the literal, moral, or spiritual sense—that mystery of circularity that worried his imagination long after his faith had left—appears as a frequent thematic structure. The dead simply do not stay dead, but return to haunt the living, as happens in "The Sisters," "Eveline," "A Painful Case," "The Dead," *Ulysses*, and *Finnegans Wake*. Even where characters shed the skin of the old life and prepare to begin anew, as in "The Dead" or *Exiles*, there is implicit the circularity of death and resurrection. With all its pessimism about the possibility of human growth, or change, or perfectability, *Dubliners* ends on a note of hope, at that magical moment where Gabriel Conroy experiences a kind of egotistical death and transfiguration that is foreshadowed by the ending of "A Painful Case."

It is no accident that the endings of "The Dead" and "The Sisters," the last and the first stories of *Dubliners*, are not merely enigmatic, but the most indeterminate in the collection. By this I mean that we cannot know their meaning with certainty: they are gnomonic; educated speculation is invited, but disagreement guaranteed.[7] Between first and last are endings that range from crystal clear ("After the Race"; "Grace"; "A Mother") to quite enigmatic ("An Encounter"; "Araby"). Joyce lopped off the ending of "The Sisters" just at the moment when, as in "Araby," boy and reader might have shared an epiphany. Given the endings of the later stories, it seems safe to say that this is the structure that fits, though the precise nature of the insight would be a matter of speculation. Sandwiched between these stories is "An Encounter," where the boy seems on the verge of an epiphany at the end, but is still quite confused. "Two Gallants" was written so that the story's central idea—that Corley and Lenehan have conspired to defraud a servant girl out of a gold sovereign to finance an evening in the pubs—eludes the reader until the final line, when Corley displays the coin. Readers are typically confused because talk belies action, and often it dawns on them but slowly that seduction is of far less importance to these gallants than alcohol, and then only if we mentally rehearse or reread the story's plot. Here the ending is tricky or enigmatic without being indeterminate. There is also a strong sense of closure in that "Two Gallants" ends at the appropriate moment; one need not, nor would one perhaps wish to, know more about the gallants or their victim, though some readers have been curious about whether the coin was stolen or earned.

Where there is a strong sense of closure in *Dubliners*, usually

[7] Here I would go beyond Florence Walzl, whose view is that "The Dead's" "great final ambiguity" (*D* 443) arises from whether the ending is seen as belonging either to the story or the *Dubliners* collection. See "Gabriel and Michael: The Conclusion of 'The Dead' " (*D* 423-44).

a character's entrapment or paralysis is emphasized, and character revelation is dominant in the design. There is little trace of heuristic design as in, say, "Clay." Eveline misses the boat; Jimmy Doyle is a loser at cards and in most other ways; Little Chandler is trapped by marriage, timidity, and artistic myopia; the Farrington family will suffer; the characters in "Ivy Day" and "A Mother" will go on being obtuse. The endings do not send us back into the text for clarification.

Joyce's interest in circular structure is responsible for what I call the heuristic ending, which denies us the resolution we expect and encourages rereading. Here the game of puzzle-solving has its rewards, though the picture that emerges may vary considerably with the reader. When I assign these stories to students, I tell them that when they finish the book they are to read the last paragraph or two of each story again to see how well they have understood. Invariably their confidence is undermined by this process, to be built up again by further study. We are expected to be suddenly jarred into a new awareness of possible meanings overlooked in the initial perusal. Joyce typically resists closure, refuses to untie knots of meaning, unravel complications, or reorder confusions. We may even feel that he creates confusions, and that his most interesting texts cannot be read, but only reread. Many of his endings seem to insure a cyclical return to an Ithaca of meaning that can never quite be reached.

Why does the boy in "An Encounter" feel penitent that he has called to Mahoney for help, thinking, "For in my heart I had always despised him a little" (*D* 28), an issue that seems quite irrelevant to the story? Why does the boy in "Araby" see himself "as a creature driven and derided by vanity" (*D* 35); what could he possibly have seen or experienced at the bazaar to open his eyes to this imperfection in himself? At the end of "The Boarding House" there is the unreported interview between Mrs. Mooney and Bob Doran, during which time Polly daydreams. The last line seems curiously inconclusive: when her mother calls for her, "Then she remembered what she had been waiting for" (*D* 69). Why does "Counterparts" conclude with "I'll say a *Hail Mary* . . ." (*D* 98)? Such heuristic endings serve to raise doubts about our comprehension, thus making us work harder at the task of interpretation.

In *Dublin's Joyce,* Hugh Kenner made a statement about the endings of *A Portrait* and its five chapters that has become a critical touchstone (or should have) for discussion of the novel's structure: "Each of the preceding chapters, in fact, works toward an equilibrium which is dashed when in the next chapter Stephen's world becomes larger and the frame of reference more complex" (122). The chapters end with Stephen's sense of fulfillment or achievement, to be followed by more complex frames of reference that show a more mature Stephen more deeply embedded in the trap of an environment that has already been defined in *Dubliners*.

At the end of Chapter One, Stephen seems finally to have won the much-desired esteem and acceptance of his peers for the courageous act of protesting his unjust punishment. That his happiness will be short-lived is evoked by the lonely sound of the cricket bats, which both echoes Father Dolan's pandybat and emphasizes Stephen's exclusion from the game. Chapter Two begins by describing the boy's dull routine and growing pessimism, goes on to show his interest in literary exiles (*AP* 62-63), and posits the image of a Mercedes figure who will touch him with a magic wand that will transform him into a strong, self-confident young man (*AP* 65). The toad does not become a prince in the arms of the prostitute who kisses him at the chapter's end. Chapter Three opens by having us view a newly debased Stephen enslaved by vices of the flesh that he continues to view in orthodox Catholic terms. The hell-fire sermons prod him to repentance and a return to the Sacraments, but the ending emphasizes his ardent, but suspect, desire to renew an innocence that is irretrievably lost. Chapter Four begins with Stephen's fanatically pious attempts to impose discipline on his five senses in accordance with the principles of the Jesuit handbook, exercises that seem to run directly counter to his artistic nature. We are reminded that the artist's tools have been given on the novel's first page. Stephen's artistic vocation will crowd out religion by the chapter's end, when vision will present him with a deeply moving image of feminine beauty in the flesh. Again he is seduced, in his imagination at least, this time by an image that may transform him from an idle dabbler in aesthetics into an artist in touch with a muse who is very much of the world around her.

The first pages of *A Portrait*'s final chapter place Stephen in the squalor of his familial environment, where his mood is a far cry from that of the previous chapter's ending. We see his dashed hopes, his lack of direction, the wasted university days, and his rejection of friends and causes that seek to claim him. The final pages must then obviously be read in light of the preceding structures, all of which measure Stephen's immaturity by showing chapters ending on lyrical notes of expectation to be followed by beginnings that describe the folly of Stephen's optimism. We cannot miss the irony inherent in the last line of his diary: "Welcome, O life! I go to encounter for the millionth time the reality of experience and to forge in the smithy of my soul the uncreated conscience of my race. . . . Old father, old artificer, stand me now and ever in good stead" (*AP* 252-53). Such great expectations seem to promise failure, and sure enough, the opening episode of *Ulysses* serves particularly well as a comment on the ending of *A Portrait*. How much more hopeless do his prospects seem than at any point in the earlier novel. For him the lyrical ending is a thing of the past, an outgrown form of adolescence.

The ending of *A Portrait* is doubly appropriate because it is itself a failure generically guaranteed: *A Portrait* is a *Bildungsroman* about a young man who aspires to become an artist. That aspiration, *not* its fulfillment, is the novel's subject. The form must therefore be incomplete or indeterminate because its autobiographical aspect can never catch up with its fictional denouement, or Joyce might have to show us Stephen beginning to write the work of which he is the subject. Early critics often commented that the novel was unfinished, but they could not see that structurally *A Portrait* was programmed to collapse before we approach too close to that epiphanic moment that will tell whether or not Stephen will actually succeed in becoming an artist.

But if Stephen falls short of success, he is not short of the talent, or power, or vision, or appropriate indignation to carry him to his goal. Still, the novel's ending mixes the modes of visionary and ironic climax, where Stephen's awareness of vocation places him on an imaginary Mount Pisgah, to behold a Promised Land of the future that can never be entered, or even clearly seen. (Ironically, Moses is forbidden to enter the homeland, while for Stephen deliverance is exile.) The ending is visionary in that it promises in ecstatic tones a new life in exile, but on another level it tells us that narration is power, and that Stephen now has the power unconsciously to end the novel of which he is the subject by allowing us to peek at his diary. He could not in any sense have controlled the novel's opening. The story about the moocow coming down the road is told by his father, who has the power to tell stories to Stephen, whose weakness is the subject of the first chapter. By the novel's end, the father will have become an insignificant character, eclipsed by a son who will not let him get a word in edgewise.[8]

If the endings of *A Portrait* show us Stephen at five stages of immaturity, while those of *Dubliners* test our powers of analysis, in *Ulysses*, where there are eighteen episodes and many literary styles to contend with, the endings are complex in still different ways. First, there is the problem of structural multiplicity: whereas the ending of "The Dead" fits both story and book, and that of *A Portrait* fits both novel and final chapter, three episodes of *Ulysses* have multiple functions. Both *Ulysses* and *The Odyssey* are composed of three sections: the Telemachiad, Odyssey, and Nostos, or Homecoming. In *Ulysses*, the third and fifteenth episodes have endings that complete both episode and Homeric section, while that of the eighteenth—Molly's monologue—concludes episode, section, and novel. For instance, the fifteenth episode—"Circe"—has an ending that functions in the following way: Bloom has a vision of Stephen as his dead son Rudy grown to maturity, which is an appropriate conclusion to an episode where hallucinations are common. It is a fitting ending for the Odyssey section because

[8] Essentially this is the argument of Edmund L. Epstein in *The Ordeal of Stephen Dedalus*.

in Homer's work a climactic scene is the tearful reunion of father and son. The title *Ulysses* promises that a parallel scene will be of major importance, that the separate odysseys of Telemachus and Odysseus will become one, that together they will head homeward to drive out the suitors. A major irony of *Ulysses* is that the son fails to recognize the father, and Molly's suitor is hardly unwelcome.

The endings of the episodes of *Ulysses* reveal considerable variety. Some ("Calypso," "Lotus-eaters," "Hades") either present no particular problems or seem unremarkable; others ("Telemachus," "Proteus," and "Lestrygonians") emphasize Homeric parallels; the remainder are heuristic or indeterminate and usually comical.

Frequently the endings of *Ulysses* simply contain jokes, where the point is to understand the "punchlines." The last lines of "Nestor" focus on the two essential points made earlier about Garrett Deasy: he is a very foolish teacher because he usually gets his facts wrong; and he is stupidly mercenary, which is curiously at odds with his brand of anti-Semitism. His joke about Ireland being the only country never to have persecuted the Jews because she never let them in is so absurd as to be puzzling, as any Dubliner would have known. (Equally absurd is the plausible meaning that they were not persecuted because they were ostracized.) "Nestor's" punchline is thus appropriate: "On his wise shoulders through the checkerwork of leaves the sun flung spangles, dancing coins" (*U* 2:448-49).

"Aeolus" ends with a humorous response to Stephen's "Parable of the Plums" (*U* 7:1072-75). Lines from Shakespeare's *Cymbeline* form an apt comment on Stephen's dishonest, if clever, theory of Shakespeare:

> *Laud we the gods*
> *And let our crooked smokes climb to their nostrils*
> *From our bless'd altars.* (*U* 9:1223-25)

In "Cyclops," Bloom's flight from the pub takes the appropriate form of an ascension of Elijah the Prophet (*U* 12:1910-18).

The clock has struck four-thirty in "Nausicaa" and loudly cuckoos Bloom, who believes he has now been cuckolded (*U* 13:1289-1306). In "Oxen" the rantings of the imaginary Reverend Dowie perhaps forecast the fragmentary, apparently chaotic quality of modernist texts as well as the afterbirth. One scarcely needs to interpret these endings.

Joyce once said, Ithaca "is in reality the end [of *Ulysses*] as *Penelope* has no beginning, middle or end" (*Letters*, 1:172), but the wordplay seems specious. "Ithaca" was finished after "Penelope," and it is there we see the last of Bloom and Stephen, but the implication seems to be that because the final episode has a circular structure, it cannot contain the ending of *Ulysses*.

This cannot be right, for the process of closure is especially powerful and moving in "Penelope." Furthermore, the large dot at the end of "Ithaca" is a good example of indeterminate form: it could represent the point at which Bloom drops off to sleep, or simply the full stop to his voyage to Ithaca, or, given Joyce's scatological taste, and the symbolic importance of Molly's posterior in "Penelope," it could represent an anus. We are invited to imagine additional possibilities, but the text will not help us here.[9]

Frequently in *Ulysses* closure does suggest the anatomical posterior. At the end of the "Sirens" episode, where Joyce entwines musical and linguistic forms, Bloom's fart is musical and serves as a comment on political rhetoric. When we reach the end of "Wandering Rocks," we are presented with a rear view of Stephen's music teacher, Almidano Artifoni, whose trousers are "swallowed by a closing door" (*U* 10:1282). (This is likely an insulting gesture, typically Italian in character, toward the twin clashers of Church and State.) "Eumaeus" ends with a horse dropping "smoking globes of turds" as Stephen and Bloom walk into the distance (*U* 16:1876-94). That Joyce came to associate endings with arses is not simply an absurd joke one can chuckle over and forget; it is a reflection of his fre-

[9] I agree with Karen Lawrence about the form of "Ithaca." See her *The Odyssey of Style in "Ulysses."*

quent association of anatomy with geography and literary form. One cannot appreciate "Penelope," which is actually the end of *Ulysses,* without understanding the implications of this parody of closure.[10]

Throughout his career Joyce was capable of envisioning the topography of "dear dirty Dublin" and Ireland of the round towers as obscene. In *Finnegans Wake,* Finn MacCool is at times supine across the Dublin landscape with his head at Howth, his feet sticking up in Phoenix Park, and his mythic potency visible on O'Connell Street. ALP is the river Liffey and at one point Shaun's navel is the center of Ireland (*FW* 474-76; Hart, *Structure* 136-37). In Appendix B of Clive Hart's *Structure and Motif in "Finnegans Wake,"* there is a map of Ireland with the familiar interlocking rings by which Shem explains ALP's anatomy; its suggestive circles resemble the way that Joyce conceived of Leopold Bloom's odyssey through Dublin's two hemispheres.[11] Look at a map of Dublin as Joyce could have, with malice ahindthought, and you see two vast buttocks, bounded on north and south by circular roads and divided in the center by a flowing river carrying sewage out to sea. Looking at a map of Dublin pornotopographically, it is easy to see why Joyce thought of eastward motion as regenerative, as he did in *Dubliners.* In anguished parturition has Ireland given birth to millions of emigrants who passed out of Dublin harbor to start new lives in the lands beyond the sea.

In a novel that begins on an omphalos, includes a suggestive story about Nelson's Pillar, treats us to a fireworks display that scatters any god's quantity of fantasy semen across the sky; in a novel where each of the eighteen episodes claims for its own one favorite organ of the body, it should hardly sur-

[10] Several of the paragraphs that follow appeared in somewhat altered form in my half-serious article "Experimentation with a Landscape."

[11] Hart says, "*Finnegans Wake* is laid out like a map of the globe—'a chart expanded' (*FW* 593.19)—for geography is as important to Joyce as history" (Structure 111). See him also on the spiraling trajectories of Bloom and Stephen (113). Despite Hart's important work on cyclic form and circles, it needs to be demonstrated that these formal concerns of Joyce in *Finnegans Wake* are ingenious extensions of the earlier works.

prise us to find Dublin belted with pornotopographical design. When Dublin's derriére and Molly's are seen numerically we have the figure 8. Eight is the number of sentences in Molly's monologue; her birthday is the eighth of September[12] and, to push mathematics toward absurdity, if we add Molly's 8 to Dublin's we get 16, which is Bloomsday. When our map is leered at laterally from across the Irish Sea what emerges is an 8 on its side, the mathematical sign for infinity. Clive Hart called this "zeroic couplet" (*FW* 284:11) the basic structure of *Finnegans Wake* (*Structure* 130). Without wishing to be reductive, I propose that this is also a basic design of *Ulysses*. The 8 or infinity sign is Dublin; in Joyce's schema the infinity sign is in the time column for "Penelope"; it reflects the circularity of that episode's structure; and it can also stand for Molly's behind, 8 if Molly is lying down and ∞ if standing up, which explains why there are eight sentences in her prostrate monologue.[13]

Hart shows the ALP diagram of *Finnegans Wake* to have significance on three levels: the anatomical, the geographical, and the cosmic (*Structure* 136-38; 248). If we assume this structure in the configuration of *Ulysses*, we can gradually see the bicircular love odyssey of Bloom merge with the imaginary quest of the Wandering Jew for the Promised Land. As in *Dubliners*, the final meaning of the pattern is frustration. Moses got no more than a glimpse of the Promised Land; and Odysseus spent just a single night with Penelope before leaving to seek out a people who knew nothing of the sea. Similarly, Bloom must be satisfied with

> the ubiquity in eastern and western terrestrial hemispheres, in all habitable lands and islands explored or

[12] See my *Joyce's "Ulysses" Notesheets* 511; 513.

[13] This topographical structure for *Ulysses* is not just fanciful; Joyce's notesheets for the novel reveal him frequently thinking of Molly's ample "hemispheres" (Herring, *Notesheets* 456). He equated her "rump" with the Promised Land (ibid. 463) and calls her the "spinning Earth" (ibid. 515; cf. *Letters*, 1:170). Though Bloom never travels that far, Molly's "centrique part" suggested "darkest Africa" in yet another note (ibid. 494), a pornotopographical insight of the first order if hardly consistent geographically.

> unexplored (the land of the midnight sun, the islands of the blessed, the isles of Greece, the land of promise), of adipose anterior and posterior female hemispheres, redolent of milk and honey and of excretory sanguine and seminal warmth, reminiscent of secular families of curves of amplitude, insusceptible of moods of impression or of contrarities of expression, expressive of mute immutable mature animality. (*U* 17:2229-36)

If Palestine, according to Bloom, contains the "sunken cunt of the world" (*U* 4:227-28), so, too, do Dublin and Molly. The "immense melonfields north of Jaffa" (*U* 4:194) are right in his bed, which moves with our celestial wanderer (*U* 17:2013-23) and his wife "westward, forward and rereward respectively, by the proper perpetual motion of the earth through everchanging tracks of neverchanging space" (*U* 17:2308-10). In recognition of much of this significance, Bloom kisses Molly's buttocks (*U* 17:2241-43).

Richard Ellmann correctly notes that "in Molly's mind Mulvey, who was her Ulysses on Calpe's mount at Gibraltar, blends into Bloom, her Ulysses on Howth" (*Ulysses on the Liffey* 172). In Molly's memory, lovers merge and nostalgic memories and places blend just as for Bloom the Promised Land becomes both his wife's posterior and his native city. If Dublin becomes Palestine for Bloom, Gibraltar becomes Howth Head for Molly as she dozes off to sleep. Pornotopographically speaking, the reason is clear: Gibraltar is like Howth Head because each perches like a clitoral eminence at its particular gateway to the sea.

Joyce gave Molly the last word so that she could through memory and imagination impose on *Ulysses*, its events and human relationships, the necessary disorder of indeterminacy that Joyce felt that a woman's mind would provide. Although this makes me uncomfortable (and I do not defend Joyce here), it seems obvious that Molly's shrewd but ignorant mind reflects the confusion of June 16 as *Ulysses* captures it. Bloom's profane kiss thus pays a comical homage to an epistemological skepticism that doubt-tormented Stephen, like the hero of *Exiles*, cannot bring himself to embrace.

The final "yes" of *Ulysses* affirms not truth or certainty, but earthiness or carnal love.[14] If Molly seems body-bound it is because on this day she has decided to end a long period of celibacy. For her, June 16 is in no way a typical day, nor should the content of her monologue be taken as the "truth" about Molly. Still, her "yes" affirms a vision of human passion powerful enough to propel us up the bottom side of that infinity sign or figure eight and over again to the episode's beginning; perhaps it even serves as a comment on Stephen's profound negativism, as seen in "Telemachus." Her curves are as close to the "melonfields north of Jaffa" (*U* 4:194) as Bloom will ever get, yet like Moses he may never again enter this place so little resembling a land of milk and honey.

Despite the linguistic complexity of *Finnegans Wake,* one learns little new about endings in the structural sense. They do not provide resolution, nor are they particularly enigmatic or heuristic; usually they come at appropriate moments given the narrative rhythm, and given the various concerns of the chapters. These narrative units seldom build toward a climactic moment or reveal an identifiable process of closure, but simply conclude. For example, in two instances there are parodies of prayers (*FW* 259; 473); in another there is a farewell (*FW* 382); *FW* 103 looks forward to ALP; *FW* 125 and 168 shift the spotlight to Shem; *FW* 195 tells us that the dumb will speak, these being the Washers at the Ford, in the following chapter, who become petrified.

Since Joyce had already used endings that range from unambiguous clarity to indeterminacy, little else would have been possible but variations on familiar forms.[15] Ending *Finnegans Wake* with a sentence fragment that invites connection

[14] Ellmann interprets the ending of *Ulysses* as Molly's countersign to the recognition of Bloom and Stephen of the importance of love. He says, "Because Molly Bloom countersigns with the rhythm of finality what Stephen and Bloom have said about the word known to all men, *Ulysses* is one of the most concluded books ever written" (*New York Review of Books* 31:16 [25 October 1984], p. 31. Cf. Beebe (181) and Schiffer.

[15] In *The Chapters in Fiction: Theories of Narrative Division,* Philip Stevick is in essential agreement about the conventionality of the chapter endings of *Finnegans Wake* when he praises their traditional closural cadences (41-42).

with the book's first sentence was but a variation on the circular form of "Penelope." There we are treated to another ecstatic vision of a woman embracing her lover—this time Anna Livia Plurabelle as the river Liffey flowing into her father the sea. One even hears echoes of Molly's "yes": "Yes. Carry me along, taddy, like you done through the toy fair! . . . Yes, tid. There's where . . ." (*FW* 628). When they are mated, this incestuous union will produce moisture in clouds that will rain down on Ireland's hills, to form streams that become Anna Liffey again. This ecological cycle, the death and resurrection of a river, takes us back not only to the book's opening, but to the endings of "A Painful Case" and "The Dead" as well, where protagonists experience similar annihilations, or even to "The Sisters," where the ellipses at the end seem to point to the death of boyhood innocence and the birth of watchful adolescence. In addition to death and resurrection, we are reminded of the themes of exile and return, sleeping and awakening, passion building and passion spent, and other human activities reflecting cyclical patterns. Structurally, Joyce's works are like a pool: a tossed stone sends ever-widening circles that only stop at the shore's edge.

SEVEN

Joyce's Meanderthalltale: *Finnegans Wake*

In a book about uncertainty in Joyce's works, all roads lead to *Finnegans Wake*, and all theories meet there to find their most extreme examples. It is no wonder then that this "meanderthalltale" (*FW* 19:25) is a favorite text of post-structuralist critics, who find language at war with itself, and the *bête noir* of take-us-or-Leavis great traditionalists, who see the *Wake* as an unsightly switchyard disaster on the novel's mainline railroad from Fielding to the future.

No responsible scholar engaged in a comprehensive study of the *Wake* can avoid wrestling with its central questions and deciding whether or not they have definitive answers, questions such as who the dreamer is or what HCE did in the park to disgrace himself, or even what, precisely, the book is all about. Most have concluded that such answers cannot be definitive, but in doing so have seldom noticed that the *Wake* sits not in a specially constructed switchyard of indeterminacy, but rather on Joyce's mainline originating with *Dubliners* and the curious idea of *gnomon*. If this present book has virtue, it is in establishing Joyce's uncertainty principle as a critical touchstone for his works early and late.

Joyce knew that he was writing a work of unprecedented obscurity, a work "dandymount to a clearobscure" (*FW* 247:33-34), which would keep the professors busy perhaps indefinitely, but he felt the need to give direction. Just as he gave *Ulysses* criticism its first major impetus by sponsoring and enriching Stuart Gilbert's book, a decade before *Finnegans Wake* was published he also gave direction to the first major work of *Wake* criticism, a book of essays called *Our Exagmination Round His Factification for Incamination of Work in Progress* by Samuel Beckett and others. From these earliest critics to the latest, most have seen humor and problem-solving to be the main rewards of wrestling with the *Wake*'s difficulty. However, essentially no progress has been made in clearly distinguishing solvable from insolvable problems.

At times a voice emerges from the clearobscure of the *Wake* to address the reader's befuddlement: "(Stoop) if you are abcedminded, to this claybook, what curios of signs (please stoop), in this allaphbed! Can you rede . . . its world?" (*FW* 18:17-19). "Now, patience; and remember patience is the great thing," (*FW* 108:08). "You is feeling like you was lost in the bush, boy? You says: It is a puling sample jungle of woods. You most shouts out: Bethicket me for a stump of a beech if I have the poultriest notions what the farest he all means" (*FW* 112:03-06).

Incertitude may be the dominant theme of the *Wake* as well as a caution to those who seek definitive answers: "Thus the unfacts, did we possess them, are too imprecisely few to warrant our certitude, the evidencegivers by legpoll too untrustworthily irreperible . . ." (*FW* 57:16-17). Incertitude is at the center of the *Wake* and will flavor the answer to every interesting question we can ask. Bernard Benstock has said:

> There remains, then, only the cold, logical realization that *Finnegans Wake* as an enigma may well go unsolved. Time, which was expected to bring all evidence eventually to the surface in an ordered pattern, so far has had the opposite effect. (*Joyce-again's Wake* 40)

Margot Norris in *The Decentered Universe of "Finnegans Wake"* puts it so well that I quote at length:

> The formal elements of the work, plot, character, point of view, and language, are not anchored to a single point of reference, that is, they do not refer back to a center. This condition produces that curious flux and restlessness in the work, which is sensed intuitively by the reader and which the *Wake* itself describes as follows:
>
> Every person, place and thing in the chaosmos of Alle anyway connected with the gobblydumped turkery was moving and changing every part of the time: the travelling inkhorn (possibly pot), the hare and turtle pen and paper, the continually more and less intermisunderstanding minds of the anticollaborators,

> the as time went on as it will variously inflected, differently pronounced, otherwise spelled, changeably meaning vocable scriptsigns ([*FW*] 118).
>
> The substitutability of parts for one another, the variability and uncertainty of the work's structural and thematic elements, represent a decentered universe, one that lacks the center that defines, gives meaning, designates, and holds the structure together—by holding it in immobility. (120-21)

Patrick McCarthy similarly stresses uncertainty in his *The Riddles of "Finnegans Wake,"* where he says that in the *Wake*, "certainty is virtually nonexistent" (16), and that "Joyce's failure to resolve all the puzzles that he sets up is an indication of his rejection of dogma, of rational certitude, of reductive or simplistic visions of reality" (46). This viewpoint would be a logical result of working with the *Wake* riddles. (See also *Riddles* 32; 46; 64; 153-54.)

McCarthy is astute in referring to earlier works as familiar examples, whereas Norris seems to view the *Wake*'s indeterminacy as interesting primarily as a precocious example of deconstruction. She sees the book as "about the quest for truth, the 'true' facts, the correct interpretation, the 'authentic' version, and . . . it purposefully levels all such pretensions" (139). This is a view with which many would agree, and I for one subscribe to her view of the *Wake* as a decentered literary universe, but her debunking of the efforts of *Wake* scholars rests on the false assumption that *all* aspects of the book are uncertain: "The greatest critical mistake in approaching *Finnegans Wake* has been the assumption that we can be certain of who, where, and when everything is in the *Wake*, if only we do enough research" (120). And, again, "The results of critical efforts are not important in the *Wake*, but rather the compulsions and motives of the questors, their styles and methods, their quarrels, their self-justifications, and their own implication in the object of their study" (139).

These statements reflect a widely held assumption about Wakean uncertainty, not addressed by Norris, that because at the *Wake*'s center truth is so elusive, because the book laughs at "compulsions and motives of questors," therefore any scholar who attempts to address any difficulties or solve any problems in *Finnegans Wake* is playing Joyce's fool. As stated, her view is too pessimistic. In order to counter the extreme position that all indeterminate problems can be solved through research, she seems to take an equally extreme one that research is totally useless, and that critical efforts achieve only attention for the critic. But perhaps her word "criticism" does not cover so much. My view is that research has taught us much about nonindeterminate problems.

Defeatism also lends impetus to the erroneous idea that the *Wake* is so slippery that the wildest interpretation of any passage might be justified. Joyce's works, more than those of any writer except perhaps Shakespeare, have suffered from wildly speculative readings and pet theories. In *Ulysses*, Haines says, "Shakespeare is the happy huntingground of all minds that have lost their balance" (*U* 10:1061-62), which is untrue of Shakespeare or Joyce, but more nearly true of them than perhaps all other writers in English. Here again is the Scylla and Charybdis of Joycean criticism, that readers are caught between Joyce's uncertainty principle and the necessity of imposing rational limits to speculation, especially in distinguishing solvable from insolvable problems.

Norris's view of the *Wake*'s uncertainty is one I could accept with qualification: "It is freeplay that makes characters, times, places, and actions interchangeable in *Finnegans Wake*, that breaks down the all-important distinction between the self and the other, and that makes uncertainty a governing principle of the work" (123). "Freeplay" and "interchangeable" are justifiable concepts, but suggest boundless whimsicality, and imply that she might agree with Clive Hart's surprising theory that "in the last of an infinite regress of planes of meaning," anything in the *Wake* may be about anything else, that in any random passage one might find "the twenty-four golden umbrellas of the King of Thailand" ("Elephant": 8).

Hart's position on exegesis of the *Wake* is actually quite an intelligent one except for this point, which is in sore need of rebuttal.[1] What he calls a "lunatic principle" surely does not refer to meaning in the *Wake,* but rather to more innocent wordplay. Hart's examples of the sort of fanciful readings one can do with given passages are exceedingly clever, but do not prove that any passage in the *Wake* may mean anything a fanciful mind compels it to mean ("*FW* in Perspective": 152-57). *Wake* language is never gibberish or nonsense, but wordplay often results in surprising puns on disparate concepts. Readers are not meant to search deeply into the logical strands connecting most puns, which leads interpretation to the lunatic fringe, but to enjoy their humor. Meaning in the larger sense is often uncertain, normally ambiguous, and, despite the uncertainty principle's invitation to explore limitless possibilities, a more *limited* range of meaning, for which Hart argues, yields more defensible interpretation. When the Prankquean asks, "Why do I am alook alike a poss of porterpease?" (*FW* 21:18-19), we understand various meanings, but they do not include references to the price of oranges in Calcutta or Wallace Stevens's "bauds of euphony."

The issues raised here are sorely in need of clarification, since they result from a view of uncertainty that fails to make any distinction between areas of critical investigation on those larger questions where the best one can hope for is to be more convincing than the previous commentators, and those areas in which real milestones of progress can and have been reached, such as in the discovery of new sources, or the more expansive and rigorous explications of influences, as is the case with J. S. Atherton's *The Books at the Wake,* or Mary Reynolds's *Joyce and Dante,* or John Bishop's illuminating chapter on the Egyptian *Book of the Dead,* or important manuscript work such as David Hayman's *A First-Draft Version of "Finnegans Wake."*

In this context it is illuminating to juxtapose, as Hugh Sta-

[1] Hart has probably done the most important work on exegesis in the *Wake* in "*Finnegans Wake* in Perspective," and "The Elephant in the Belly." His attempts to define the limits of meaningful exegesis in the *Wake* make for stimulating reading in conjunction with my theory of Joyce's uncertainty principle.

ples does in a book review, the positions of Margot Norris and of Grace Eckley in *Children's Lore in "Finnegans Wake,"* a theorist against a more traditional scholar. Eckley must have been precisely the kind of "dedicated explicator" (1) in reaction against whom Norris wrote her *Decentered Universe,* a scholar in the tradition of the late J. S. Atherton who spends most of his/her life in libraries searching for sourcebooks, who pores over the *Wake*'s text with dictionaries at hand, and who at any given moment has in mind a limited range of meanings for a given passage. Traditional researchers will often have little to do with indeterminacy because of their faith in intelligence, hard work, and luck.

Such scholars often see theorists as followers of critical trends that will be discredited tomorrow, wordmongers of theoretical jargon that throws up a screen of obfuscation, and are themselves frequently viewed condescendingly by theorists as old-fashioned hewers of wood and drawers of water who lack the training necessary to handle difficult philosophical ideas. One senses this attitude in *The Decentered Universe* in the binary opposition initially set up between "conservative" and "radical" scholarship (2), terms value-plagued and inflammatory as critical terms in the sense she uses them. Still, Norris does have the edge on Eckley in clarity and conceptualization, in part because Eckley seems unwilling to omit any part of her harvest even if it means that critical contours blur or theoretical implications suffer. She also emphasizes the nonblurring distinctiveness of Wakean character, especially in *Narrator and Character in "Finnegans Wake"* (Begnal and Eckley), which opposes the concept of indeterminacy of character endorsed by Norris.

Eckley pointedly disagrees with Norris's position that research is useless: "The viewpoint that research will not pay off—that no one can know anything—seems to me extremely futile; moreover, it blinds the vision. . . . My view *almost* diametrically opposes this, because I find logic and order where Margot Norris finds chaos . . ." (xi-xii). Both positions are misstated, and Eckley argues at cross purposes, because neither adequately distinguishes indeterminate problems from solvable ones. Whatever logic and order is contained in the *Wake* does not produce certainty. Norris would seem to support my position on the undecidability of central issues, which no amount of research can make decidable, whereas Eckley seems to understand Norris to mean that no amount of research on any Wakean subject can prove fruitful. This dubious idea is belied by the Wakean scholarship without which Norris's book itself would have been impossible. Eckley has certainly contributed to our knowledge with her discovery of William T. Stead as an historical original of HCE's dominant persona and, among other things, her fascinating work on Richard F. Burton's translation of *The Book of the Thousand Nights and a Night*. But neither Eckley nor Norris seems to have searched for the demarkation line between mysteries, which are to be experienced, and problems, for which one may hope to find solutions.

Eckley addressed herself to the problem of whether or not Joyce had one particular historical character in mind when he created HCE; the answer was "yes," and the character was William T. Stead. She intends to write a book about Stead that will "prove" her point, but since she believes that Joycean problems normally have just one solution, her book may ultimately be an extended demonstration of the uncertainty principle in character that will please only M'Intosh sleuths. Eckley has made exciting discoveries that ought to influence future scholarship on the *Wake*, but that leave undecidable issues untouched. As for Norris, she is right about undecidability, but states her position in an imprecise manner. In their respective positions, though, one clearly sees the larger debate between theory and traditional scholarship.

Another widely held misconception, which this book has sought to address, is that the *Wake* alone among Joyce's works undermines the reader's efforts at solving problems of interpretation, a tacit assumption in Norris because she ignores similar problems in the earlier works. Joyce's last work is not an isolated instance of fundamental uncertainty. Even *Exiles*, which has not been considered a very experimental work technically, highlights at its conclusion Richard Rowan's uncertainty as to his wife's fidelity, and strongly implies that his developing moral philosophy will be founded on the realization that fidelity of the spirit—an irrevocable commitment of the self—will diminish the perceived importance of sexual indiscretion. Out of the ashes of the egotistical devastation caused by his uncertainty as to whether or not Bertha has slept with Robert, and self-scrutiny into his own responsibility for this, phoenix-like, a new moral being will presumably arise. *Exiles* predicts a new covenant between man and woman, founded upon incertitude, "upon unlikelihood" (*U* 9:842).

Issues discussed in earlier chapters are usually relevant to Joyce's uncertainty principle in the *Wake*. As we have seen, *gnomon*, when understood as a critical tool, helps us focus on undecidable issues, juxtapose absence and presence, see synecdoches of relationship. What may have begun as a political maneuver in *Dubliners* became in the dream world of the *Wake* normal obscurantism. As Hugh Staples said, "It is as though Joyce were anxious on the one hand to conceal his meaning from the uninitiated but equally anxious to reveal it to the adept on the other" ("Joyce and Cryptology": 168-69). This has been the view of many readers.

In my section "On Joycean Difficulty," nullity as a mathematical and philosophical subject was discussed, and we have seen how double-null, or the infinity sign, and Molly's posterior come to be associated with Dublin's two hemispheres and the Promised Land in *Ulysses*. This sexual geometry recurs in somewhat altered form in Book II, ii in the children's lessons, where Dolph draws for Kev the overlapping double null (*FW* 293) which forms the "zeroic couplet" (*FW* 284:10), "the whome of your eternal geomater" (*FW* 296-97), the nether parts of ALP. On view is mother's void, which father will fill in Book IV. Clive Hart extends this geometrical figure to describe the "Irish Universe" (*Structure and Motif* 249; see also Margaret Solomon's analysis of sexual geometry in her chapter "Plain Geometry").

The lessons are filled with mathematical allusions to nether parts and sexual intercourse: "Ainsolph, this upright one, with that noughty besighed him zeroine" (*FW* 261:23-24).

"Quarrellary. The logos of somewome to that base anything, when most characteristically mantissa minus, comes to nullum in the endth . . ." (*FW* 298:18-21). HCE is a phallic *1* and ALP a *0*.

The void and its functions in the *Wake* have been covered in John Bishop's chapter "Nothing in Particular: On English Obliterature" (40-63), though he does not connect the void to issues of uncertainty or indeterminate meaning. He is more interested in the common theme of "Real Absence" (*FW* 536:05-06), a concept of importance because of the *Wake*'s dream language, the language of *nat* (*FW* 83:12), as the Scandinavians say, or night, or nought, with its "Nichtian glossery which purveys aprioric roots for aposteriorious tongues this is nat language at any sinse of the world . . ." (*FW* 83:10-12).

Bishop says that "the book represents nothing; or to modulate the phrase one degree, much of it represents much the same kind of nothing that one will not remember not having experienced in sleep last night" (41). The events of the *Wake* suggest "real absence" in that they resemble experience, history, imagination, or literature, but are expressed with the jumbled imprecision of dreams. Sleeptime is noughtime, nought is absence, uncertainty is the rule. (Even if by this time Joyce had forgotten *gnomon*, it is still a perfect symbol for the waking and sleeping consciousness.) One might well argue, then, that the uncertainty principle of *Finnegans Wake* is traceable directly to the dream process, which of necessity distorts meaning.

Uncertainty and the quest for meaning as we decipher the record of HCE's unconscious are what the *Wake* is about. This we see clearly if we frustrate ourselves by trying to read it as a novel. On the other hand, identifying the major conventions of the novel in their murky Wakean forms does enable us to see how each is undermined. Character is based on types that are identified in the *Wake* manuscripts and at *FW* 299 as sigla (see McHugh and Glasheen, especially Glasheen's diagram "Who's Who When Everybody's Somebody Else").[2] An im-

[2] In Glasheen's *Third Census* (lxxii ff.). Manfred Pütz says that indeterminate

portant aspect of indeterminate character in the *Wake*, Joyce's interest in documented cases of multiple personality, has been discussed by Adaline Glasheen ("*Finnegans Wake* and the Girls from Boston, Mass.") and Morris Beja ("Dividual Chaoses: Case Histories of Multiple Personality and *Finnegans Wake*").

Plot is unstable in that there is no one plot from beginning to end, but rather many recognizable stories and plot types with familiar and unfamiliar twists, told from varying perspectives. Still, trustworthy plot synopses have been written, and at the moment John Gordon is writing a book-length synopsis. What is uncertain is *precisely* what happens to whom and when. One may continue to test novelistic conventions with the same result: at the center of each is uncertainty. Consequently, the *Wake* requires that "ideal reader suffering from an ideal insomnia" (*FW* 120:14) to make (non)sense of the (w)hole.

Women's Letters and Uncertainty

As we turn to examine women's letters and uncertainty, for contrast, let us look first at letters by men.[3] In *Ulysses*, Denis Breen receives a mysterious unsigned postcard, with "U.p: up" on it, which so infuriates him that he wishes to sue the unknown author (*U* 12:258). Who wrote the card and precisely what it means have been the subject of much speculation in Joyce studies. The issue is a mystery, and is best left so, for it is a minor puzzle. Another letter initiates a motif in *Ulysses*, but is otherwise unremarkable except as an example of ped-

identity in characterization ("centuple celves" [*FW* 49:33]) has become a feature of "post-modernist" fiction: "Today, figures of this sort will seem all too familiar to readers of fiction, since disintegration of character, blurring of fixed outlines, and merging of one personality with another have become essential features of modern narrative art" (387).

[3] See the special number of the *James Joyce Quarterly* 19 (Summer 1982) on letters. Especially relevant are articles by Wilhelm Fuger and Shari Benstock. Two intelligent articles on this subject have appeared more recently, by Claudine Raynaud ("Woman, the Letter Writer; Man, the Writing Master") and Shari Benstock ("The Letter of the Law"). Cf. Richard Ellmann, *Golden Codgers* 132-54.

antry: Stephen skims Garrett Deasy's letter on "foot and mouth disease" in cattle, which he is to have published, but it is never reproduced in its entirety (*U* 2:324-30). With all Deasy's factual mistakes about Irish history, one wonders whether the disease might not have reached the Dalkey shore in disguised form.

Rudolph Bloom's last letter (actually a suicide note) to his son Leopold is filtered through Leopold's consciousness as he spots it in the drawer, but only a few phrases are communicated to us (*U* 17:1883-86). One has the impression, though, that the letter might have been written in unidiomatic English, given the German phrases therein and the imagined Yiddish-flavored English he speaks in "Circe" (*U* 15:253-79). Rumbold the hangman barber's letter of application in "Cyclops" reveals as much its author's callousness toward human life as it does his grammatical ignorance. We never see Blazes Boylan's note to Molly, indicating his proposed visit that afternoon, but Molly's tells us, "He's bringing the programme" (*U* 4:312).

While in Joyce's fiction males occasionally create epistolary enigmas, female writing is more specifically linked with uncertainty, a subject Begnal discusses briefly as mystery (400). Letters and confessional narratives by women form a discrete Joycean subgenre pointing to an author who often seemed amused at their efforts to write. Milly's letter to her father (*U* 4:397-414) is repetitive and often ungrammatical, perhaps a typical missive of an Irish teenager, but it is the only unmediated encounter we have with Milly's language in *Ulysses*, which shows no evidence of intelligence or seriousness of purpose; her interests go no further than chocolate, picnics, popular music, and young men, a view not contradicted by the perspectives of her parents. The card to her mother we do not read, but Molly says that "she got the things" (*U* 4:260) mailed to her.

The only other complete letter printed in *Ulysses*, in addition to those of Rumbold and Milly, is by Martha Clifford, who is basically an older Milly (*U* 5:241-59) with a narrowed range of interests extending no further than men and extramarital intrigue. Here, too, Martha's ungrammatical letter tells all there is to know about her, the speculations of Begnal notwithstanding. Whereas the thoughts of the Blooms on their daughter may well be accurate, Bloom's fantasies about Martha have nothing to do with reality.

In "U.p.: up" and one line of Martha's letter ("I do not like that other world"), we have mysteries that were designed to generate controversy.[4] Does the postcard imply that Breen is sterile, that his time on earth is up, or is it perhaps a slur on his Protestant background? Is Martha's "world" merely a misprint for "word," or is there a deeper meaning? Such speculation is akin to inquiring after M'Intosh.

In an earlier chapter I argued that Synge's plays might have heightened Joyce's sensitivity to the oppression of women in Ireland; here I balance my view of his progressivism on women's issues by supplying some evidence that Joyce enjoyed representing female writing as ludicrous. On the other hand, if true, it should also be remembered that Joyce's women are not more foolish than Deasy the schoolmaster, who in *Ulysses* is the human yardstick in that category. Letters in *Ulysses* thus form a subgenre made comical, regardless of the author's sex, like the drama in "Scylla and Charybdis" or "Circe," and though grammatical ignorance may be a feature of Rudolph Bloom's letter, and is strikingly obvious in Rumbold's letter, I cannot see that this warrants conclusions about the way men write in *Ulysses*. When we look at women's letters separately, however, we see something different. The comedy of women writing takes on considerable significance in *Ulysses* if one extends the category of examples to the narrative of "Nausicaa" and "Penelope." In *Finnegans Wake,* ALP's letter becomes a major aspect of Joyce's uncertainty principle.

Two of the cleverest remarks I have heard about women writing in *Ulysses* were by Edmund Epstein (to me orally) and Adaline Glasheen in *The Third Census* (xxxviii). About Samuel Butler's misogynic *The Authoress of "The Odyssey"* (1897), first discussed in relation to *Ulysses* by Stuart Gilbert, Epstein speculated that Joyce exposed Gerty MacDowell's thoughts in the

[4] In the Garland edition of *Ulysses* we find another error: "So now you know what I will do to you, you naughty boy, if you do not wrote" (5:252-53). In response Bloom thinks, "Wonder did she wrote it herself" (5:268-69).

style of the penny novelette in "Nausicaa" to illustrate the absurdity of Butler's thesis that *The Odyssey* was written by a woman.[5] Only loyalty to one's sex, Butler stated, could have been the author's motive for whitewashing the character of Penelope, who was obviously promiscuous with the suitors. (Butler's candidate for authorship was, of course, Nausicaa herself.) In his "Nausicaa" episode, Joyce's object seems thus not a denigration of silly Gerty or young women, but rather Butler's thesis, whatever the effect.

The connection with women's writing is clear, though: Gerty's section of "Nausicaa" is written in pseudo-autobiographical form as she could have written it about 1904, in the prose style of the romance novels for frustrated young women that presumably define her romantic view of herself and the world. Poor Gerty doesn't realize the triteness of her literary language; she is held captive on her ventriloquist's knee, laboriously scribbling her letter to the world while her master howls with laughter.

Glasheen's point about "Penelope" is precisely that Molly Bloom's monologue is her letter to the world (*The Third Census*, xxxviii). I agree, but would extend the thesis to include all women's writing in Joyce. "Nausicaa" and the letters of Milly and Martha are, in effect, miniature autobiographies. Gerty and Molly write letters as revealingly intimate as they are stereotypical. The narrative styles are, of course, different, Gerty's reflecting a literary style, and Molly's being conversational. Assuming that Gibraltar has left no trace on Molly's accent, she and Milly write as they would speak, the one through interior monologue, the other by letter. Let us hope this is not the case with Gerty.

My argument here is that in terms of effect, there is no important difference between letter, interior monologue, and ventriloquism—that the purpose is basically the same, the revelation of supposedly female secrets or essence more for amusement than instruction. The origin may be found in the letters and memoirs by and about women in the eighteenth

[5] *The Authoress of the Odyssey* was listed by Thomas E. Connolly as part of Joyce's personal library.

century. Joyce was not ignorant of the number of important women novelists in that period, and he was aware too that English novels then were often composed as a series of letters, often from and about women. Famous examples are, of course, Richardson's *Pamela* and *Clarissa*, and Fanny Burney's *Evelina*. In Defoe's *Moll Flanders* and Cleland's pornographic *Memoirs of Fanny Hill*, which Joyce asked Frank Budgen to send him while he was drafting "Penelope" (*Letters*, 1:171), letters gave way to memoirs as a first-person narrative technique for telling an unfortunate woman's story to the world at large. In the case of Moll and many of her lower-class sisters, the story was usually one of seduction and humiliation told in the language of the uneducated. Whether in the form of letters written to specific recipients, or first-person narratives or confessions addressed to the world at large, the subject matter often had to do with the exploitation of women.

On one level Joyce seems to have had in mind parody of this epistolary tradition in the cases of Milly, Martha, Molly, Gerty, and ALP. In naming the hen who scratches ALP's letter out of the middenheap Belinda of the Dorans, a hen "ladylike in everything she does [who] plays the gentleman's part every time" (*FW* 112:16-17), Joyce probably had in mind Maria Edgeworth's novel *Belinda* (1801), a critique of English society by an Irish woman.[6]

Influence also came from a direction other than the novel. These often ungrammatical letters to the world in Joyce's works reveal his interest in ridiculing uneducated women's writing as the product of stereotypically illogical and untutored minds rather than a dig at female novelists in general. In particular they show an awareness of the epistolary style of the women in his own family, which may well be the most important single influence on the style of "Penelope." At times, though, Joyce's knowledge of women seemed to go little beyond Nora. Here is a sample of her writing:

> My darling Jim since I left Trieste I am continually thinking about you how are you getting on without me or do

[6] Deirdre Bair says Joyce named the hen after Belinda Duncan (96).

> you miss me at all. I am dreadfully lonely for you I am quite tired of Ireland already well I arrived in Dublin on Monday night your father charley Eva Florrie were at the Station all looking very well we all went on to Finn's Hotel I stayed two nights in the Hotel but I got very sick of Dublin its a horrible place its quite true what you said I would soon get tired of it, now I am in Galway I find everyone here very well my Mother is very fat and looking very well also all my sisters and brother I feel very strange here but the time wont be long slipping round till I am going back to you again. . . . (*Letters*, 2:296-97)

Bonnie Scott makes the important point that these run-on sentences are also the epistolary style of Joyce's Aunt Josephine and his mother (70-71), thus seeming to justify Joyce's generalization to his brother: "Do you notice how women when they write disregard stops and capital letters?" (*Letters*, 2:173). Ungrammatical letters by women continued to interest Joyce in *Finnegans Wake*, where Book IV, the ALP chapter, and ALP's letter are linear descendants of the episodes and documents previously discussed. ALP's letter is especially interesting because it became an exercise in the uncertainty principle, and in terms of interpretive problems, as Füger has said (407), a microcosm of the *Wake* itself. We now have a context for understanding Joyce's bemused attitude toward female writing, judge him how you will.

ALP's Mamafesta

The *Wake*'s fifth chapter (I, v) is mostly a long analysis of ALP's "mamafesta" (*FW* 104:04) in defense of her husband, wrongfully accused of vague crimes and moral lapses. If "manifestoes" have a male origin, the "mamafesta" is Joyce's term for a female document that characteristically begins as a manifesto or protest letter to the authorities, but that through various drafts, and through hearsay and reference in the text, gradually becomes so unstable and self-referential as scarcely to be recognizable in its final form. This process of change undermines original intent, purpose, and subject matter, so that the end result is a more experimental manifestation of the uncertainty principle.

What we have is an extension of Molly's contradicting confessional letter to the world, which in the *Wake* becomes the understandable desire of a wife to defend her husband against slander. The effect of ALP's letter is precisely the opposite of her intent; once it is published it becomes like a rumor at the royal court: the wording continually shifts, and the meaning is obscured by commentary and digression. The more ALP defends her husband in her letter, the more scandal attaches to him. References to female writing often become tainted with lascivious comment: "Who in his heart doubts either that the facts of feminine clothiering are there all the time or that the feminine fiction, stranger than the facts, is there also at the same time, only a little to the rere?" (109).

The eventually notorious letter of ALP, which rises to the surface in humorous ways throughout *Finnegans Wake,* is worth examining in some detail, for it is here that Joyce's uncertainty principle, and his attitude toward it, are most clearly stated. Chapter Five (I, v; 104-125) is especially interesting since it is an analysis of various possible critical tools and approaches to the letter or the *Wake* (none of which will help), where Joyce casts his ventriloquist's voices into a mock-pedantic lecturer who sounds suspiciously like Shem. Difficulties of interpreting unstable texts are alternately explored, parodied, and dismissed until we gradually see that the uncertainty of the letter is the uncertainty of the *Wake,* and that our scholarly efforts to solve these puzzles are being mocked.

Following the chapter's invocation to "Annah the Allmaziful" (104) is a three-page catalog of titles for the "mamafesta" strongly reminiscent of the catalogs of "Cyclops" and "Circe" (*U* 12:559-69; 12:927-38; 12:1268-78; 12:1679-1712; 15:1402-40, etc.), but since the document has been known by so many titles, we are confused as to which one is correct. The titles seem to be "readings," fruitless attempts to label the letter and thus limit its meaning.

If we have no title, authorship is also problematic, to say the least. Perhaps the signature is missing, perhaps it has been obliterated by a tea stain, and even if it is there it may be a forgery. At the chapter's end it is hinted that Shem wrote it, possibly taking dictation, but, as Glasheen says (xxxvii), elsewhere it is suggested that he stole it (*FW* 125:21-22) either from his mother or from Shaun (*FW* 424:35-425:2). In any case it is hers and not hers: "The original document was in what is known as Hanno O'Nonhanno's unbrookable script, that is to say, it showed no signs of punctuation of any sort" (*FW* 123:32-33). Here, possibly in consequence of male assistance in the authorship, Anna Livia's name becomes masculine (as Bella's does in "Circe") and combined with that of the Carthaginian explorer Hanno the Navigator (see Glasheen). Close inspection reveals evidence of "a multiplicity of personalities inflicted on the documents or document" (*FW* 107:24-25), which undermines the notion of single authorship or even a single document. So much for title and authorship, about which we are told not to worry: ". . . Why, pray, sign anything as long as every word, letter, penstroke, paperspace is a perfect signature of its own?" (*FW* 115:07-09).[7]

As for factual authenticity, that too is untrustworthy. The "mamafesta" was penned as a "True Account" concerning Earwicker *"by a Woman of the World who only can Tell Naked Truths about a Dear Man and all his Conspirators how they all Tried to Fall him Putting it around Lucalizod about Privates Earwicker and a Pair of Sloppy Sluts plainly Showing all the Unmentionability falsely Accusing about the Raincoats"* (*FW* 107:03-07). But the letter as printed in Chapter Five doesn't actually say this or anything like it; what we find on page 111 is a newsy letter to Maggy from Boston. Still, "All schwants (schwrites) ischt tell the cock's trootabout him" (*FW* 113:11-12) and, as in the fe-

[7] Here Joyce seems to anticipate a number of post-structuralist preoccupations. See Roland Barthes, "The Death of the Author," in *Image, Music Text*, trans. Stephen Heath (New York: Hill and Wang, 1977), pp. 3, 142-48; Michel Foucault, "What Is an Author," in *Textual Strategies*, ed. Josue V. Harari (Ithaca, N.Y.: Cornell University Press, 1979); and Jacques Derrida, "Signature Event Context," in *Margins of Philosophy*, trans. Alan Bass (Chicago: University of Chicago Press, 1982), 307-330.

male writing in *Ulysses*, we find grammatical innocence, which no male collaborator has sought to correct, to bolster our faith in the author's honest intentions. "We must vaunt no idle dubiosity as to its genuine authorship and holusbolus authoritativeness" (*FW* 118:03-04), says the pedantic voice of Shaun, origin unknown.

Joyce must have been aware of the growing tendency of literary criticism in the twentieth century to overshadow the literary works critics examine, especially difficult works, and especially in academia. Students cannot help but be strongly influenced by what is said and written about the literature they encounter (the more so if they come to class unprepared), so that with time pressures, what they learn about a work read often has a greater impact than the work itself. Text is thus overpowered and obscured by context. This is precisely our experience in the *Wake*'s fifth chapter. Before we can actually read the letter, an absurdly pompous lecturer, sounding very much as if he is addressing an annual meeting of the Bibliographical Society of America, heaps upon the reader such a mass of confusing and contradictory evidence that the subject is hopelessly obscured. In "Penelope," Molly Bloom is careful to contradict herself on nearly every viewpoint expressed; here a male lecturer provides a similar service for his female author.

The letter to Maggy from Boston dated January 31, which Belinda scratched out of a middenheap, is clearest in one of its forms at *FW* 111, where the absence of punctuation recalls the style of Nora and "Penelope," though the breeziness is like Milly's:

> well & allathome's health well only the hate turned the mild on *the van* Houtens and the general's elections with a *lovely* face of some born gentleman with a beautiful present of wedding cakes for dear thankyou Chriesty and with grand funferall of poor Father Michael don't forget unto life's & Muggy well how are you Maggy & hopes soon to hear well & must now close it with fondest to the twoinns with four crosskisses for holy paul holey corner holipoli whollyisland . . .

On page 308 there is a "nightletter," really a Christmas message, which seems unconnected to other forms of the letter:

> With our best youlldied greedings to Pep and Memmy and the old folkers below and beyant, wishing them all very merry Incarnations in this land of the livvey and plenty of preprosperousness through their coming new yonks
>
> from
> jake, jack and little sousoucie
> (the babes that mean too)

It is impossible to say what relevance the letter in this form or the one on page 111 has to ALP or her defense of HCE, except that through commentary they all seem linked. As with the M'Intosh mystery in *Ulysses*, the more evidence one gathers, the less one understands, or as our lecturer says: "The farther back we manage to wiggle the more we need the loan of a lens to see as much as the hen saw" (*FW* 112:01-02). Soon we realize that the letter has faded into the tapestry of the *Wake* itself, and all its interrelated themes. This scattering of parts McCarthy compares to the scattering of Osiris's body ("Structures and Meanings": 576-77), to which I would add, this presumably makes the reader an Isis figure who looks in vain for enough of the remains to identify.

Our lecturer, of course, keeps insisting that the letter (book) will finally yield definitive meaning: "we ought really to rest thankful . . . we have even a written on with dried ink scrap of paper at all to show for ourselves . . ." (*FW* 118:31-34), that "things will begin to clear up . . . within the next quarrel of an hour" (*FW* 119:05-06). But "when all is zed and done" (*FW* 123:04), we are still not sure. ALP was surely never in Boston.

A second letter, which is said to be connected to the first, does seem to be authored by ALP, and does contain some defensive statements about HCE. It finally emerges in the last pages of the final book of *Finnegans Wake*, on pages 615-19, but it is far too long and digressive to merit quotation, and it is necessary to approach it from another angle.

Our subject is not so much the letter's content, as how that content becomes obscured, and how we are urged to embark on what is tantamount to an archaeological investigation so as to piece its meaning together. This task is carefully made impossible in the *Wake* itself, but by extending such an investigation to the manuscripts, one sees more. Manuscripts are also especially helpful in limiting speculative readings. Some would view this as a futile strategy. Norris admiringly quotes Kenner's frustrated remark that "it is worse than useless to push this toward one or the other of the meanings between which it hangs; . . . it is equally misleading to scan early drafts for the author's intentions, on the assumption that a 'meaning' got buried by elaboration. Joyce worked seventeen years to push the work away from 'meaning,' adrift into language; nothing is to be gained by trying to push it back" (Norris 124-25; *Dublin's Joyce* 304).

While I do argue for a large measure of uncertainty in the case of all major issues and many minor ones, one gains nothing by adopting a defeatist attitude toward textual meaning in the *Wake*. The reader was meant to live with uncertainty, not surrender. Whatever yields results should be tried—dictionaries, criticism, intelligence, knowledge, imagination, and manuscripts. One learns more, narrows the range of possibility, contemplates with amusement the pseudo-authorities such as our lecturer in Chapter Five.

Our lecturer fails to mention that the manuscripts of *Finnegans Wake* tell us more than does the *Wake* about ALP's letter, for they reveal a constant development toward the ever more obscure. We see how the letter becomes a fascinating example of displacement, or gnomonic absence, for it nearly disappears, but not quite. One can't tell for sure, but there really seems to have been something like an original letter by ALP in manuscript form that Joyce carefully excluded until ALP's chapter (*FW* 615-19), where it appears so changed, so digressive, that the defense of HCE, which was the letter's original purpose, is hopelessly obscured. Yet remembering Molly, who had the last word in *Ulysses*, we should not be surprised to find ALP babbling on in a confused manner at the *Wake*'s end.

If the point of reading the *Wake* is to read it, a familiar tautology, the point of the letter is to search for it, to speculate about it. In order to do that, or to read the *Wake*, it is necessary to extend the context to include all that is relevant to interpretation, and that includes seeing the book (or any Joycean work) as a continuity from earliest surviving notes to final printed text(s).

This approach to the letter is especially rewarding, because it leads us to a document that is as close to the original letter in prehenscratch and preteastain condition as we are ever likely to get. What Joyce intended here was presumably to draft the letter as a document to which he could frequently refer, but to keep it hidden until Book Four, a strategy of absence guaranteed to heighten reader interest. This *Urbrief* can be found in David Hayman's *A First-Draft Version of "Finnegans Wake"* (81-83), where it is prefaced by a fragment that both hints at Shem's authorship and reinforces the theme of uncertainty: "Alone one cannot know who did it for the hand was fair. We can suppose it that of Shemus the penman, a village soak, who when snugly liquored lived, so."

The *Urbrief*, if it is that, does indeed read like a "mamafesta," in this case a letter of protest to a royal figure about the slanderous attacks on her husband in the shrill voice of a semiliterate harridan who undermines her own cause through comic ignorance. The document is indisputably sophomoric ("The Honourable Mr Earwicker, my devout husband, is a true gentleman which is what none of the sneakers ever was . . . " [81]; "I hereinafter swear by your revered majesty that he gave me the price of a ~~new~~ bulletproof dress with angel sleeves" [82]). This is not the ALP we come to know in the *Wake*, but her comic missive is another letter to the world by a Joycean woman who unwittingly calls a great deal more attention to herself than she does her cause. The uncertainty was added later.

This example of Joyce's uncertainty principle, the intentional exclusion of vital evidence, a central text, must seem startling until one realizes that this is precisely the sort of evidence the boy in "The Sisters" lacked (and readers of Joyce lack) to reach certainty on important issues. If the letter and the *Wake* run along parallel lines of uncertainty, and the original letter is missing, the shopworn phrase that *Finnegans Wake* is really about *Finnegans Wake* gradually begins to take on new meaning: from our perspective in this present study, ALP's letter and the *Wake* are themselves *gnomons,* each absent or decentered from its respective context. All readings must take this into account.

Conclusion

From early to late in Joyce's work one finds an uncertainty principle responsible for obfuscation; its effect is to make readers think harder, to question what is missing, and with absence in mind to interpret what is present in the text. In the process of interpretation we find that in important questions the evidence for decidability is usually ambiguous, of dubious veracity, or missing. I have not begun to exhaust the possibilities in this line of interpretation. My purpose, rather, has been to describe the origin and development of Joyce's principle in its earlier forms, providing appropriate examples, and to trace its effect on character and structure as it grew in complexity. Ultimately this principle became perhaps the central topic of *Finnegans Wake* (not to mention modern literary theory), which questions how validity is possible in the interpretation of world or text.

Gnomon, which in Euclid means an incomplete geometrical structure, in *Dubliners* was a heuristic concept designed to control perspectives so that a maximum of political and moral impact could be attained with a minimum risk of censorship. In creating gnomonic strategies, Joyce probably hoped readers would share his sense of pity or grief or outrage at inadequate human beings, largely self-condemned, who fail to understand the nature of power and oppression. *Gnomon* could also be seen as an early endorsement of a kind of reader response theory that assumes that readers will bring to the text a range of perspectives. The effect was somewhat more complicated, and to Joyce surely more exciting: readers brought their perspectives, but they confused mysteries with problems, mostly believing that mysteries were simply more complicated problems having real solutions. That careers have been made and bibliographies padded with arguments that purport to give us the final word on unsolvable problems or mysteries would not have bothered our mischievous Mr. Joyce, who welcomed attention in whatever form.

Occasionally cruces are actually solved, as with the meaning of the "word known to all men" (*U* 15:4192-93; cf. *U* 9:429-31), a motif in Stephen's thoughts which a hitherto unknown passage in the Garland edition of *Ulysses* now makes clear. Whether mysteries or problems, we are normally pleased to read arguments that are more convincing than others we have read, and that is as it should be. What has been troublesome in Joyce studies is our inability to identify cruces that were obviously designed to entrap us into gathering specious evidence in the service of unsolvable problems. There are cases no good lawyer would voluntarily accept; some Joyceans, forgetting Leopold Bloom's impossible attempt to square the circle, have been most enticed by the hopeless ones.

What is the nature of the mystery surrounding Father Flynn? Why is "An Encounter's" ending so elliptical? What is the subject of the bantering conversation near the end of "Araby," and why precisely does it disturb the boy? Why does Eveline not board the ship? Has the housemaid in "Two Gallants" stolen or earned the gold coin? Has there possibly been no sexual intercourse between Bob Doran and Polly Mooney in "The Boarding House"? We are told that during Bob's confession, "the priest had drawn out every ridiculous detail of the affair and in the end had so magnified his sin . . ." (*D* 65). How is the sin of fornication magnified? What precisely is happening to Gabriel Conroy during the conclusion of "The Dead"? Convincing evidence that would lead us to certainty in the above cases is missing.

"Missing pieces" itself is the subject of "The Sisters," "Clay," and "Ivy Day in the Committee Room," stories in which a boy fails to reach certainty in interpretation, a series of missing items defines the nature of a romantic middle-aged woman, and a missing political leader, whose memory is being celebrated, defines the moral poverty of certain political flunkeys.

Has Bertha of *Exiles* been to bed with Robert Hand? This ought to be *the* central question of the play, certainly for Bertha's husband Richard, yet the evidence has been arranged so that we cannot know the answer. As spectators we are carefully absented during the evening hours when consummation would have taken place. On the morning after, the conversation between Bertha, Robert, and Richard is tantalizingly ambiguous throughout.

In *A Portrait* we see the uncertainty principle at work in characterization: we witness the growth of a young man who is defined in terms of his presumed vocation. Paradoxically, though, Stephen Dedalus seems not to be becoming what he is destined to become, given the book title *A Portrait of the Artist as a Young Man*. He may be the first of a series of Joycean characters who somehow cannot be what they are, whose essence is ultimately indeterminate. As we have seen, a major reason for this in Stephen's case may be that he is blocked in the apprentice stage by an experimental forebear he cannot go beyond.

The focal point of vocation has revealed another paradox in Stephen's character. If he is trapped in the tradition of Rimbaud and the decadents of the 1890s, sinking ever deeper into interior realms that lead away from the social conscience that sparked Joyce's own career, his path diverges from his autobiographical model. Joyce's own social conscience was very active at Stephen's age; it surely prompted the writing of *Dubliners*, a work that Stephen would seem incapable of writing.

We have seen that other major characters of *Ulysses* also contain paradoxes at the center. Molly is a Dublin woman (very Irish-Catholic indeed) who is having a love affair but secretly prefers her husband; but she is also a woman of Gibraltar, legally Jewish according to Jewish law, who was raised in a garrison (highly uncustomary) until she left for Dublin at the age of sixteen. She knows little Spanish, seems unaware of what became of her mother or that her mother's family was in Gibraltar during her girlhood. An excellent example of indeterminate character, Molly cannot be what she is, being of sociologically mismatched parts. One is hardly surprised to find her married to an indeterminate husband, who loves her and shares her, a Protestant-Catholic Jew who suffers from anti-Semitism, even though at birth he was probably not legally Jewish.

Small wonder, then, that minor mysteries of character have been so troublesome to interpreters of Joyce: from those like the Man in the Macintosh, whose identity was never meant to be discovered, to characters who seem to be somebody other than who they say they are, we have seen that Joyce's texts are peopled with identities that seem to pose questions for which there are no reliable answers.

Joyce's uncertainty principle poses difficulties, proliferates error, so that these concepts have required redefinition in the Joycean context. We often say that some sections of his work are more difficult than others, but what, precisely, makes them so? What happens to authority in interpretation when there is an authorial intent to promote perspectivism? Is it possible to find a defensible middle ground between the naive tolerance of all interpretations and the dogmatic insistence upon one "true," perhaps authorially sanctioned, reading of any given passage?

We have looked at intentional error in Joyce's works and have found that error itself is a subject. Mistakes are nearly always a source of comedy there, but it is quite a serious matter when, as in Stephen's case, a character chooses to fall into error. We saw that in most Joycean contexts the word *error* means *sin*. Sin and opposition to authority have a paralyzing effect upon Stephen, who seems self-condemned in this world and the next.

If the uncertainty principle affects character, it also affects structure, which has been the subject of my chapter on endings. Joyce is famous for his circular endings, one kind of structural indeterminacy, but from the enigmatic endings of the *Dubliners* stories, which return us to the text for clarification, to *Finnegans Wake,* where the last sentence flows into the first, we also find an implicit theory of closure.

In *Finnegans Wake* we have seen that the uncertainty principle produced Joyce's most radical experimentation in language, character, plot, structure—in short, every traditional aspect of the novel becomes indeterminate. In the *Wake,* Joyce discusses his principle most openly and directly, especially in those sections where ALP's letter appears in defense of her husband. There we arrived again at *gnomon* and absence: although snippets of the letter's content appear in the *Wake*, the letter in its most genuine form does not. Though it generates much controversy, and large parts of it are scattered through Book Four, its content is least unadulterated in manuscript form. Even in his last work we saw Joyce teasing his readers with absence and presence, using the letter to address most directly, though with heavy irony, the problems he foresaw readers having with literature's most radical experiment.

Works Cited

Abrams, M. H. *Natural Supernaturalism: Tradition and Revolution in Romantic Literature*. New York: Norton, 1971.

Adams, Robert M. *Nil: Episodes in the Literary Conquest of Void during the Nineteenth Century*. New York: Oxford, 1966.

———. *Strains of Discord*. 1958. Reprint. Freeport: Books for Libraries Press, 1971.

———. *Surface and Symbol: The Consistency of James Joyce's "Ulysses."* 1962. Rev. ed. New York: Oxford University Press, 1967.

Alexander, Jean. "Synge's Play of Choice: *The Shadow of the Glen.*" In *Sunshine and the Moon's Delight*, edited by S. B. Bushrui. Gerrards Cross: Colin Smythe, 1972.

Atherton, James S. "Araby." In *James Joyce's "Dubliners": Critical Essays*, edited by Clive Hart, 39-47. New York: Viking, 1969.

———. *The Books at the Wake*. London: Faber and Faber, 1959.

Bair, Deirdre. *Samuel Beckett: A Biography*. New York: Harcourt Brace Jovanovich, 1978.

Baudelaire, Charles. *Baudelaire: Selected Poems*. Translated by Joanna Richardson. Harmondsworth: Penguin, 1975.

Beck, Warren. *Joyce's "Dubliners": Substance, Vision, and Art*. Durham, N.C.: Duke University Press, 1969.

Beebe, Maurice. "*Ulysses* and the Age of Modernism." In *"Ulysses": Fifty Years*, edited by Thomas F. Staley, 172-88. Bloomington: Indiana University Press, 1974.

Begnal, Michael H. "The Unveiling of Martha Clifford." *James Joyce Quarterly* 13 (1976): 400-407.

Begnal, Michael H., and Grace Eckley. *Narrator and Character in "Finnegans Wake."* Lewisburg, Pa.: Bucknell University Press, 1975.

Beja, Morris. "Dividual Chaoses: Case Histories of Multiple Personality and *Finnegans Wake*." *James Joyce Quarterly* 14 (1977): 241-50.

Bell, Archie. *The Spell of Ireland*. Boston: Page, 1928.

Benstock, Bernard. *Joyce-again's Wake*. Seattle: University of Washington Press, 1965.

———. "The Kenner Conundrum: Or Who Does What with Which to Whom." *James Joyce Quarterly* 13 (1976): 428-35.

———. "On the Nature of Evidence in *Ulysses*." In *James Joyce: An International Perspective*, edited by Suheil Bushrui and Bernard Benstock, 46-64. Gerrards Cross: Colin Smyth, 1982.

Benstock, Bernard, ed. *The Seventh of Joyce*. Bloomington: Indiana University Press, 1982.

Benstock, Shari. "The Letter of the Law: *La Carte Postale* in *Finnegans Wake*." *Philological Quarterly* 63 (1984): 163-85.

———. "The Printed Letters in *Ulysses*." *James Joyce Quarterly* 19 (1982): 415-27.

Benstock, Shari, and Bernard Benstock. *Who's He When He's at Home*. Urbana: University of Illinois Press, 1980.

Bishop, John. *Joyce's Book of the Dark: "Finnegans Wake."* Madison: University of Wisconsin Press, 1986.

Blasco Ibáñez, Vicente. *Luna Benamor*. Valencia and Madrid: Prometeo, 1909. Translated by Isaac Goldberg. Boston: Luce, 1919.

Bloom, Harold. *The Anxiety of Influence: A Theory of Poetry*. New York: Oxford University Press, 1973.

Bowen, Zack. "After the Race." In *James Joyce's "Dubliners": Critical Essays*, edited by Clive Hart, 53-61. New York: Viking, 1969.

Bowen, Zack, and James F. Carens, eds. *A Companion to Joyce Studies*. Westport, Ct.: Greenwood, 1984.

Boyle, Robert, S.J. *James Joyce's Pauline Vision: A Catholic Exposition*. Carbondale and Edwardsville: Southern Illinois University Press, 1978.

———. "A Little Cloud." In *James Joyce's "Dubliners": Critical Essays*, edited by Clive Hart, 84-92. New York: Viking, 1969.

Brandabur, Edward. *A Scrupulous Meanness: A Study of Joyce's Early Work*. Urbana: University of Illinois Press, 1971.

Brivic, Sheldon. *Joyce the Creator*. Madison: University of Wisconsin Press, 1985.

Brooks, Cleanth, Jr., and Robert Penn Warren. "The Chalice Bearer." In *James Joyce's "Dubliners": A Critical Handbook*, edited by James R. Baker and Thomas F. Staley, 93-96. Belmont, Calif.: Wadsworth, 1969.

Bushrui, Suheil, and Bernard Benstock, eds. *James Joyce: An International Perspective*. Gerrards Cross: Colin Smyth, 1982.

Byrne, J. F. *Silent Years*. New York: Farrar, 1953.

Calpensis, Flora [pseud.]. *Reminiscences of Gibraltar*. London: 1880.

Čapek, Milič. *The Philosophical Impact of Contemporary Physics*. Princeton: Van Nostrand, 1961.

Card, James Van Dyck. *An Anatomy of "Penelope."* Rutherford, N.J.: Fairleigh Dickinson University Press, 1984.

———. "A Gibraltar Sourcebook for 'Penelope.' " *James Joyce Quarterly* 8 (1971): 163-75.

Carroll, Lewis. *Alice in Wonderland*. Edited by Donald J. Gray. Norton Critical Edition. New York: Norton, 1971.

Clayton, Jay. *Romantic Vision in the Novel*. New York: Cambridge University Press, 1987.

Clemens, Samuel. *Innocents Abroad*. London: 1881.

Collins, Ben L. "Joyce's 'Araby' and the 'Extended Simile.' " In *Twentieth Century Interpretations of "Dubliners": A Collection of Critical Essays*, edited by Peter K. Garrett, 93-99. Englewood Cliffs, N.J.: Prentice-Hall, 1968.

Connery, Donald S. *The Irish*. New York: Simon and Schuster, 1970.

Connolly, Thomas E. "Joyce's 'The Sisters': A Pennyworth of Snuff." *College English* 27 (1965): 189-95.

———. *The Personal Library of James Joyce: A Descriptive Bibliography. University of Buffalo Studies* 22 (1955).

Curran, C. P. *James Joyce Remembered*. New York and London: Oxford University Press, 1968.

Day, A. Grove, and Edgar C. Knowlton, Jr. *V. Blasco Ibáñez*. New York: Twayne, 1972.

Day, Robert Adams. "Joyce's Gnomons, Lenehan, and the Persistence of an Image." *Novel* 14 (1980): 5-19.

Degnan, James P. "The Reluctant Indian in Joyce's 'An Encounter.' " *Studies in Short Fiction* 6 (1969): 152-56.

DiBattista, Maria. "*Women in Love*: D. H. Lawrence's Judgment Book." In *D. H. Lawrence: A Centenary Consideration*, edited by Peter Balbert and Phillip L. Marcus, 67-90. Ithaca, N.Y.: Cornell University Press, 1985.

Dolch, Martin. "Eveline." In *James Joyce's "Dubliners": A Critical Handbook*, edited by James R. Baker and Thomas F. Staley, 96-101. Belmont, Calif.: Wadsworth, 1969.

Donoghue, Denis. *The Arts Without Mystery*. Boston: Little, Brown, 1983.

Eckley, Grace. *Children's Lore in "Finnegans Wake."* Syracuse: Syracuse University Press, 1985.

Eggers, Tilly. "What Is a Woman . . . A Symbol Of?" *James Joyce Quarterly* 18 (1981): 379-95.

Ellicott, J. T., and D. M. Ellicott. *An Ornament to the Almeida: Being the Story of Gibraltar's City Hall*. Portsmouth: Grosvenor, 1950.

Ellmann, Richard. *The Consciousness of Joyce*. New York: Oxford University Press, 1977.

———. *Golden Codgers: Biographical Speculations*. London: Oxford University Press, 1973.

Ellmann, Richard. *James Joyce*. New York: Oxford University Press, 1982.

———. *Ulysses on the Liffey*. New York: Oxford University Press, 1972.

Empson, William. *Using Biography*. Cambridge: Harvard University Press, 1984.

Epstein, Edmund L. "James Augustine Aloysius Joyce." In *A Companion to Joyce Studies*, edited by Zack Bowen and James F. Carens, 3-37. Westport, Ct.: Greenwood, 1984.

———. *The Ordeal of Stephen Dedalus: The Conflict of Generations in James Joyce's "A Portrait of the Artist as a Young Man."* Carbondale: Southern Illinois University Press, 1971.

Esslin, Martin. *The Peopled Wound: The Work of Harold Pinter*. Garden City, N.Y.: Doubleday, Anchor Books, 1970.

Fabian, David R. "Joyce's 'The Sisters': Gnomon, Gnomic, Gnome." *Studies in Short Fiction* 5 (1968): 187-89.

Fennell, Nuala. *Irish Marriage How Are You?* Dublin and Cork: Mercier, 1974.

Field, Henry. *Gibraltar*. New York: 1888.

Ford, Richard. *A Hand-Book for Travellers in Spain* [1845]. Reprint. London: Centaur, 1966.

French, Marilyn. "Missing Pieces in Joyce's *Dubliners*." *Twentieth Century Literature* 24 (1978): 443-72.

Friedman, Alan. *The Turn of the Novel*. New York: Oxford University Press, 1966.

Friedrich, Gerhard. "The Gnomonic Clue to James Joyce's *Dubliners*." *Modern Language Notes* 72 (1957): 421-24.

———. "The Perspective of Joyce's *Dubliners*." In *James Joyce's "Dubliners": A Critical Handbook*, edited by James R. Baker and Thomas F. Staley, 71-78. Belmont, Calif.: Wadsworth, 1969.

Füger, Wilhelm. " 'Epistlemadethemology' (*FW* 374.17): ALP's Letter and the Tradition of Interpolated Letters." *James Joyce Quarterly* 19 (1982): 405-413.

Garvin, John. *James Joyce's Disunited Kingdom and the Irish Dimension*. Dublin: Gill and Macmillan; New York: Barnes and Noble, 1976.

Ghiselin, Brewster. "The Unity of Joyce's *Dubliners*." In James Joyce, *Dubliners*, edited by Robert Scholes and A. Walton Litz, 316-32. Viking Critical Edition. New York: Viking, 1969.

Gibraltar Guide. Sussex: Service Publications, n.d.

Gifford, Don, and Robert J. Seidman. *Notes for Joyce: An Annotation of James Joyce's "Ulysses."* New York: Dutton, 1974.

Gilbert, Martin. *The Jews of Arab Lands*. London: Board of Deputies of British Jews, 1976.

Gilbert, Stuart. *James Joyce's "Ulysses": A Study*. 1930. Reprint. New York: Vintage, 1960.

Glasheen, Adaline. *The Third Census of "Finnegans Wake."* Berkeley: University of California Press, 1977.

Gogarty, Oliver St. John. "They Think They Know Joyce." *Saturday Review of Literature* 33 (18 March 1950): 8-9; 35-37.

Gordon, John. *James Joyce's Metamorphoses*. Dublin: Gill and Macmillan; New York: Barnes and Noble, 1981.

———. "The M'Intosh Mystery." *Modern Fiction Studies* 29 (1983): 671-79.

Gose, Elliott B., Jr. *The Transformation Process in Joyce's "Ulysses."* Toronto: University of Toronto Press, 1980.

Greenburg, Sidney Thomas. *The Infinite in Giordano Bruno*. New York: Octagon, 1978.

Greene, David H. and Edward M. Stephens. *J. M. Synge: 1871-1909*. New York: Collier, 1961.

Groden, Michael, et al. *The James Joyce Archive*. 63 vols. New York: Garland, 1978.

Hannay, John. "Coincidence and Fables of Identity in 'Eumaeus.' " *James Joyce Quarterly* 21 (1984): 341-55.

Hart, Clive. "The Elephant in the Belly: Exegesis of *Finnegans Wake*." In *A Wake Digest*, edited by Clive Hart and Fritz Senn, 3-12. Sydney: Sydney University Press, 1968.

———. "Eveline." In *James Joyce's "Dubliners": Critical Essays*, edited by Clive Hart, 48-52. New York: Viking, 1969.

———. "*Finnegans Wake* in Perspective." In *James Joyce Today: Essays on the Major Works*, edited by Thomas F. Staley, 135-65. Bloomington: Indiana University Press, 1966.

———. *Structure and Motif in "Finnegans Wake."* Evanston, Ill.: Northwestern University Press, 1962.

———, ed. *James Joyce's "Dubliners": Critical Essays*. New York: Viking, 1969.

Hayman, David. *Joyce et Mallarmé*. 2 vols. Paris: Lettres Modernes, 1956.

———. *A First-Draft Version of "Finnegans Wake."* Austin: University of Texas Press, 1963.

Heisenberg, Werner. *The Physical Principles of Quantum Theory*. Translated by Carl Eckart and Frank C. Hoyt. Chicago: University of Chicago Press, 1930.

Herr, Cheryl. "Irish Censorship and 'The Pleasure of the Text': The 'Aeolus' Episode of Joyce's *Ulysses*." In *Irish Renaissance Annual III*, edited by Dennis Jackson, 141-79. Newark: University of Delaware Press, 1982.

Herring, Phillip F. "Comment Joyce finit ses chapitres et ses livres." *Europe: revue littéraire mensuelle* 62 (janv.-fév. 1984): 65-73.

———. "Experimentation with a Landscape—Pornotopography in *Ulysses*: The Phallocy of Imitative Form." *Modern Fiction Studies* 20 (1974): 371-78.

———. "Joyce and Rimbaud." In *James Joyce: An International Perspective*, edited by Suheil Bushrui and Bernard Benstock, 170-89. Gerrards Cross: Colin Smyth, 1982.

———. "Joyce y el fantasma de la gabardina." *Quimera* (Barcelona) 6 (April 1981): 34-37.

———. "Recent Joyceana." *Contemporary Literature* 24 (1983): 387-94.

———. "Structure and Meaning in 'The Sisters.' " In *The Seventh of Joyce*, edited by Bernard Benstock, 131-44. Bloomington: Indiana University Press, 1982.

———. "Toward an Historical Molly Bloom." *ELH* 45 (1978): 501-521.

———, ed. *Joyce's Notes and Early Drafts for "Ulysses." Charlottesville: University Press of Virginia, 1977.*

———, *ed. Joyce's "Ulysses" Notesheets in the British Museum.* Charlottesville: University Press of Virginia, 1972.

Hertslet, Lewis. *A Complete Collection of the Treaties and Conventions . . .* 31 vols. London: 1820.

Howe, Irving. *Literary Modernism*. New York: Fawcett, 1967.

Howes, H. W. *The Gibraltarian: The Origin and Development of the Population of Gibraltar from 1704*. Colombo, Ceylon: City Press, 1952.

Hunting, Claudine. "La Voix de Rimbaud: Nouveau point de vue sur les 'naissances latentes' de 'Voyelles.' " *PMLA* 88 (1973): 472-83.

"An Interview with John Fowles." *Modern Fiction Studies* 31 (1985): 187-203.

James, Henry. *The Art of the Novel*. Edited by R. P. Blackmur. 1907. Reprint. New York: Scribner's, 1962.

Joyce, James. *The Critical Writings of James Joyce*. Edited by Ellsworth Mason and Richard Ellmann. New York: Viking, 1959.

———. "Daniel Defoe." Edited and translated by Joseph Prescott. *Buffalo Studies* I (1964).

———. *Dubliners*. Edited by Robert Scholes and A. Walton Litz. Viking Critical Edition. New York: Viking, 1969.

———. *Exiles*. New York: Viking, 1961.

———. *Finnegans Wake*. New York: Viking, 1939.

———. *The Letters of James Joyce.* Vol. 1. Edited by Stuart Gilbert. New York: Viking, 1957; reissued with corrections, 1965. Vols. 2 and 3. Edited by Richard Ellmann. New York: Viking, 1966.

———. *A Portrait of the Artist as a Young Man.* Edited by Chester G. Anderson. Viking Critical Edition. New York: Viking, 1968.

———. *Stephen Hero.* New York: New Directions, 1963.

———. *Ulysses: A Critical and Synoptic Edition.* 3 vols. Edited by Hans Walter Gabler, with Wolfhard Steppe and Claus Melchior. New York and London: Garland, 1984.

Joyce, P. W. *A Social History of Ancient Ireland.* 2 vols. London: Longmans, Green, 1903.

Joyce, Stanislaus. *My Brother's Keeper: James Joyce's Early Years.* New York: Viking, 1958.

Kenner, Hugh. *Dublin's Joyce.* 1956. Reprint. Boston: Beacon, 1962.

———. *Joyce's Voices.* Berkeley and Los Angeles: University of California Press, 1978.

———. "Molly's Masterstroke." *James Joyce Quarterly* 10 (1972): 19-28.

———. *The Pound Era.* Berkeley and Los Angeles: University of California Press, 1971.

———. "Pound on Joyce." *Shenandoah* 3 (1952): 3-8.

———. "The Rhetoric of Silence." *James Joyce Quarterly* 14 (1977): 382-94.

Kermode, Frank. *The Genesis of Secrecy.* Cambridge: Harvard University Press, 1979.

———. *The Sense of an Ending.* New York: Oxford University Press, 1966.

Kronegger, M. E. "Joyce's Debt to Poe and the French Symbolists." *Revue de Littérature Comparée* 39 (1965): 243-54.

Langbaum, Robert. *Mysteries of Identity.* New York: Oxford University Press, 1977.

Laredo, Abraham I. *Berebes y Hebreos en Marruecos.* Madrid: Instituto de Estudios Africanos, 1954.

———. *Les noms des juifs du Maroc.* Madrid: Consejo Superior de Investigaciones Científicas, Instituto "B. Arias Montejo," 1978.

Laredo, Isaac. *Memorias de un viejo Tangerino.* Madrid: Bermejo, 1935.

Lawrence, D. H. *The Fox. Four Short Novels of D. H. Lawrence.* New York: Viking, 1965.

Lawrence, Karen. *The Odyssey of Style in "Ulysses."* Princeton: Princeton University Press, 1981.

Leavis, F. R. *The Great Tradition.* New York: New York University Press, 1967.

Loss, Archie K. "Presences and Visions in *Exiles, A Portrait of the Artist,* and *Ulysses.*" *James Joyce Quarterly* 13 (1976): 148-62.

MacCabe, Colin. *James Joyce and the Revolution of the Word.* London: Macmillan, 1978; New York: Barnes and Noble, 1979.

McCarthy, Patrick A. "Joyce's Unreliable Catechist: Mathematics and the Narration of 'Ithaca.' " *ELH* 51 (1984): 605-618.

———. *The Riddles of "Finnegans Wake."* Rutherford, N.J.: Fairleigh Dickinson University Press, 1980.

———. "The Structures and Meanings of *Finnegans Wake.*" In *A Companion to Joyce Studies,* edited by Zack Bowen and James F. Carens, 559-632. Westport, Ct.: Greenwood, 1984.

Macherey, Pierre. *A Theory of Literary Production.* Translated by Geoffrey Wall. London: Routledge and Kegan Paul, 1978. (*Pour une théorie de la production littéraire.* Paris: François Maspero, 1966.)

McHugh, Roland. *The Sigla of "Finnegans Wake."* Austin: University of Texas Press, 1976.

MacKenzie, Alexander Seidell. *A Year in Spain* [By a Young American]. London: 1831.

Maddox, James H., Jr. *Joyce's "Ulysses" and the Assault upon Character.* New Brunswick, N.J.: Rutgers University Press, 1978.

Meakin, Budgett. *The Moors: A Comprehensive Description.* London: Sonnenschein; New York: Macmillan, 1902.

Mercier, Vivian. *The Irish Comic Tradition.* Oxford: Clarendon, 1962.

Miller, Henry. *Time of the Assassins: A Study of Rimbaud.* Norfolk, Ct.: New Directions, 1956.

Mitchell, Susan L. *George Moore.* 1916. Reprint. Port Washington, N.Y.: Kennikat, 1970.

Morse, J. Mitchell. "Baudelaire, Stephen Dedalus, and Shem the Penman." *Bucknell Review* 7 (1958): 187-98.

Norris, Margot. *The Decentered Universe of "Finnegans Wake."* Baltimore: The Johns Hopkins University Press, 1976.

O'Connor, Ulick. *The Times I've Seen: Oliver St. John Gogarty, A Biography.* New York: Obolensky, 1963.

Patrides, C. A., ed. *Milton's "Lycidas": The Tradition and the Poem.* Rev. ed. Columbia, Mo.: University of Missouri Press, 1983.

Peake, C. H. *James Joyce: The Citizen and the Artist.* London: Edward Arnold; Stanford: Stanford University Press, 1977.

Perloff, Marjorie. *The Poetics of Indeterminacy.* Princeton: Princeton University Press, 1981.

Power, Arthur. *Conversations with James Joyce.* New York: Harper and Row, 1974.

Pütz, Manfred. "The Identity of the Reader in *Finnegans Wake*." *James Joyce Quarterly* 11 (1974): 387-93.

Raynaud, Claudine. "Woman, the Letter Writer; Man, the Writing Master." *James Joyce Quarterly* 23 (Spring 1986): 299-324.

Reid, B. L. "Gnomon and Order in Joyce's *Portrait*." *Sewanee Review* 92 (1984): 397-420.

Reynolds, Mary T. *Joyce and Dante*. Princeton: Princeton University Press, 1981.

Rickword, Edgell. *Rimbaud: The Boy and the Poet*. 1924. Reprint. Castle Hedingham: Daimon, 1963.

Rimbaud, Arthur. *Rimbaud: Complete Works, Selected Letters*. Edited and translated by Wallace Fowlie. Chicago and London: University of Chicago Press, 1966.

Ronan, Myles V. *Glendaloch and Its Ruins*. Enniscorthy: Redmond, 1957.

Roscher, W. H. *Ausführliches Lexikon der griechischen und römischen Mythologie*. 6 vols.; 2 supp. vols. Leipzig: Teubner, 1884-1937.

Russell, Bertrand. *Introduction to Mathematical Philosophy*. London: Allen and Unwin; New York: Humanities Press, 1919.

Saddlemyer, Ann. *The Collected Letters of John Millington Synge*. Vol. 1 (1871-1907). Oxford: Clarendon Press, 1983.

Schiffer, Paul S. " 'Homing, upstream': Fictional Closure and the End of *Ulysses*." *James Joyce Quarterly* 16 (1979): 283-98.

Scholes, Robert. "Counterparts." In James Joyce, *Dubliners* edited by Robert Scholes and A. Walton Litz, 379-87. Viking Critical Edition. New York: Viking, 1969.

Scholes, Robert, and Richard M. Kain, eds. *The Workshop of Daedalus*. Evanston, Ill.: Northwestern University Press, 1965.

Scott, Bonnie Kime. *Joyce and Feminism*. Bloomington: Indiana University Press, 1984.

Seidel, Michael. *Epic Geography: James Joyce's "Ulysses."* Princeton: Princeton University Press, 1976.

Senn, Fritz. " 'An Encounter.' " In *James Joyce's "Dubliners": Critical Essays*, edited by Clive Hart, 26-38. New York: Viking, 1969.

———." 'He Was Too Scrupulous Always': Joyce's 'The Sisters.' " *James Joyce Quarterly* 2 (1965): 66-72.

———. *Joyce's Dislocutions: Essays on Reading as Translation*. Baltimore: The Johns Hopkins University Press, 1984.

Serfaty, A.B.M. *The Jews of Gibraltar*. Gibraltar: 1933; reprinted 1958.

Skelton, Robin. *The Writings of J. M. Synge*. Indianapolis and New York: Bobbs-Merrill, 1971.

Smith, Barbara Herrnstein. *Poetic Closure*. Chicago: University of Chicago Press, 1968.

Solomon, Margaret C. *Eternal Geomater: The Sexual Universe of "Finnegans Wake."* Carbondale: Southern Illinois University Press, 1969.

Staley, Thomas F. "A Beginning: Signification, Story, and Discourse in Joyce's 'The Sisters.' " In *Critical Essays on James Joyce*, edited by Bernard Benstock, 176-90. Boston: G. K. Hall, 1985. First published in *Genre* 12 (Winter 1979), 533-49.

Staples, Hugh B. Book Review. *James Joyce Quarterly* 22 (1985): 435-39.

———. "Joyce and Cryptology: Some Speculations." *James Joyce Quarterly* 2 (1965): 167-73.

Starkie, Enid. *Arthur Rimbaud*. Norfolk, Ct.: New Directions, 1961.

Steinberg, Erwin R. "The Religion of Ellen Higgins Bloom." *James Joyce Quarterly* 23 (Spring 1986): 350-55.

Steiner, George. "On Difficulty." In *On Difficulty and Other Essays*, 18-47. Oxford: Oxford University Press, 1978.

Steppe, Wolfhard, and Hans Walter Gabler. *A Handlist to James Joyce's "Ulysses."* New York: Garland, 1985.

Stevick, Philip. *The Chapters in Fiction: Theories of Narrative Division*. Syracuse, N.Y.: Syracuse University Press, 1970.

Stoddard, Charles Augustus. *Spanish Cities*. London: 1892.

Stone, Harry. " 'Araby' and the Writings of James Joyce." In James Joyce, *Dubliners*, edited by Robert Scholes and A. Walton Litz, 344-67. Viking Critical Edition. New York: Viking, 1969.

Symons, Arthur. *The Symbolist Movement in Literature*. 1899. Reprint. New York: Dutton, 1919.

Synge, John M. *The Complete Plays of John M. Synge*. New York: Vintage, 1960.

Thackeray, William [M. A. Titmarsh, pseud.]. *Notes of a Journey from Cornhill to Grand Cairo*. London: 1846.

Thomas, Brook. *James Joyce's "Ulysses": A Book of Many Happy Returns*. Baton Rouge: Louisiana State University Press, 1982.

Thornton, Weldon. *Allusions in "Ulysses."* Chapel Hill: University of North Carolina Press, 1968.

Tindall, William York. *James Joyce: His Way of Interpreting the Modern World*. New York: Scribner's, 1950.

———. *A Reader's Guide to "Finnegans Wake."* New York: Farrar, Straus and Giroux, 1969.

Torgovnick, Marianna. *Closure in the Novel*. Princeton: Princeton University Press, 1981.

The Traveller's Hand-Book for Gibraltar by An Old Inhabitant. London: 1844.

Valente, Joseph. "Beyond Truth and Freedom: The New Faith of Joyce and Nietzsche." *James Joyce Quarterly,* forthcoming.

Voelker, Joseph. "Molly Bloom and the Rhetorical Tradition." *Comparative Literature Studies* 16 (1979): 146-64.

Walzl, Florence. "Gabriel and Michael: The Conclusion of 'The Dead.' " In James Joyce, *Dubliners,* edited by Robert Scholes and A. Walton Litz, 423-43. Viking Critical Edition. New York: Viking, 1969.

———. "Joyce's 'The Sisters': A Development." *James Joyce Quarterly* 10 (1973): 375-421.

Weir, David. "Moore's Young Man." *James Joyce Broadsheet* 16 (1985): 4.

———. "Stephen Dedalus: Rimbaud or Baudelaire?" *James Joyce Quarterly* 18 (1980): 87-91.

Wellington, Frederick V. "A Missing Conversation in *Ulysses.*" *James Joyce Quarterly* 14 (1977): 476-79.

Welsh, Alexander. "Opening and Closing *Les Misérables.*" *Nineteenth-Century Fiction* 33 (1978): 8-23.

Wilson, Edmund. *Axel's Castle.* New York: Scribner's, 1931.

Index

Library of Congress Cataloging-in-Publication Data

Herring, Phillip F.
Joyce's uncertainty principle.

Bibliography: p.
Includes index.
1. Joyce, James, 1882-1941—Technique.
2. Experimental fiction—Ireland—History and criticism
3. Uncertainty in literature. I. Title.

PR6019.09Z5824 1987 823'.912 87-3438
ISBN 0-691-06719-8 (alk. paper)

Lightning Source UK Ltd.
Milton Keynes UK
UKHW021146050223
416481UK00007B/1043